THE ROUGH GUIDE TO

Cuban Music

by

Philip Sweeney

There are more than two hundred Rough Guide titles
covering destinations from Alaska to Zimbabwe
and subjects from Acoustic Guitar to Travel Health

www.roughguides.com

ROUGH GUIDES

Rough Guide Credits

Text editor: Joe Staines, James McConnachie
Series editor: Mark Ellingham
Production: Michelle Draycott, Julia Bovis
Design and typesetting: Katie Pringle
Proofreading: Ken Bell
Cartography: Maxine Repath, Ed Wright

Publishing Information

This first edition published June 2001 by
Rough Guides Ltd, 62–70 Shorts Gardens, London WC2H 9AH

Distributed by the Penguin Group

Penguin Books Ltd, 27 Wrights Lane, London W8 5TZ
Penguin Putnam Inc., 375 Hudson Street, New York 10014, USA
Penguin Books Australia Ltd, 487 Maroondah Highway,
PO Box 257, Ringwood, Victoria 3134, Australia
Penguin Books Canada Ltd, 10 Alcorn Avenue,
Toronto, Ontario, Canada M4V 1E4
Penguin Books (NZ) Ltd, 182–190 Wairau Road,
Auckland 10, New Zealand

Typeset in Bembo and Helvetica to an original design by Henry Iles.
Printed in Spain by Graphy Cems.

Contents

Introduction

Argentinian tango and Brazilian samba may have provided strong competition, but it's the sounds of Cuba that have dominated the Latin music world throughout the twentieth century and seem set to continue to do so well into the twenty-first.

Cuban music has proved influential in two distinct ways. The great richness of traditional forms still preserved on the island continues to fascinate new generations – witness the Buena Vista Social Club phenomenon. At the same time, much pan-Latin dance music, notably salsa, has developed from Cuban music more than any other ingredient.

The Rough Guide to Cuban Music describes the full range of this thriving musical melee, from its historic origins to its very latest hit manifestations in Havana, Miami, Paris and London. Each chapter highlights a particular aspect of the story – son, trova, boleros, etc – and culminates in a series of profiles of the most significant performers and the pick of their available recordings.

The primary aim in writing this book was to focus on popular music of a Cuban style played by artists of Cuban origin. Thus, purely classical or totally folkloric musics are described only to the extent to which they overlap with popular styles, or when they have exercised a traceable influence on the development of popular musics: Ernesto Lecuona, for example, features quite prominently as his work comprised both classical and popular. In the area of traditional music, the range of African-origin percussion is sketched in concisely as background, but the emphasis is on its wider popular developments, like rumba.

Limitations of space have meant the exclusion of some performers, while occasionally a relatively minor artist has been profiled, in

order not to neglect a noteworthy but peripheral style or trend. Comments, favourable or otherwise, will be gratefully received and may well influence future editions – if Cuban musical and political development continues as dynamically as it has for the last decade, a new and fascinating chapter is even now in the making.

Acknowledgements

I owe enormous gratitude and appreciation for the instruction, inspiration and general help of the many musicians, writers and other professionals who made my research possible. Prominent among them are:

UK
Lucy Duran, Sue Steward, Tomek, John Child, John Armstrong, Nick Gold, Jenny Adlington, Mo Fini, Dominique Roome, Richard Williams, Andy Wood, Bruce Bastin, Nelson Batista, Elder Sanchez, Homero Gonzalez, Leoncio and Luz Elena Caicedo, Phil Manzanera, Jan Fairley.

France
François-Xavier Gomez, Antoine Chao, Veronique Mortaigne, Claire Hénault, Remy Kolpa-Kapoul, Alfredito Rodriguez, Oscar Lopez, Laude Menéndez.

Cuba
The late Elio Revé, Odelquis Revé, Helio Orovio, Marina Rodríguez López, Santiago Alfonso, Pablo Menéndez, Jorge Gómez, Cary Diez, Pedro Luis Rodríguez, Juan de Marcos González and Gliceria Abreu,

v

Jesús Alemañy, Ibrahim Ferrer, Orlando "Cachaíto" López, Omara Portuondo, Compay Segundo, Salvador Repilado, Mauricio Vicent, Papi Oviedo, Lyng Chang, Paulito FG, Manolín (el Médico de la Salsa), Demetrio Muñiz, members of the cast of the Tropicana, Havana and the Tropicana, Santiago.

Spain
Howell Llewellyn, Fietta Jarque, Nacho Saenz de Tejeda, Diego Manrique, Mingus Formentor, Teddy Bautista, Enrique Romero, Jordi Pujol, Abilí Roma, Peret, Alex van Loy, Mario Pacheco, Jaime Stinus, Manuel Domínguez, Cristina Mantecón.

USA/Puerto Rico/Mexico
Max Salazar, Larry Harlow, Andy González, Ralph and Debra Mercado, Jimmy Bosch, Verna Gillis, Rudolph and Yvette Mangual, Nelson Rodríguez, Johnny Falcones, Isidro Infante, Jessie Moskovitz, John Lannert, Roberto and Marlena Torres, Emilio Estefan, Willy Chirino, Patty Vargas, Rachel Faro, Patricia Jaramillo, Raúl Alfonso, Hánsel Martínez, Hugo Cancio, Valerie Cox, Cristóbal Díaz Ayala, Javier Santiago, Charlie Dos Santos, Judy Cantor, Celeste Frazer Delgado, Fernando González, Dita Sullivan, Marti Cuevas, Manny Gonzalez, Eduardo Llerenas and Mary Farquharson.

And finally... Mark Ellingham, Joe Staines and Katie Pringle at Rough Guides, Verdine Lewis Stevens, and, as always, Liz Vibert.

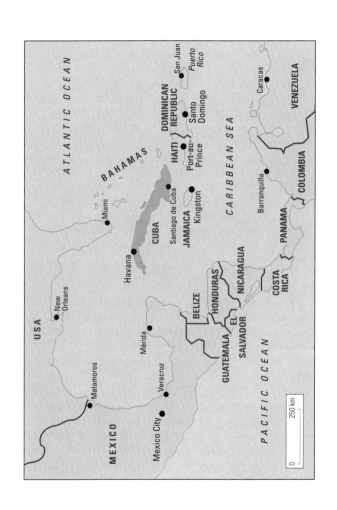

1
Background

For a nation of only eleven million people, and just under half the size of the UK, **Cuba** has tremendous musical clout. The products of Cuba's old Buena Vista-style *soneros*, its modern salsa and rumba bands, its jazz stars, its rappers and fusionists cram music stores across the world and its name is as pre-eminently identified with Latin dance music as France is with gastronomy or Italy with sports cars.

The story of how this came to be is one of wood and leather, of geography and history, but primarily one of people. The chief players were **Spanish** and **African**, but minor roles extend further – even the English have a distant input, via the eighteenth-century country dances, transmuted into French *contredanses* and then Creole *contradanzas*, the early ancestor of modern Cuban music. The **Chinese** who arrived in the nineteenth century also contributed touches such as the Chinese cornet of Havana carnival, not to mention the references to Chinese girls in Cuban songs. More distantly traceable is the music of the original inhabitants of the island, the **Siboney** and **Taíno Indians**. Less than a century after colonization began the Taínos had been exterminated, and although later generations of Cubans reclaim their memory in product titles – Hatuey beer (named after one of the chiefs who attempted to resist the conquistadores),

Areíto Records (after the Taíno
drumming celebrations), the
Orquesta Anacaona (a leg-
endary female warrior) –
no Taíno equivalent of
the indigenous musics
of Peru or Colombia
exists in Cuba.
However, the musi-
cologist Eduardo
Sanchez de Fuentes
has conjectured that
the last Taíno women,
made pregnant by the
overwhelmingly male
Spanish settler contingents,
may well have hushed their mes-
tizo babies with Taíno lullabies and
implanted a seed of the old melodies now long since lost.

The Spanish Conquest

The **conquistadores** who first arrived in Cuba had set off from
Andalucia and Estremadura – **Columbus** left Huelva, home of the *flamenco fandango*, to arrive on the island in October 1492. In 1511,
Diego Velasquez brought a small military force to the eastern end of
the island, near the present-day US base of Guantánamo Bay, and
formally colonized Cuba. However, the gold which the Spanish had
been seeking soon ran out, and for two centuries the island was
developed for small-scale agriculture; settlers were granted plots of
land and contingents of conquered Taínos helped them cultivate the

plots – until the dreadful working conditions and cruel treatment killed them off. The smallholders who came to rear cattle and grow sugar and tobacco, as well as the craftsmen and merchants, were predominantly from **Galicia** in the northwest of Spain (Fidel Castro's father was a Galician plantation owner, hence Castro's nickname "El Gallego") or **Catalonia** (many Cuban surnames, from the great rum dynasty the Bacardis to the Abreu brothers who form the modern rumba quartet **Los Papines**, are Catalan in origin). Many settlers also came from the **Canary Islands**, another Spanish colony halfway between Spain and the Caribbean, hence the continued strong affinity between the Canaries and Cuba, and the great popularity of Cuban-based musics in La Palma and Tenerife today.

The different regions of Spain all had distinct musics – the flamenco songs from the south, the Castilian *jota* – but the colonizers' major contribution to Cuban music was the use of stringed instruments, the decima verse pattern of songs, and a whole range of melodies.

Slavery

As a result of the loss of the indigenous population, the Spanish colonizers were faced with the necessity of finding workers to exploit the gold and copper mines and the agricultural settlements. The result was the introduction of slaves. Initially these were indigenous Indians from **Venezuela** but soon the Spanish were turning their attention to another continent. **African slaves** had been shipped to Europe by the Portuguese as early as 1441, and by the early sixteenth century the trade in human cargoes across the Atlantic had begun in earnest. The Spanish monarchy granted the supply monopoly to Dutch slavers, who in turn bought captives from the West and Central African kingdoms of modern day Senegal, Guinea, Ghana, Nigeria, Congo, Angola and adjoining countries. The horrific condi-

tions of the ocean crossing and the harsh work regime on arrival led to the deaths of many of the captives, but for two centuries a constant supply of new slaves flowed into the Caribbean.

The origins of the clave

Cuba's people, their customs and arts were the result of a continuous process of hybridization. But Cuban music is more than simply the combination of its ingredients: it also contains unique new elements. An interesting example of the complexities of this cultural cross-fertilization can be found in Fernando Ortiz's *Instrumentos de la Música Afrocubana* in which he attempts to unravel the origins of the **clave** – the paired wooden sticks central to the island's percussion. The clave isn't exactly modelled on the Andalusian castanets, nor is it based on any of the African percussion instruments, even though the high musical resonance of its wood (taken from the trunk of a hardwood) resembles the sound of a single key of a *marimba* or a *balafon*, the African proto-xylophone. Nor does it derive from the similar-sounding *ku-chó* found in traditional Chinese theatre which came to Havana with the Chinese labourers who augmented Africans in the nineteenth century.

On the other hand, there does seem to be a connection between the clave and the music of a number of Cuba's early settlers, in particular the inhabitants of the port of **Havana** between the sixteenth and eighteenth centuries. During this period, Havana became the chief meeting place and stopping-off point for the transatlantic convoys between Spain and its rich silver-producing colonies, Peru and Mexico. As the Caribbean's biggest centre of ship repairing and provisioning, Havana's port

Unlike the British, who discouraged intermarriage between colonizers and slaves, and prohibited African religious and cultural expression, the Spanish interbred with slaves and also allowed them

and surrounding suburbs were home to a population of sailors, workmen, small traders and prisoners from both Africa and Spain. These included freed African slaves – the *negros curros* – who formed an important part of the artisans of Havana. Both the slow mournful *martinetes* of the flamenco canon, traditionally sung with only a hammer-on-anvil slow percussion accompaniment, and the work-song rhythms of slave-gangs straining at ships' oars or cane-cutting in the fields, lend themselves to a clapped wood-block beat.

In colonial Havana there existed not only the people and the musical inclinations most perfectly suited to create the clave, but also the materials. The variety and quality of the hardwoods used in Havana's shipyards were the best in the Americas, and among the items produced in huge quantities were the long hardwood pegs and studs used for assembling wooden structures. Havana ship-building pegs, known in Spanish as *claves*, were renowned for their quality – as hard as iron but resistant to water. A couple of modifications would transform two of these parts into the instrument known as a clave, and this, concludes Ortiz, is exactly what happened, giving rise to the form of percussion whose short, crystalline, fluid tapping Federico García Lorca was to encapsulate in the lovely phrase, "gota de madera" ("a drop of wood"). The clave, then, key to Cuban rhythm, is not an adapted Spanish or African instrument but a uniquely Cuban one, just as the rich texture of Cuban music is not merely a mixture, but a new genre.

to use drums and organize to a limited extent in societies of similar ethnic provenances. Spain did not abolish slavery nominally until 1880, and slaves were still tied to their masters for a further six years: thus, some black Cubans today still remember grandparents who were slaves and the African element of Cuban culture remains a powerful presence.

The nineteenth century

Although sugar was introduced into Cuba by the first Spanish invaders, the island lagged behind its Caribbean neighbours in terms of production and manufacture. With the **Haitian revolution** of 1791 Cuba took over as the leading sugar producer, thus fuelling an ever-increasing need for slave labour. The revolution also led to an exodus of Haiti's French and Creole élite (and some of their slaves) across the narrow stretch of sea which separates Haiti from eastern Cuba. The musical result was the injection of French formal dance music and dress, copied by African servants, into Santiago's carnival, and the creation of the *tumba francesa* music of **Oriente province**. It's interesting that the proximity to eastern Cuba of Hispaniola – the island shared by Haiti and the Dominican Republic – still has musical repercussions: Dominican *merengue* and *bachata* from radio stations across the water are much listened to on the streets of **Santiago de Cuba**, but hardly ever in Havana, six hundred miles away.

During the nineteenth century, Cuban music evolved into a number of distinctive forms, guided by a series of notable composers and musicians whose careers already oscillated between the cities of Cuba and European capitals, notably Paris. **José White**, a composer and multi-instrumentalist born in Matanzas in 1836, studied at the Paris Conservatoire and wrote classics of the **danza** genre, notably

the famous "La Bella Cubana". The danza, based on European orchestral music which had been creolized, was rivalled in popularity by the equally sprightly **contradanza**. The latter was the dance and salon music favoured by Havana high society until the last decades of the century, when it was eclipsed by a slower but more varied and more heavily rhythmic development, the **danzón**. The danzón was the creation of another Matanzas musician, **Miguel Failde**, the son of a trombonist, who began his career as an apprentice cornet player in the Matanzas Fire Brigade Band and went on to become one of Cuba's top bandleaders and the composer of the first recognised danzón, "Alturas de Simpson". But the best known form outside Cuba during this period was the **habanera**, another rhythmic style based on creolized European dance music, which was frequently employed by European composers, most famously Bizet in his opera *Carmen*.

In *fin de siècle* Havana, **musical theatre** also flourished, and European forms were giving birth to Cuban offspring. Classical opera was rivalled in popularity by the Spanish light operatic form *zarzuela*, which was a good training ground for early popular singers, notably the great star **Rita Montaner** (see p.116). The Italian comic theatre tradition gave rise to a strong presence in Havana of *teatro bufo*, while Southern US music hall troupes were also popular. The sketches of the *teatro bufo* were interspersed with *guarachas*, originally colourful burlesque songs full of satire and references to the characters and morals of the period. Later the *guaracha* evolved into a dance form, and although its popularity waned greatly during the twentieth century, it is regarded as an important element of the ethos of **salsa**: use of the term *guarachero* to describe particularly spicy salsa singers, such as the great **Celia Cruz**, confirms this.

Independence

By the beginning of the twentieth century, Cuba had taken major steps in the creation of distinctive indigenous musical forms. The different elements of the population, and their musics, still existed separately, but they also mingled. The island was divided between a wealthy white and Criollo bourgeoisie in Havana cultivating primarily European tastes, a slightly more mixed rural population, and a segregated black sub-class practising its own rites and celebrations.

The cause of independence was gradually espoused by those Criollo notables exasperated by the virtually exclusive power of the *peninsulares* – the Spanish-born élite. A quarter of a million Cubans died in the **Ten Years War** launched in 1868 by Carlos Manuel de Céspedes, Maximo Gomez and Antonio Maceo before they were defeated. Seven years later, the struggle was resumed by **José Martí**, whose persuasive oratory in the United States and cleverly-waged guerrilla war was on the verge of success in 1898, when a US expeditionary force stole the victory and accepted the surrender of Spain. For three years, sovereignty of Cuba was passed to the US, and even after the declaration of the Republic of Cuba in 1902, the giant neighbour to the north still dominated trade and cultural interchange. American companies ran Cuba's railways, electricity supply and telephones, while ever greater areas of the countryside were converted to sugar production to supply the American market.

The entertainment boom

The first fifty years of independence saw the Cuban entertainment industry boom, greatly helped by the growth of North-American tourism. This occurred during the presidencies of two men, **Gerardo Machado** (1924–33) and **Fulgencio Batista** (1933–40 and 1952–59), both of whom started out as populist, and popular, reformers in the

classic Latin American mould, and ended up as corrupt and cruel dictators. Batista, in particular, was an enthusiastic sponsor of the American mafiosi who set up gambling operations in Havana at the end of Prohibition. In return he received substantial rake-offs, ranging from ten percent of Florida hood Santo Trafficante's roulette and crap profits at the Sans Souci and the Hotel Comodoro to fifty percent of the Jewish gang boss Meyer Lansky's slot-machine profits at the Montmartre and the casino of the Hotel Nacional.

A Havana bar in the 1950s

By the 1950s, Havana's pleasure industries – hotels, casinos and brothels – had made the city the playground of choice for North-American hedonists. The music industry benefited, with armies of entertainers required, from the on-board son quartets who serenaded passengers on the evening cocktail-hour flight from Miami to the chorus girls and orchestra members of the flagship Tropicana night-club, which opened in 1939 in the grounds of a villa in the smart new suburb of Miramar. Not only Cuban musicians filled the stages. Frank Sinatra, Nat King Cole and Edith Piaf all played Havana. In 1957, Meyer Lansky built the extravagant 21-storey Hotel Riviera, with an egg-shaped casino, a grand cream marble lobby and a circular night-club, The Copa Room, which opened with a show by Ginger Rogers.

Revolution

The boom in Havana nightlife contributed nothing to the lives of the Cuban working class, who were ill-paid and only too aware of the fla-

Fidel makes another point

grant corruption and luxury of the élite. **Fidel Castro**'s bid to oust Batista therefore met with popular support. Castro, born in 1927 in eastern Cuba, studied law at Havana University and began a career in conventional opposition politics, but espoused armed uprising as the only practical option when Batista staged his coup and return to power in 1952. In a catastrophic first attempt in 1953, Castro, accompanied by one hundred and twenty men, attacked the Moncada barracks in Santiago, resulting in most of the group being killed or imprisoned. Castro, his brother Raul, the Argentinian doctor-turned-revolutionary **Ernesto "Che" Guevara** and a small group of guerrillas returned from Mexican exile two years later in the yacht *Granma* and recommenced their war from the haven of the Sierra Maestra mountain range, helped by a campaign of bombings and subversion in the cities.

By the end of 1958, with the under-motivated army demoralized and unable to crush the rebels, Batista decided the game was up. On New Year's Eve, he and his family fled to the Dominican Republic and eight days later Castro's *barbudos* (bearded ones) drove tri-umphantly into Havana to cheering crowds. Although mobs ran-sacked the casinos, hurling slot-machines into the streets, and the new rulers closed down the brothels, the Castro regime posed no ideological threat to Cuba's music scene. Indeed, Che Guevara insisted the new order was to be "socialism with *pachanga*" – the then current popular dance genre. Many musicians had supported social reform before the Revolution, and many more applauded, and still applaud, the improvements in their working lives that resulted from it. These entailed a classic socialist combination of state sup-port – all musicians would receive salaries, musical education was free, etc – with rigid control and restrictions on freedom of expres-sion and movement. Within a decade of the Revolution, all Cuban musicians were obligatory members of one of the State *empresas*

(agencies) that regulated all aspects of their working lives, from the allocation of instruments to arranging the exit visas necessary to perform abroad.

The isolationist years

As Castro's regime moved from its initial vaguely liberal reformist position towards strict **Communism** over the first six years, its once close links with the US music business were severed. Along with all private businesses, Castro appropriated the Cuban studios and installations of American record companies such as RCA, and in return the US refused to pay performing and publishing rights to the Cuban State for the works of Cuban songwriters. As Cuba's regime became more hard-line, and the American embargo on trade and aid correspondingly more rigid, Cuba turned to the **Soviet bloc** for support. By the mid-1980s the Cuban economy was reliant on the massive sale of overpriced sugar to, and the receipt of cheap oil from, the Soviet Union. Cuban musicians were denied access to the huge US market, which had meanwhile developed Cuban-based music into what the world began to call salsa. Instead, they made rare trips to perform at Polish and Bulgarian pop festivals, while increasing numbers of Cuban musicians joined the half-million exiles who had left, mainly for Miami, by the end of the first decade after the Revolution.

The combination of isolation and socialism on Cuban popular music had two pronounced effects. One was to keep a large body of state-supported musicians active and in good health, so that the tradition of longevity in Cuban bands was even further accentuated, with institutions of up to eighty years of age regularly surviving. Many of these musicians played traditional forms such as son or *trova*, leading to the music's preservation. The other effect was to lead the vanguard

of Cuban popular dance music to pursue a totally distinct path to the rest of Latin America, at once modernizing yet out-of-date.

The 1990s revival

The removal of the Soviet bloc's aid at the beginning of the 1990s had a shattering effect on Cuba. The government's siege austerity measures, for what it described as a **Special Period in Peacetime**, filled the streets with bicycles and the petrol stations with queues of Ladas. With no transport for either musicians or audiences to get to concerts and lengthy power cuts, the professional life of Havana's entertainers was dramatically curtailed.

Relief, when it came, was due to the combined and mutually promoting phenomena of a huge upsurge in **tourism** to Cuba and a boom in international interest in Cuban music. The latter, due to both the World Music and the salsa dance crazes across the globe, meant that Cuban bands were more in demand than ever before, and able to play to non-Latin audiences in a parallel circuit to that of the Latin public. The desire to employ Cubans was enhanced at

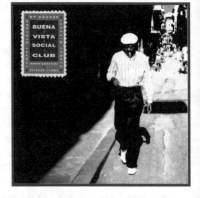

first by the low rates of pay they were willing to accept, although by the end of the millennium, with the huge commercial success of the **Buena Vista Social Club** project, this situation was changing.

At the same time, aided by the romantic and fashionable image of its music on one hand, and its affordability as a holiday destination within the Caribbean on the other, Cuba became, once again, a major tourist attraction, welcoming thousands of French, Italians, Germans, a good many Canadians and British, and an increasing number of US citizens willing to disregard their Government's ban on non-essential travel to Cuba. Desperate for finance, Castro embraced both tourism and music as new hard currency generating industries and, while vociferously rejecting any *glasnost* or *perestroika* for Cuba, introduced liberalizing reforms to encourage business. These included signing joint venture agreements with Spanish hotel and catering groups, which resulted in a dramatic expansion and renovation of Havana's decrepit Iron Curtain hotel stock, legalizing the possession of dollars (once punishable by five years imprisonment), allowing musicians much greater freedom in arranging to tour and record abroad, and facilitating the needs of foreign record companies in Havana.

The beginning of the new millennium, then, saw Cuban music in excellent shape. Abroad, Cuban bands toured more than ever before, including in the US. The 25-year ban on commercial Cuban concerts in the US crumbled to the point where a group such as **Cubanismo**, led by the trumpeter **Jésus Alemañy**, was able to spend almost three-quarters of the year successfully touring the US, while still based in Havana. At home, the worst rigours of the Special Period had been alleviated, with the music business having played a significant role in the country's salvation. The Copa Room of the Hotel Riviera, briefly renamed El Palacio de la Salsa, buzzed again with international music tourists. At Havana's "International Record Fair" **Cuba disco 2000**, the talk was of Cuba transforming its founding role in Latin-American music into real music business leadership. Optimistic perhaps, but by no means an impossible dream.

2

The African Heritage

African culture in modern Cuba is a kaleidoscopic mixture of history and myth, tradition and improvisation, the most secret lore and the most flagrant kitsch. Anyone who's attended one of Havana's cabarets, from the glossy tourist-haunt **Tropicana** down to the little Cuban-audience version in the basement of the **Teatro Nacional**, will have witnessed Afro-Cuba in all its most gloriously sequin-spangled extravagance.

Sandwiched between some Soviet-era acrobatic troupe and a medley of classic boleros, the regulation chorus of G-string-clad dancers will flock on stage caparisoned in swathes of gauze and ostrich feathers in the colours of one or other of a series of deities of the religious cult known as **santería**. Meanwhile, a squad of three or four drummers playing tall vertical conga drums augments the house band and a male lead singer wails out complex chants in a clearly non-European language and is answered by a massed chorus.

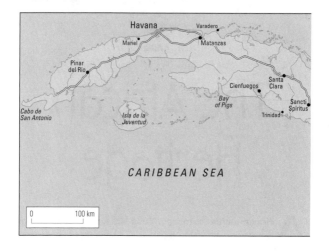

Africa's religious cults

Often a central feature of the choreography is a stylized representation of some of the *orishas* of santería, a religion based on the religious cults of the **Yoruba** peoples of West Africa, origin of many of Cuba's slaves. The orishas are divinities, each distinguished by human character traits, specific histories, areas of activity, emblematic colours, favourite foods and individual gaits, mimicked in dance. **Yemayá**, queen mother and ruler of the seas, sumptuous in blue and white, sways on, rippling her long skirts like the waves. **Ogún**, the god of war, forges and metalwork, in black and green clashes his twin machetes fiercely, followed by **Changó**, the god of thunder, passion and virility, leaping with erotic aggression in red and white, and

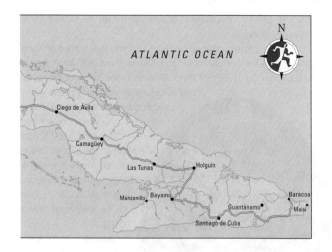

Ochún, the Yoruba Venus, flirtatious and feminine in golden yellow with a crown of brass.

Santería, also known as *La Regla de Ocha*, or the rule of the gods, is based on a synthesis of different elements of Yoruba religion, which itself consisted of a range of similar but distinct cults. All share the central tenet of a distant, uncommunicative supreme being, equivalent to the Christian God named **Olofí** or **Olodumare** in santería whose intermediaries with humanity are the orishas. The orishas can interact with men by taking possession of human acolytes during the **bembé** ceremonies, the Cuban equivalent of Haitian voodoo, or Brazilian *candomblé*. Like voodoo and candomblé, santería fuses **Christianity** with Yoruba religion. Partly by assimilation, and partly to placate, or simply deceive, the slave-mas-

ters and priests, the slaves' orishas came to be twinned with Christian saints.

Changó's Christian alter ego is Saint Barbara: the duo are celebrated in one of the country music star **Celina Gonzalez'** most famous songs, while Ogún is Saint Peter. Yemaya is the Virgin of Regla, the old harbour-side barrio of Havana whose church contains a much-venerated statue of the Virgin copied from one in Chipiona, near Cádiz, point of origin of many Spanish ships arriving in Cuba, and Ochún is the *Virgin de la Caridad del Cubre*, the patron saint of Cuba.

Babalú-ayé, the orisha of illness, depicted on crutches with sore-covered legs licked by dogs, is twinned with St Lazarus. One of Havana's most impressive manifestations of santería occurs every December 17, St Lazarus' feast day, when a huge procession winds its way through the outskirts of Havana, some of the participants on their knees, to the chapel of the former leper hospital of St Lazarus, now an epidemiological clinic. Bubonic pustules notwithstanding, Babalú-ayé has also forged a career as one of the

JULIO ETCHART

Showgirl and saint

most prolific showbusiness *santos*. The orishas have appeared in commercial Cuban music for much of the twentieth century. The singer **Miguelito Valdés**, who brought the conga to New York in the 1940s, acquired the nickname "Mr Babalú" with his version of a song to Babalú-ayé written by Margarita Lecuona, before the young **Desi Arnaz** usurped his position and became even more successful with it. The most recent show at the Tropicana features a Cuadro Negro (Negro Tableau) – consisting of this song, plus folkloric songs to Babalú-ayé and Oddua and a Lucumí Dance by **Ernesto Lecuona**, Cuba's most eminent composer, and a pioneer in the 1920s of incorporating what came to be known as Afro-Cuban themes into serious music.

Afro-Cuban religion was not in fact studied properly until the twentieth century. The great jurist, historian and ethnographer **Fernando Ortiz** is generally credited with having first analysed Cuba's negro society seriously with the publication of his book *Hampa Afrocubana, Los Negros Brujos* (Afro-Cuban Underworld, Negro Witchcraft) in 1906. It was as a result of Ortiz's work that the term Afro-Cuban came into usage. In 1936 Ortiz arranged for the first public exhibitions and performances of the sacred **batá drums** used in Yoruba ceremonies.

The world of African-based culture which Ortiz and his successors began to describe is extremely complicated. Slaves were imported from a range of ethnic groups throughout West and Central Africa, and time had a double effect in mutating this complex mix. Firstly, the original tribal languages were gradually forgotten; although many African words and phrases exist in modern Cuba, very few Cubans can speak, say, Yoruba. Secondly, the process of creolization meant that elements of different cults and languages began to mingle, so that a pure line of descent of, for example, a musical style is almost impossible to trace.

Nonetheless, various distinct broad traditions still exist in Afro-Cuban culture. The **Lucumí** tradition of the big Yoruba population of the Ulkumi area of what is modern Nigeria is supported by a similar strand descending from emigrants from old Dahomey, modern-day Benin, but speaking the Arará language. Both Yoruba and Arará phrases might occur in one santería ceremony, while further cults exist mixing Yoruba and other non-African beliefs, for example, *lucumí cruzado*, which mixes santería with spiritualism. A third part of the pre-Nigeria region, near the river Calabar, was the source of the **Carabalí** population of Cuba, whose culture is the chief ingredient of one of the most striking Afro-Cuban sects, the **Abakuá** secret societies. Adherents of these all-male groups, also known as *ñañigos*, wear striped pointed-topped, all enveloping *diablito* (little devil) costumes which represent spirits called *ireme*, for their ceremonial dances, and, like the Masons, place loyalty to fellow-members above obligations to society and the law.

Partly due to this policy, and an association in the minds of the authorities with crime and insurgency, the ñañigos' history is chequered with interdictions and police persecution, both colonial and independent. Like all Afro-descended clans, groups and religions, the Abakuá have their own drums, the most sacred of which, the *ekué*, a rubbed drum, is played concealed behind a curtain. In spite of their secrecy, elements of the Abakuá's lore have entered Cuban culture in general, not least linguistically: the ubiquitous modern Latin American phrase "*Chévere!*" meaning, roughly, "Great!" is ñañigo in origin.

South of modern Nigeria, the tribes of the Congo Basin, linguistically classed together as **Bantú**, provide another important strand of Afro-Cuban lore, particularly prevalent in the sugar provinces of **Matanzas** and **Las Villas**. Here, some of the most directly African

percussion is still found, the *yuka* drums used in the rural *makuta* dance. Other early Cuban *guajira* instruments such as the *marimbula* (metal-pronged thumb piano) or the spectacular *tumbadera* (earth-bass) are of Congolese origin. Also proceeding from the Bantú tradition, the syncretic religious cults equivalent to santería are known variously as the **Regla de Palo Monte**, in which the Yoruba orishas have equivalents such as Sarabanda (of Ogun), Balaundé (Yemaya), El Viejo

Santería altar and offerings

Luleno (Babalú-ayé) and Siete Rayos, or Seven Rays, the paleros' version of Changó/Santa Barbara. Also known as Kimbisa and Mayombé, the Palo Monte rites include much more emphasis on the invocation of evil spirits to harm enemies than does santería, and the santero *babalawos* (priests) consequently devote a significant part of their repertoire of spells and divination to counteracting *mayombero brujería* (witchcraft).

21

Bembés

Among the musical manifestations of santería, the most important occur in the ceremonies referred to as **bembés** and *toques para los santos*, in which the initiates of the congregation dance and are possessed by the orishas to whom they owe obeisance. They are directed by three drummers, known as *olubatá*, playing the rhythms of the different orishas to call them down, while a lead singer, the *akpwon*, chants the liturgy of the saints, answered by the *ankorí*, or chorus. The three long slim drums of santería are called batá drums, and in Africa, were dedicated to one orisha, Changó, but later came to dominate santero ceremony in general. True batá drums were always constructed by dedicated drum-makers, anointed for sacred use, and kept only for this purpose. The rhythms they play mimic the intonations of Yoruba phrases, and in this sense they are "talking drums".

Fernando Ortiz traces the appearance of genuine batá drums in Cuba back to the early nineteenth century, three hundred years after the first Lucumí slaves arrived, and considers this occurred as a result of the defeat of the Lucumí by the Fula, when enslaved Lucumí drummakers began to be sold for shipment to Cuba. In this way sets of the three slim double-headed drums, the small *okónkolo*, the mid-sized *itótele* and the big *iyá*, or mother drum, began to appear among the burgeoning santero groups. It was more than a century before batá drums began to make an appearance in secular dance music, in groups such as the Orquesta of **Elio Revé**, by which time santería had become a frequent theme in Cuban popular music, promoted by such artists as Miguelito Valdés, and later **Celia Cruz**, who recorded Homenaje albums to Yemayá and to Los Santos in the 1960s. By the 1990s, santería was booming in Cuban popular music, with the small coloured bead wristbands indicating allegiance to an orisha common among bandmembers, and great hits like Adalberto Alvarez' huge "¿Y

Que Tu Quieres Que Te Den?" (What do you want them to give you?),
the "them" referring to the saints. By the end of the millennium, santería had named its first rap group, the Cuban-French **Orishas**.

Cuba's secular music

The slowly coalescing musical life of Cuba's Africans also gave birth
to **secular styles**. Key institutions for both sacred and profane
music-making were the **cabildos** (associations) which the slaves
were permitted to set up. Originally these were meeting places in the
churches where slaves could congregate during their minimal free
time. Later the slaves began to occupy their own buildings, usually
by law, outside town boundaries, where the members, generally of
similar ethnic origin, could meet to hold religious ceremonies, organize basic mutual aid activities, and celebrations for feast-days. At
the end of the nineteenth century, the Law of Associations obliged
the cabildos to adopt Catholic names such as Society of Saint
Lazarus. This Christianization was reinforcing pressure on the syn-
cretization of santería. Cabildo houses can still be found in the suburbs of Cuban cities, often a simple, one-room building with a table-
altar at one end, a niche where drums are kept, perhaps some
benches, the walls adorned with flags and inscriptions.

The most important non-religious musical activities of the members
of the cabildos were the occasions when slaves were allowed to cele-
brate in public. These centred round the nascent **carnivals**, and the
Catholic feast of the Epiphany, also known as the **Day of Kings**, on
January 6. Nineteenth-century accounts of the Day of Kings festivities
in Havana and Matanzas, and a much-referred-to canvas by the *cos-
tumbrista* painter **Landaluze**, describe groups of black Cubans,
dressed in an assortment of African costumes and imitations of the
bourgeoisie's finery, dancing and playing for alms on tall conga-like

drums outside the houses of the rich. Among the dance movements recorded is a sort of restrained demonstration of female modesty in which the cockerel-like attentions of a courting male dancer are warded off by the female chastely holding her voluminous crinolined skirts in front of her. This, according to the musicologist Raúl Martínez Rodriguez, was an early example of a *rumba de calle*, street rumba – the forerunner of the genre of Afro-Cuban music whose name (often mis-spelt rhumba) was wrongly attached to son-based Cuban music and which became a craze across the world in the 1920s.

If the rumba de calle was a relatively decorous affair, its private version, held in a cabildo house, a sugar-estate workers' dormitory

CRISTINA PIZA

A street rumba

or, later, a *solar* (the central patio of a city tenement block), was more boisterous. With the abolition of slavery, poor blacks had more opportunity to meet and make music, although rumba dances still required the permission of the police.

The birth of rumba

According to the writer and percussionist **Tony Evora**, rumba percussion grew out of multiple traditions, including the yuka drums, ceremonial marches of the Abakuá societies and the various Congo musics. In fact, the traditional rumba drums were not drums at all, but *cajones* – crates that had been used to import *bacalao* (salt cod) and candles from Europe. The use of large, thus deeper, bacalao crates and smaller, high-pitched candle crates eventually became formalized, with the boxes taken apart, fine-tuned and reassembled. Modern professional rumba groups still use specially made versions but the lack of an alternative was the original reason for their use.

Rumba grew up originally in the communities around the great sugar mills of **Matanzas** and **Havana**. The dockers of Matanzas later provided another fertile rumba breeding ground and Matanzas is still regarded as the home of the rumba. The term rumba covers three groups of dances, with their own musical accompaniments, always combinations of lead and choral voices, cajones or drums, a *cata* (a slit cane played with sticks), a *maraga* (a sort of iron rattle), and often a wood block played with spoons. The drums which replaced cajones were either special *tambores de rumba*, tall curved barrel drums with single nailed-on leather heads, or later, the *tumbadoras*, similar but with tension screws, which also came to be called congas. Whatever the style of instrument, the important lead improvising drum is called the *quinto*.

The less practised styles of rumba are known as the **columbia** and the **yambú**. The columbia is probably the oldest form, born in the late eighteenth century in the countryside, around the sugar town of Unión de Reyes, south of Matanzas. It is a dance for men only, designed to show off virtuosity, and to enhance its macho character dancers sometimes balance glasses of beer on their heads, or fasten knives to their ankles like the spurs of fighting cocks. The columbia was also known as *timba*, the term adopted in the 1990s by a new wave of Havana dance bands to describe their sound. The yambú, another old form of the genre, is a couple dance, relatively slow and sauntering, in which the movements are often said to mimic those of old people.

The form of rumba which has come to dominate the genre is **guaguancó**, a couple dance in which the male, with explicit pelvic thrusts, attempts a symbolic sexual possession of the female, who avoids his advances with graceful twirls, and handfuls of skirt gathered in front of her groin. The aim of the man is to consummate the *vacunao*, "vaccination" of the woman. A guaguancó always begins with a solo voice singing the *diana*, a long wailing series of meaningless syllables taken

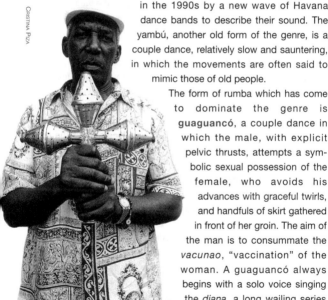

CRISTINA PIZA

Agogo, traditional rumba percussion

up by the chorus, before the percussion gradually begins, and, having reached a certain point of momentum, the rumba "breaks out".

Rumba was traditionally an amateur activity, although legendary rumberos of the past fill the lore. The most famous is **Malanga**, a dancer named José Rosario Oviedo from Unión de Reyes whose death in 1923 is supposed to have been due to poisoning with ground glass by jealous rivals. The great jazz percussionist **Chano Pozo** is among Cuban musicians who have written songs about Malanga. Although compositions such as Pozo's in the fields of jazz and dance music were sometimes influenced by guaguancó, it was not until the 1950s that rumba began to be performed professionally by government folkloric troupes and by special rumba bands. The first, and still the most famous of these, is the **Muñequitos de Matanzas**, but many now exist. In May 2000, several dozen, including an all-women band in mini-skirts and stiletto heels, took part in a 24-hour attempt to perform "the world's longest rumba" at the Tropical outdoor dancehall in Havana. Modern rumba is in fact a flourishing art form, practised at a variety of levels. The old informal Sunday afternoon solar rumbas, with improvised percussion, still exist, but are not widespread. There are regular public rumba displays, partly for tourists but still authentic, such as the long-standing *Sábado de la Rumba* (Saturday Rumba) near Havana Cathedral.

Government ballet and folkloric troupes incorporate rumba into their repertoires, as do the numerous cabarets from the Tropicana down, and the personnel of the latter two often overlap. The top professional rumba groups, such as the Muñequitos de Matanzas, who were one of the few groups to play in the US at the height of the embargo, or **Los Papines**, who starred in the international touring version of the Tropicana show, have serious showbusiness careers.

The Cuban musical panorama still includes other forms descended from activities of the Africans' cabildos. The *coros de clave* (clave choirs) have now almost died out, except as part of the names of rumba groups such as **Clave y Guaguancó**. These groups met, like the early rumberos, in cabildo houses or solares, but placed increasing emphasis on singing rather than dancing, partly as a response to the difficulty of obtaining permission to hold drumming fiestas from suspicious authorities. The repertoire of late-nineteenth-century coros de clave such as **El Pañuelo Blanco**, **Los Jovenes Lindos** and **La Dulzura de Amalia**, included African-descended chants and songs, but also songs taken from the *teatro bufo* and the patriotic songs relating at that time to the Cuban War of Independence.

CRISTINA PIZA

Rumba dancers with tumbadora drummers

While the last full clave choirs died out in the 1960s, the *tumba francesa*, a form of African-derived percussion peculiar to the city of Santiago, still survives. The adjective *francesa* (French) relates to the language of the drums' owners, rather than their nationality: they were the slaves brought from Haiti after the Haitian Revolution, often therefore descended predominantly from the Fon and Ewe tribes of what is now Togo, Benin and Ghana. The colourfully decorated sets of big squat drums they constructed were used in societies, which, like the other cabildos, combined social, religious and musical functions.

Carnivals and conga bands

While the slave celebrations centred around the **Día de Reyes**, and the pre-Lent period slightly later, developed into private rumba gatherings, they also gave rise, after the abolition of slavery, to major street festivities, the fore-runners of the *carnavales*, or **carnivals**. By the end of the nineteenth century, the cabildos would parade through the streets drinking cane spirit, extravagantly costumed and playing a wide variety of drums, scrapers and rattles, whistles, blown conch shells, donkeys' jawbones and beaten frying pans and competing with each other in colour and élan. Eventually the groups formalized into what became known as *comparsas*, carnival bands more or less along present-day lines. These recruited members who met throughout the year to make costumes and props and rehearse for their annual outings. By the early decades of the twentieth century, the two great carnivals of **Havana** and **Santiago** were major civic events, attracting sponsorship from alcohol manufacturers such as Bacardi in Santiago and Cristal Beer in Havana. The Bacardi bat symbol was omnipresent in the street decorations of the pre-Revolution Santiago Carnival. Sponsors also paid for the floats which began to parade with the comparsas, and which began to carry their own popular

bands: in the 1950s and 1960s, the singer **Ibrahim Ferrer**'s most immutable annual booking was on a float in Havana Carnival with the group Los Bocucos and later at the great dinner given for the revellers and entertainers by the Cristal Brewery.

Among the street-level carnival comparsas, the chief source of music was, and still is, the massed groups of percussionists known as **congas**, and the word conga came to denote both one of the most common drums of general use in Cuba, and the main dance step performed by the comparsas as they marched. The tall, slim conga drum is more correctly described as a *tumbadora*, since the drums used for conga were originally large flat discs, suspended by bands around the players' shoulders, and known as *bombos*, *galletas* or *piloneras*. The tumbadora, originally with its single hide head tensioned by a spirit lamp, later modernized with screw tensioners, was adapted for convenience and, because of its association with carnival conga use, has come to be referred to generally in the non-Latin world as a conga, even though that name applies in theory only to a drum specifically for carnival conga use.

The conga bands were augmented with two brass instruments: the **trumpet** and the **Chinese cornet**, the latter originally adapted by the members of the great nineteenth-century immigration of Chinese labourers to Havana, but whose strident, bagpipe-like skirl is nowadays more associated with Santiago's big July 25 Carnival.

The **conga dance** was both simple and visually striking, with its three steps followed by a kick to the side, and for this reason spread far beyond its Cuban carnival context, when popularized internationally by stars such as **Desi Arnaz** in the 1930s and 1940s, and the **Miami Sound Machine** in the 1980s.

Within Cuba, the conga remains essentially a street fiesta music, although certain groups such as the **Hermanos Bravo** have devel-

oped the rhythm into a more sophisticated arranged style. As for the Cuban carnival, it survives, as elsewhere in the Caribbean and Latin America, as a rich multi-level people's art form, despite having almost perished during the financial crisis of the early 1990s. The orishas continue to be part of it – just as they are of the great cabarets, and of a regular seam of popular music – one of the many manifestations of Africa in Cuba.

Artists

Hermanos Bravo

The original brothers Bravo – Juan, Felix and Tony – were three members of a Santiago family who started their musical career in the 1950s, playing the full range of popular styles, before deciding to focus on the conga in the early 1960s, when the percussionist Marcos "Marquitos" Barnet joined the group. At the time this was novel: although the conga was a vital part of carnival, and conga songs had been part of the repertoire of great artists such as Miguel Matamoros and Miguelito Valdes, no popular professional groups made it their principal repertoire, partly due, no doubt, to its rather simplistic rhythmic formula, which without considerable subtlety can be boring on stage.

The Hermanos Bravo used a line-up of conga drums and traditional Oriente conga percussion, the bombo bass drum, the flat galleta pan drum, the sharp improvising quinto, cowbells plus an

acoustic guitar, alto saxophone and the Chinese cornet typical of Santiago carnival, along with harmony vocal choruses to create a lively, danceable sound, but one with sufficient melody and sophistication to work as a stage performance. The Bravo's act became highly successful: songs such as "Hasta Santiago A Pie", "La Batea" and "Tirala por el Balcón" became nationally known and the band began to tour regionally and as far as Europe, the US and Japan.

In 1992, with the death of two members, the band stopped performing for several years, but soon re-formed under the leadership of Tony Bravo, with a new generation of Bravo brothers – **Esteban**, **Juan**, **Alfredo** and **Jorge** – handling percussion and vocals, and adding an inventive and distinctive new saxophonist, **Enrique Delgado Garro**. The new Hermanos Bravo seem to have timed their formation well; the song

Bravo brothers with conga percussion

YOURI LENQUETTE

"Que Baila La Habana" was immediately popular, winning first prize at Havana Carnival in 1997 and inspiring something of a conga revival.

⊙ **Conga Tu Carnaval**   Tumi, UK

The first new recording for over a decade, containing a selection of classic old hits and new numbers, including the 1997 hit "Que Baila La Habana", with its thudding bombo drum, galloping conga rhythm, curious male voice choir vocals and Enrique Delgado's enchanting sax playing. Other tracks are arcane hybrids, such as merengue-conga, conga-calypso, conga-sones and chachacha-congas, or sub-strands of conga, such as the Santiago *cocuyé*, which features the wild skirl of a Chinese cornet played by one Emilio "Yucayo" Hechavarría. Other guests on this unusual and enjoyable record include the eminent conga-player (in the non-carnival sense), Tata Güines, and members of the Orquesta America on bass, piano, violins, flute and extra percussion.

Grupo AfroCuba

If the Muñequitos de Matanzas were the pioneers in performing rumba professionally, their fellow Matanceros, the group nowadays called **AfroCuba**, makes a powerful claim to being the first to incorporate rumba and a whole range of other percussion forms into a repertoire of great scope and depth. The twelve members of AfroCuba, who also take costume to spectacular heights – now in brilliant flounced *guarachera* sleeves, now in white sailor's or santero's outfits – perform not only the three styles of rumba, but other styles, notably *arará*, *iyesá*, *bantú*, *abakuá* and *güiro* music, all using the special instruments associated with each genre.

Their speciality is **batárumba** – a combination of rumba cajones and the sacred batá drums – which they claim to have invented in 1973, when the most recent reorganization of the group took place.

Although earlier experiments incorporating batá drums into secular music had taken place, these had always simply placed sections of batá music quotes, as it were, in new settings. AfroCuba, however, use the section of batás as fully integrated elements of the percussion range. Batárumba was the innovation of artistic director **Francisco "Minini" Zamora Chirino**, who also sings lead voice, while other members include former Muñequitos star **Esteban Lantriz "Saldiguera"**.

The group was founded in the town of Pueblo Nuevo in Matanzas province in 1957 by a nucleus of members from a carnival comparsa named Los Guajiros who were impressed by the success of the group now known as Los Muñequitos. AfroCuba were successively known as Guaguancó Neopoblano, Conjunto Cuba and Folklore Matancero before arriving at their present name.

⊙ **Raíces Africanos**   Shanachie, US

The first full-length studio album by AfroCuba, made in 1996 at Egrem in Havana, showcasing a full range of the group's rhythms, from their famous batárumba to guaguancós, yambús and columbias, and including a güiro (a style of music using *shekeres* – cowry-strung gourds), a piece for bembé drums (unusual and distinct from batá), an ensemble of abakuá drums, and a rare example of a *brikamo* rite – an ancient Carabalí ritual regarded as an antecedent of the abakuá's culture and nowadays restricted (according to the excellent CD booklet) almost to a single family.

Clave y Guaguancó

A long-standing Havana-based group, the **Conjunto Clave y Guaguancó** began to achieve its present prominence in the 1980s, under the directorship of current leader, **Amado de Jesús Dedeu**

Hernández. Dedeu was born in 1945 in Havana and learned to sing rumba, according to Helio Orovio, from local rumba notables, Miguelito "Cheo el Muerto" and Santos Ramirez "El Niño". At the same time he was initiated into the santería religion, eventually reaching the rank of babalawo (see p.21). The third element of his training was academic, studying music at the Escuela de Superación Profesional Ignacio Cervantes and taking ethnological advice from the major Afro-Cuban studies figures Argeliers León and

Odilio Urfé, among others. Dedeu began performing with the rumba group Armandito y su Grupo, moved to the directorship of the Coro Folklórico, then Clave y Guaguancó, at which point he succeeded – with the aid of two of his musical children – in transformng the dozen-strong group into a powerful and progressive presence, and an active international touring operation.

⊙ **Dejala en La Puntica**   The Music Network, Germany

Eleven good tracks, mainly guaguancós, but also variations including guarapachanga, bataguacolumbia, guanbatá, a nice leisurely melodic yambú and a guanpoliritmo, or rap-guaguancó.

| ⊙ Noche de la Rumba | Tumi, UK |

A star-studded 1998 production, including even more arcane hybrids: batácompoli, catumba, a tonadaguaguancó "para Celina", presumably dedicated to the guajìra star Celina Gonzalez, whose repertoire included the old Spanish-derived tonada form, and a flameguambatá, which is not an exotic ice-cream concoction, but a combination of flamenco, courtesy of the guitarist Nolberto Rodriguez Gonzalez, with guaguancó and batá drums. This is an interesting experiment, given that some theorists see in rumba's vocal line an Africanized interpretation of flamenco song. Special guests include the top percussionist Changuito, Celeste Mendoza, in one of her last recordings before her death, and the poet and actor Eloy Machado, "El Ambia", whose verse in memory of Mendoza, "daughter of Ochún and tambolera (drummer) from Heaven", adorns the sleeve.

Celeste Mendoza

A remarkable singer with an extraordinary life, **Celeste Mendoza** acquired the tag "Queen of Guaguancó" in the early 1960s at the height of her popularity, when, in the middle of a tour of the US and Latin America, she returned to Havana and appeared as a guest of Beny Moré at the Ali Bar, where his band was resident. With a power-ful and agile contralto voice, Mendoza excelled at the guaguancó, but she was a showbusiness all-rounder who also recorded good sones and boleros. She also pioneered a range of new hybrids, notably the *bolero-guapachá* and the *ranchera-mambo*, the latter a response to the fashion in 1950s Cuba for Mexican ranchera music. Mendoza was born in 1903 in Santiago and began to sing in her early teens. Shortly after her family moved to Havana in 1943, she appeared on *CMQ radio* singing the popular Orlando Guerra guaracha "El Marañon". Soon afterwards she found professional

work as a dancer in the seaside cabaret, "Mi Bohio", in Marianao, then in the pioneering Afro-centric company Batamú, finally graduating to the spectacular shows of top choreographer "Rodney" Neyras at the Tropicana, where she appeared on stage with Josephine Baker and Carmen Miranda.

In 1956, Mendoza had great success, recording and appearing with the **Ernesto Duarte orchestra** on the top Havana station *Radio Progreso*, and touring internationally. In 1965 she appeared with the **Orquesta Aragon** and **Los Zafiros** as part of the show *Gran Music Hall de Cuba* at the Olympia in Paris, one of the most important post-Revolution demonstrations of Cuba's popular music in Europe.

At the end of the 1960s, Mendoza's career flagged and, amid persistent rumours that she was an alcoholic and had been placed under house arrest for killing a lover, Mendoza spent a number of years out of the public eye. She returned in the 1980s to perform at festivals and then to record with considerable success in 1990 with the son revival group **Sierra Maestra**. In 1992 she performed in Spain with a similar group, **Raisón**. At the end of the decade, she continued to record, completing guest appearances on the album *La Noche de la Rumba* with 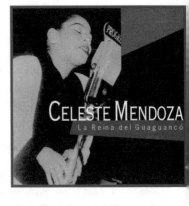 **Clave y Guaguancó**, taking part in the sessions armed with rum and a succession of cigars, and always coiffed in one of her trademark

turbans. She was preparing for another record with Los Papines when she was found dead alone in her eighteenth-floor apartment in Central Havana in November 1998.

⊙ **La Reina del guaguancó**   Virgin, Spain

An excellent compilation of highlights from Mendoza's later career, including plenty of guaguancós, but also sones, guarachas and boleros, recorded with a first-class Egrem house big band in 1989, with Sierra Maestra in 1990 and with Los Papines in 1996. Good sleeve notes and a short montage of vintage photos.

⊙ **Boleros Con Aché**   Musica del Sol, Spain

A classic album from the mid-1950s' height of Mendoza's career, recorded with the Orquesta of Bebo Valdés, at that time on superb form. A mix of guaguancós, boleros and the interestingly wide variety of marginal genres that characterized Mendoza's repertoire, a merengue, a tango-bolero, a Peruvian waltz and a Mexican-Cuban hybrid corrido-guaguancó, "Que Me Castigue Dios", which was one of the greatest hits of her career.

Los Muñequitos de Matanzas

The little dolls of Matanzas' critical role in the history of the rumba of their city, Matanzas, was to make it a professional, public style of music: in the early 1950s, when the group was formed, rumba was still a private, amateur affair. At that time, Cuba possessed one other rumba group, based in Havana, named Vive Blen. The **Muñequitos** were created originally under the name Guaguancó Matancero in 1956 by the songwriter **Florencio Calle**, the singer **Esteban "Saldiguera" Lantri**, the choral singers **Juan Mesa** and "Virulilla", and drummers including **Gregorio Diaz** (who is still with the group). The new name was a result of the Muñequitos' first local hit record, "Muñequitos de Matanzas", released on a small Cuban label Puchito,

which left audiences calling out the phrase at their performances, and the change of name was inevitable.

The Muñequitos' repertoire includes many songs written by the members, particularly **Juan Mesa**, and the fluctuating personnel of the dozen-strong group is always recruited from the cream of the crop of family-linked rumberos. The Muñequitos were one of the first pure rumba groups to visit Europe, playing in London in 1989. They were prominent among the rare Cuban groups to perform in the United States at the height of the embargo in the early 1990s.

⊙ Los Muñequitos de Matanzas   Qbadisc, US
and Folklore Matancero

A repackaged album, originally recorded in 1970 in Havana, re-mastered in the 1990s and equipped with an outstanding new cover illustration by one José Rodriguez. Features both the Muñequitos, on excellent form, with some nice harmonies and a strong clear sound, and the group Folklore Matancero, which was the name until three years later of Gruop AfroCuba (see p.33).

⊙ Congo Yambumba   Qbadisc, US

Exciting virtuoso percussion, full of heavy shekeres, babbling quinto drums, plus voices, recorded originally in the then new Siboney studio in Santiago in 1983, including among the selection

of guaguancós (mainly), yambús, columbias and abakuá songs, a few verses of one of the most improbable Afro-Cuban themes imaginable, "Jingle Bells".

Los Papines

A quartet of brothers who have taken rumba to its heights of night-club success, **Los Papines** have managed to retain their authenticity without concentrating unduly on the ethno-musicological aspect of things (although on occasion they have given workshops outside Cuba, for example, in Puerto Rico). In the 1950s, **Luis**, **Alfredo** and **Jesús Abreu** were playing in a variety of different bands in the Marianao district, while the eldest brother, **Ricardo**, nicknamed "Papín", ran his own group, Papín y sus Rumberos, which eventually took on the other three brothers. Shortly after this, when the group appeared on the television programme *Noche Cubana*, it was suggested they change their name to Los Papines. In 1959 they began working with the orquesta of Havana's top hotel, the Nacional, under the musical direction of the trumpeter **Leonardo Timor**. Within a decade, their slick, expert, entertaining performances, usually in bow-ties and sequinned dinner jackets, led to considerable demand at home and abroad, always playing a pared-down virtuoso rumba: they also began to perform as backing for singing stars of the stature of Celeste Mendoza. In 1969, they were the first group to take live rumba to Japan, where they played for a highly successful three-month season using batá drums. Unusually, however, they do not regard themselves as experts in Yoruba sacred music. In 1998, the Papines appeared as a guest act in the cast of the Tropicana touring revue, which included performances at London's Royal Albert Hall.

The Abreu brothers, or Los Papines

⊙ **Tambores Cubanos**   Egrem, Cuba

The Papines have never been prolific solo recording artists, although they crop up regularly on rumba and percussion compilations, and guesting on other people's records. This relatively early record is still theoretically in print, with the foursome posing over their stacked multi-hued conga drums on the cover, typical of Cuban-style sleeve art. There is a good range of rumbas here plus rarer items of repertoire such as a *chambelona*.

Lázaro Ros

Lázaro Ros, the "Akpwon of Cuba" (see p.22), is the country's best-known public practitioner of santería music, and a researcher, teacher and innovator of great renown. He was born in Havana in 1925, attended ceremonies from his childhood at the santería house of Otilia

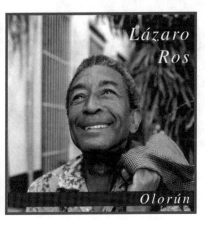

Lázaro Ros

Olorún

Mantecón, and was initiated into the Regla de Ocha in 1950, receiving the name Osha Nieve, meaning "saint of the mountain". He was instructed in the cantos by the akpwon Eugenio de la Rosa, and practised Yoruba sacred singing throughout the 1950s, supporting himself as a cook and shop assistant. Soon after the Revolution, Ros received government support as a cultural researcher, and

worked with the famous ethnologist **Argeliers León**. In 1962 he was one of the founding artists of the **National Folkloric Ensemble**, with which he still works: the Cuban government, though keen to support previously denigrated Afro-Cuban rites, was committed to official atheism and the fight against what it regarded as superstition, so Yoruba sacred ritual was officially regarded as "folklore".

Ros lives in Guanabacoa and continues to perform with the Folkloric Ensemble, as well as the National Ballet of Cuba, and to co-

operate with institutions such as the National Symphony Orchestra of Matanzas. In addition to performing and recording purely ritual music, often with the group of young acolytes he founded, Olorún, Ros has been adventurous in recording traditional cantos with experimental backing, including with the jazz-rock groups **Sintesis** and **Mezcla**, and with **Chucho Valdés** and his group **Irakere**.

⊙ **Olorún**   Xenophile, US

A well-produced and recorded traditional cycle of cantos to eleven orishas, opening as always with Elegba and concluding with Changó. The batá drum section is directed by Carlos Aldama, a pupil of the early master Jesús Perez, one of the drummers who served as a vehicle for Fernando Ortiz to introduce santería music to the outside world, and a large ankorí of mixed adults and children.

⊙ **Cantos**   Intuition, Germany

Ros's 1992 collaboration with the jazz-rock-traditional group Mezcla and batá drummers including the well-known Eddie Bobé. Here, Elegba is saluted in 1970s Weather Report mode, Ogún receives a jaunty World Music setting, with hints of calypso and soukous, while Changó, appropriately enough, gets the heavy metal treatment. Informative and unusual sleeve notes.

Merceditas Valdés

Like her contemporary Celeste Mendoza (see p.36), **Merceditas Valdés** managed to combine religious and secular Yoruba-based musics with a successful career in international popular entertainment. In the former sphere, she collaborated with Fernando Ortiz for his illustrated lectures on Afro-Cuban music: it was Ortiz who gave her the nickname, "Little Aché", using the Yoruba word for a kind of god-granted personal force or luck. As a secular artist she gave

43

numerous and varied performances in the US, from the Carnegie Hall and the Apollo Theatre in New York where she participated in early Afro-Cuban concerts, to the Hotel Flamingo in Las Vegas.

Valdés was born in the black barrio of Cayo Hueso in Havana in 1928 to a father who sang with the early rumba ensemble Los Roncos, directed by the son pioneer Ignacio Piñeiro. Like Celeste Mendoza, Valdés began to sing in her early teens, appearing on the *Corte Supremo de Arte* (Supreme Court of Art) radio show on *CMQ* at the age of twelve, and later in the 1950s in *Rapsodia Negra* (Negro Rhapsody), the show on *Radio Cadena Suaritos* which controversially pioneered prime-time broadcasting of pure Afro-Cuban music.

Valdés appeared in nightclubs including the Sans Souci and the Tropicana where she worked with major figures from **Bola de Nieve** to **Joseíto Fernandez** and **Beny Moré**, and in the 1970s, with **Los Amigos**, a group including her husband, the timbalero **Guillermo Barreta**, the pianist **Frank Emilio Flynn**, the conga-player **Tata Güines** and the bassist **Cachaíto López**. Valdés died in June 1996.

⊙ **Merceditas Valdés, Volume 2**   Tumi, UK

A traditional chant, percussion and chorus cycle of 14 cantos to orishas, showcasing Valdés' light, mellifluous voice, with some interesting harmonies.

3

The Origins of Son

The first-time visitor to **Havana** may be slightly puzzled by all the references to mountains in Cuban song, given the fact that the city is built on a plain. **Son montuno** (mountain son) for example, is the name commonly given to the island's major song form, although *montuno* also has a less obvious connotation of "wild" or "rustic". It would be remarkable if twenty-four hours passed by in any of the big tourist hotels without a perambulant quartet singing the famous Matamoros number "Son de la Loma" (The Son of the Hills). "Mama, where are the gallant singers from?" asks the verse, and the chorus chimes in, with a word-play on son, "Son – they are – *de la loma* – from the hills, and they sing on the plains."

Then there are the groups named after mountains, like **Sierra Maestra**, the former band of **Juan de Marcos González** (the brains behind the **Buena Vista Social Club** recordings), or the **Septeto Turquino**, named after the Pico Turquino, highest peak in the great Sierra Maestra range. It's no coincidence that both these groups are practitioners of pure old-style son, because the foothills of the Sierra

Maestra, stretching across the eastern foot of Cuba between the cities of Guantánamo, Santiago, Bayamo and Manzanillo, comprise the birthplace of son, the most important genre of Cuban music.

Guajiros

Son came into existence in the nineteenth century, one of a group of styles created among the rural population of *guajiros*, the mulatto peasant farmers. The name guajiro originally applied to the mainland Amerindians who were the first slaves to be imported to Cuba, but subsequently came to denote not only these people, but also descendants of Spanish settlers, the last of the Taínos, and freed or escaped African slaves, who became the new indigenous population of Cuba's eastern hill country. The guajiros lived in little thatched homesteads called *bohios* and were farmers, smoking the fragrant home-made cigars the Taínos had introduced them to, celebrating their *guateques* (parties) with rum, the roasted pig, or the *bacalao* (salt-cod) beloved of their Iberian cousins. Images of the life of the guajiro – straw hats, little chestnut horses, machetes, the setting sun over the cane-fields – still adorn CD sleeves from Havana to New York whenever an old-time country nostalgia is to be evoked.

African and Spanish influences

The musical traits and instruments available to nineteenth-century guajiros came primarily from either **Spain** or **Africa**. From Spain came a variety of song and verse forms, including *coplas* (couplets) and *décimas* (ten-line verses). Both of these developed into improvisational forms, giving rise to the tradition of *controversias* (competitions between improvising versifier-singers). The Spanish also contributed the *zapateo* dance style, a rapid toe-and-heel stamping

dance once performed to the music of stringed instruments, accordions and even the mechanical organs common throughout the countryside but nowadays almost extinct. A variety of stringed instruments came from Spanish stock, apart from the Spanish guitar itself. The Iberian *bandurria* gave rise to the Cuban *laúd*, a sort of mandolin with six sets of double strings. The *tres*, a small guitar with three sets of double strings, was created, according to tradition, in the town of Baracoa, the first models made of wood from boxes of imported salt-cod.

The African antecedents of eastern rural music were predominantly vocal and percussive. The call-and-response style of singing, in

Laúd player

which a lead vocalist's line alternates with a choral one, is usually attributed to Africa. A classic example of this style can be found in the montuno section of a son – the repeated solo set against the rhythmic build-up of the chorus which follows the mellower introductory solo singer's largo. Call-and-response vocal is also present, however, in some Spanish traditional song forms.

The basic percussion elements of son were *clave*, maracas, *güiros* and bongos. The **clave**, two hardwood sticks, one held horizontally across the left hand, beaten with a second held vertically by its tip, seems to have been a genuine Cuban innovation (see p.4). Its function – to pick out the essential anchor rhythm (also known as *clave*) of the music – has become more important as the complexity of Cuban-based tropical music has increased, so that two centuries after its popularization, big salsa orchestras still include the steady syncopated metronome-clop of a *clave*, almost the only instrument never used for improvisation, so fundamental is its regular presence.

If the *clave* was the first new, purely Cuban instrument, the **maracas** represent a legacy from the island's first population. Maracas were used by the Taíno Indians as indeed they were, and are, in traditional societies over a large part of the globe. "Oh Cuba! Oh ritmo de semillas secas!" – rhythm of dry seeds – wrote Federico García Lorca about the rustling, rattling, whispering sway of the maracas, among whose associations Fernando Ortiz discerns sensuality, magic and witchcraft, mystery, the sound of fountains and breeze-stirred fronds.

Originally made of hollowed seed-pods filled with dried seeds, subsequent developments included carved wooden receptacles filled with everything from pebbles to lead shot – an unsuccessful modification as the hard shot rapidly destroy the interior of the maraca – to

An early son septeto

the smart red and black leather-covered items like musical boxing gloves latterly commercialized in New York.

The **güiro** is another musical vegetable, also probably used by both the Caribbean's indigenous population and Africans. An elongated calabash, or piece of wood shaped like one, the güiro's body is striped with horizontal ridges, struck and rubbed with a stick. A metallic version, the guayo, also exists.

Finally, the **bongos**, the linked pair of little drums whose high rattling *repique* (improvisation) has inspired so many onomatopoeic lyrics in Latin songs, from the 1940s' "El Bongosero", noted by Ortiz, "Priquitipó priquitipó po po priquitipó!", to the Willie Chirino hit,

MICHAEL OCHS ARCHIVES

"Bongo", so familiar to late 1990s' salsa dance floors: "Cu cu prá, cu cu prá, cu cu prá." The bongo, too, seems to be a Cuban innovation (although of African origin) which in the reduced size and convenient coupling of the two drums makes transport and playing easy. Originally tensioned by heat – traditional bongo players carried candles or little spirit burners – the hide playing heads were later made taut by screw tighteners, and, as in other drums, hide was replaced by plastic. If the bongo is Cuban, it is a major export success, spreading from its rustic home-made origins, across the entire globe as the virtuoso Afro-Latin percussion instrument par excellence and the star of jazz bands. The bongo is built to be a virtuoso – light, fast and agile, it is capable of playing the complex rhythms of both mambo and Latin jazz.

Regional variations of son

At the beginning of the twentieth century regional and racial variations on the son already existed. A more African sound, known as **changüi**, developed around the cities of Guantánamo and Santiago. The relation between *changüi* and the guajiros' son is likened by the American writer Morton Marks to the situation in Louisiana, where the similar but distinct forms of black *zydeco* and white Cajun music existed in close proximity. *Changüi* used a different line-up: the tres, clave and bongo were accompanied by a *marímbula* – a large thumb-piano similar to a Central African *mbira*, in which the big plucked metal keys produced a sort of early syncopated bass sound – and sometimes by a *botija*, an earthenware jug containing water into whose neck the player blows. *Changüi* sounded denser and rougher than conventional son, and still does. Modern *changüi* groups do not necessarily conform to the old instrumentation, though they do still

tend to come from Guantánamo, the epicentre of *changüi*. The orquesta of the late **Elio Revé**, for example, the top *changüi* purveyor of the late twentieth century, was in charanga format, containing flutes and violins, but also slack-tuned timbales and the semi-sacred African batá drums, giving an unmistakable *changüisero* flavour to the music.

If the tres, guitar, *clave*, *güiro* and bongo were the main instruments of conventional early son, they were joined at times by other, more exotic items: a donkey's jawbone, rubbed with a stick like a *güiro*; the *tumbadera*, or earth bass, consisting of a long bowed stick fixed in the ground, with a cord stretched between its top end and the bottom of a circular resonator-pit in the ground, which is covered by a palm-leaf skin – the pitch of the deep dull note is varied by increasing or lessening the tension on the bowed string.

While Oriente province is universally regarded as the cradle of son, there are other regional son-variants, often created by the movement of agricultural labourers in search of work. A notable example is the *sucu sucu*, from the **Isla de la Juventud**, the big comma-shaped island due south from Havana once known as the Isla de los Piños. Two factors attracted migrant workers to the island and its adjoining area of mainland Cuba. The first was the presence of extensive grapefruit plantations, run by North American firms. The second was the major construction project of the 1920s, the big Modelo Prison (where Fidel Castro was subsequently incarcerated following his first failed coup attempt). Both of these recruited considerable numbers of non-Cuban labourers, primarily from Jamaica and the Cayman Islands. The resultant musical mix included Spanish décima verses, but also sections of lyrics in English, an influx of sharper, choppier non-Cuban rhythms, and an instrumentation based on tres, guitar, bass and bongos but also

Keeping it in the family

By the late 1930s son had spread from Oriente province to Havana and on to New York and Paris. Earth basses and clay jugs didn't make the trip – the new son bands were slick and evolved. Nonetheless, they remain in the memory and even repertoire of certain modern musicians. The **Familia Valera**

including items such as a fruit-cutter's machete used as a scraper, bottles played with spoons, and maracas made of dried flame-tree pods. Like early son, *sucu sucu* is still played today: a notable example is another family-based group, **La Tumbita Criolla of Mongo Rives**.

Miranda is a fascinating example of a living repository of the history of son in one family group, and as such has been much sought after by musicologists. The present-day Valera Miranda Family, a group of six musicians from two generations, is based in Santiago, from where it travels regularly to play abroad. But the wider family is scattered over the farmland of the Cauto valley, which runs between Bayamo and Manzanillo, one of the real heartlands of son. One branch of the family descends from Andalusia and the Canary Islands, another indirectly from African ancestors, primarily Bantú but also secondary immigrants from Haiti and Jamaica. Virtually all of the family's repertoire was passed on at big guateque get-togethers over the decades, and direct links from generation to generation were provided by the presence in the group of figures such as the mother and daughter Catalina and Milla Miranda who jointly passed on a mass of original, hermetic family musical lore from the turn of the twentieth century to the present performers. The Familia's present international repertoire, then, consists of direct transcriptions of old tumbadera parts to double bass, of montunos in Afro-French dialect from eighteenth-century Haiti, regional micro-variations of son such as the *nengón* and the birdsong, songs recounting everything from bohío fires to the departure of Spanish colonial troops.

Son hits Havana

The first step on the path which took classic son from the red-neck culture of eastern Cuba to the basis of Latin dance music worldwide was its implantation in Havana. This is generally regarded as having

occurred at the end of the first decade of the twentieth century, with the movement of troops of the newly constituted Cuban Permanent Army. According to **Helio Orovio**, author of the *Dictionary of Cuban Music*, son was brought to Havana in 1909 in this way. Fernando Ortiz notes that the bongo was brought back to Havana by soldiers sent to Oriente in 1912 to suppress one of the real or exaggerated insurrections that eastern blacks were supposed to have fomented at that period. The musicologist **Radames Giro** finds the army theory simplistic and comments that local musics actually travelled more quickly and regularly around the country than generally acknowledged, with the movements of individual travellers. For example, son was to be heard in the city of Matanzas in 1906, while *sucu sucu* songs were already played in the relatively distant cities of Holguin and Cienfuegos in the 1920s, virtually at the time of their creation in the Isla de los Piños.

Whatever the case, by 1910 son had reached Havana, and it received a mixed reception. For the authorities, it was part of the unruly musical manifestations of Negro culture, along with the various drum musics, and to be strictly controlled. It was necessary to apply for permission to put on popular music events, and this was rarely granted, especially in sensitive areas such as black suburbs like Guanabacoa. Illegal son parties were raided by the guardia civil and the participants arrested. For this reason, son actually became widespread among the black population of Havana only after it had penetrated the higher strata of society.

It did this by virtue of two factors. The first was sheer musical attractiveness. The second was the fact that the new small son groups, with their few inexpensive instruments, were much cheaper than the *orquestas típicas* then in vogue. This was the era of the **danzón**, the stately but rhythmic dance music played by orquestas

composed of violins, flutes, clarinets, brass and timpani (kettle drums) or *pailas*, a smaller version. In the hands of bandleaders such as **Antonio María Romeu**, **Miguel Failde** and **José Urfé**, the danzón had dominated Havana's bourgeois dance parties for nearly three decades. It was Urfé, a clarinettist, bandleader and prolific composer of danzones, who first incorporated elements of the lively new Oriente son into his music, with his piece "El Bombín de Barretto" in 1910. Within a decade, the doors of hitherto snobbish Havana salons had opened to son and it was the new craze.

Son's triumph in the capital was largely due to three star groups, beginning with the one still known today as the **Septeto Habanero**. Originally a four-piece, formed in 1917 as the Quarteto Oriental, led

The Septeto Habanero

by a Santiago tres player **Ricardo Martinez**, backed up by clave, maracas and *botija*, the group expanded to a sextet in 1920 with the addition of a guitarist and *bongosero*, while the botija gave way first to a *marímbula* and then to a double bass. In 1927, the Habanero became a Septeto, with the addition of a cornet (later changed to trumpet). With the opening of the first radio station in Havana in 1920, and the arrival on the scene of the American record company RCA Victor, which began to bring Cuban son bands back to New Jersey to record shortly thereafter, son began to be seriously diffused.

The great trova singer **Maria Teresa Vera** (see pp.179–181) began to incorporate son into her repertoire and formed her own Sexteto, the **Occidente**, to do so. In 1927, the bassist of this group, **Ignacio Piñeiro**, left to form his **Sexteto Nacional**, which duly expanded into a Septeto with the arrival of the trumpeter **Lázaro Herrera** soon afterwards. While the Sexteto/Septeto Habanero in its early days had produced a very simple son, featuring little more vocally than repeated group choruses, the Nacional was more sophisticated. Piñeiro hired fine lead singers, beginning with the great star **Abelardo Barroso**, and gave them a new central virtuoso role in the sound. He wrote more complex and adventurous songs and experimented with hybrids of son with Afro percussion, with the bolero, and with the street-vendors' cries known as *pregones*. One of Piñeiro's songs, "Echale Salsita!" (Put Some Sauce On It), prefigured by half a century the use of the word salsa to describe son-based dance music. Indeed, the creation of septets with their trumpets was one of the milestones in the slow transmutation of son into salsa.

During the 1920s and 1930s several dozen popular groups established son as a staple of Havana's popular music scene, among them the **Sexteto Boloña**, **Tipico Oriental**, the **Estudiantina Invasora**, **el**

Jiguaní, Grupo Apolo and the nascent Sonora Matancera, of whom more later. During this period, a third great son popularizer appeared, in the form of the singer, guitarist and songwriter Miguel Matamoros. Matamoros was born in Santiago, started his first trio there in 1925, and rapidly became a star throughout the Latin world by virtue of the simple but sublime sound mix of the trio – Matamoros' own intricate and savoury guitar playing accompanied by that of Rafael Cueto, a former tailor and baseball player, and the maracas of Siro Rodriguez, backing three beautifully attuned voices. Matamoros was another pioneering exponent of the art of creating attractive combinations of son with boleros, trovas and guarachas. At the head of his trio, later expanded into septeto or conjunto form, he was one of the greatest group leaders in the history of Cuban music.

Conjuntos and the development of son

By the late 1930s, son was ready for its next remodelling, and this again came about by expansion of the groups. The septeto began to add an extra trumpet or two, creating a brass section, piano, and the tall conga drums known as *tumbadoras*. The conjuntos were born. Early examples were the Conjunto Casino and the Conjunto Kubavana, but in 1940 the most influential of them all was formed by a blind tres-player from Matanzas named Arsenio Rodriguez. Rodriguez' great Cuban period lasted a mere ten years – in the 1950s he emigrated to the US where his career foundered (see p.71) – but his effect was electrifying. He combined a deep, raw Afro-roots approach, particularly in his own exciting virtuoso tres-playing, with innovative and sophisticated brass parts, especially in the work of his trumpeter Felix Chapottín. As well as this he introduced major changes of structure to the son format, notably dropping the intro-

ductory largo, and proceeding straight to a dense, exciting montuno. Throughout the 1940s, the bulky figure of Rodriguez led his band weekly at the Tropical beer-garden and dancehall in Marianao, while

Arsenio Rodriguez

other vogues – mambo and cha-cha-cha – came to challenge pure son's popularity.

Another great figure who took son to its mid-twentieth-century apogee was **Beny Moré**, the most revered star in Cuban musical history. Moré was born in the country near Cienfuegos to a poor family of slave descent.

He grew up among the drum cults of his Bantú mother's ancestors and arrived in Havana avid for music and possessing an extraordinary natural skill in all aspects of it. After several years practising as a small-time trovador around Havana cafés, he began to get minor radio work and was recruited to the Matamoros conjunto, then moved on as singer to the orquesta of **Pérez Prado**, the great mambo popularizer. When Moré eventually set up his own **Banda Gigante** in 1953, he combined the sound of a big mambo or jazz band, his own superb voice and stage personality, new and exciting arrangements, but also a deep black guajiro feel to his material. In the hands of the *bárbaro del ritmo* (rhythm barbarian), as Moré became known, son reached the peak of a certain period of development from which it would proceed to diversify.

While artists such as Arsenio Rodriguez and Moré developed son into a dynamic modern style played by ever bigger bands, the old guajiro styles were not superseded. The trios and quartets of **Oriente**, practitioners of trova and son, continued to perform, and in the 1990s returned to spectacular world success with the rediscovery of old artists such as **Compay Segundo**, and of newer heirs to the tradition, notably the **Cuarteto Patria** led by **Eliades Ochoa** (see p.67). **Guillermo Portabales** developed the *guajira de salon*, which was rough country music played with finesse and melodic sophistication in a style influenced by the Trio Matamoros. In 1928, a former danzón singer from Havana named **Joseíto Fernández** adapted a rural-style guajira-son, about a country girl from Guantánamo, "Guajira Guantanamera", which made its way around the world and eventually became one of the standards of Cuban music. And in the continued fame of the singer **Celina Gonzalez**, the *campesina* (country) sound of the guajiros continued to be nationally popular. Gonzalez was brought up in Santiago, where she met her husband and first stage partner, and from 1948 onwards forged an

MARIO GARCÍA JOYA

Beny Moré, rhythm barbarian

increasingly successful career performing the medium-paced, semi-acoustic son of the countryside, with much emphasis on the old décima verses, both conceived as poetic lyrics and improvised. Fifty years on she is still starring on campesina radio programmes, now partnered by her son Lázaro, bringing the sound of the mountains of Oriente to nostalgic Habaneros everywhere.

Artists

Familia Valera Miranda

The group formed by members of this extended family from **Oriente province** (see pp.52–53) began to come to international attention in 1983, when the musicologist **Danilo Orozco** first recorded them: a decade later, British and French record companies picked up on their fascinatingly preserved body of work and equally fascinating history. The various branches of the family trace their genealogy back over two centuries and include remarkable figures such as the resistance fighter **Vicente Cutiño** (see p.61) and his daughter **Catalina**, who was a central member of the music group until her death in the mid 1960s at age 110, according to the family.

Although the various branches of the **Valera Mirandas** lived in scattered farmsteads throughout the Cauto Valley, the present nucleus of the group, led by **Felix Valera Miranda** and his wife **Carmen**, live in Santiago de Cuba, where their house in the Calle Santa Rosa is a meeting place for local musicians and visiting music tourists. Although their line-up – guitar, tres or *cuatro*, double

bass, bongo, clave and voices – and their repertoire are deeply traditional, their music incorporates more self-consciously artistic elements, notably the virtuoso *cuatro* playing of **Enrique "Quique" Valera**, Felix' son, who also plays in the Santiago salsa group Los Karachi.

⊙ **Music from Oriente de Cuba**   Nimbus, UK

The Family's first international release, recorded in Santiago in 1994 by a team from Nimbus, is a delight, rich in beautiful metal strings and quiet old-fashioned voices. With songs by Compay Segundo and his former partner, Lorenzo Hierrezuelo-Chicharrones, as well as Huellas del Pasado, Macusa, Pena – four years before their huge return to fashion and performed just as beguilingly as in the old composer's versions.

⊙ **A Cutiño**   Naïve, France

Five years after their debut CD, Orozco was back in the studio with the Family, accompanied by Antoine Chao, brother of the French Latin *bricoleur* and songwriter Manu Chao, to produce this beautiful sequel, dedicated to Colonel Vicente "Cutiño" Marquez, eminent ancestor of the Valera Mirandas. There's a smattering of more arcane song styles than the first disc – *nengones*, for example – and extracts of recordings of the voices of the late Catalina Miranda and her daughter Milla.

Joseíto Fernández

Born in 1908 in Havana, **Fernández** would have been a minor singer and composer of campesina music and danzones, if it had not been for his role in the popularization of the song, "La Guajira Guantanamera", better known simply as "Guantanamera". Fernandez began his career singing in trios and orquestas típicas, including the orchestra of **Raimundo Pia y Rivero**, with whom he performed in the 1930s on *Radio CMCO*. For the show's signing-off number, Fernández adapted an existing guajira-son, attributed to an Oriente tresero named Diablo Wilson, in praise of a country girl (guajira) from Guantánamo, over which Fernández would improvize on topically themes. The elevation of the song to major Cuban popularity occurred some years later, when it was augmented by the composer **Julián Orbón** with extracts from the independence hero **José Martís**' poem *Versas Sencillas* – "Yo soy un hombre sincero, de donde crece la palma" (I'm a sincere man, from where the palm grows). In 1963, "Guantanamera" was adopted by the American folksinger **Pete Seeger**, who had either heard the song while in Cuba, or been introduced to it by a Cuban music teacher resident in New York. Seeger's version was then taken up by other acts, from the Californian trio The Sandpipers to the French pop balladeer Joe Dassin. It was not until 1971 that Fernández was able to inform Seeger of the true authorship of the song, by which time the American trade embargo precluded paying him authors' rights. He died in 1979 having received a fraction of the financial benefits his song should have accrued.

⊙ **Joseíto Fernández y su guantanamera**   Egrem, Cuba

A rare Fernández record, kept in print by Egrem doubtless for the potential tourist sales attracted by the title song, which features in two different versions among the 18 compositions.

Celina Gonzalez

Born in Jovellanos, near Matanzas, in 1928, **Celina Gonzalez** moved to Santiago, where she met her singing partner, **Reutilio Dominguez**, later to become her husband. The duo **Celina y Reutilio** became a popular campesina music radio act, first on the local station *Cadena Oriental* and then, when they moved to the capital, on Havana's *Cadena Suaritos*. Celina soon began to write songs, usually in the

Cuba's Queen of country song

traditional Spanish-based décima verse form, often drawing on the Afro-Christian syncretic religion **santería**, of which she became a devotee. In 1964, the duo split up and Celina became a soloist. Reutilio Dominguez died in the early 1970s, and a decade later, as her international career became more successful – Celina began to capitalize on the great success of her records in Colombia and Venezuela – she began to sing as a duo with her son, **Lázaro Reutilio Dominguez**, often billed as Reutilio Jr. She remains the Queen of Cuban country music.

⊙ Celina y Reutilio	Bongo Latino, US

Recorded in the studios of *Radio Progreso*, Havana, in 1956, and adorned with a cover watercolour of the young Celina in lemon and fuchsia guarachera dress, standing beside a white-suited, guitar-wielding Reutilio, this gives a good impression of the original duo's sound.

⊙ Fiesta Guajira	World Circuit, UK

An excellent compilation of 1980s work, recorded at Egrem in Havana, with Lázaro (aka Reutilio Jr) partnering the grande dame – in flowing white lace on the back cover – on a selection of classics, including the anthems "Santa Barbara", which celebrates the dual Catholic/Yoruba animist deity Saint Barbara/Changó, and "Yo Soy El Punto Cubano", Celina's guajira mission statement.

⊙ La Rica Cosecha	Tumi, UK

A more recent recording made in Colombia in 1996, containing "Yo Soy El Punto Cubano", with the great Bárbaro Torres on laúd.

Beny Moré

If one man had to be singled out as the greatest Cuban musician of the twentieth century, it would be **Bartolomé Maximiliano Moré** –

"El Bárbaro del Ritmo" (The Wild Man of Rhythm). Moré was born in 1919 in Santa Isabel de las Lajas, a small town near Cienfuegos. The name Beny was acquired later, when he worked in the conjunto of the great Miguel Matamoros, who told him Bartolomé was a name you gave donkeys.

Moré was a completely self-taught musician, who never learnt to read music, even when directing a big band in his own rich and dynamic arrangements. He immersed himself in Afro percussion in his childhood and during his early years in Havana, when he lived in the barrio of Pueblo Nuevo, a centre of guaguancó and santería. His musical experience was acquired in the Havana of the 1940s, a hive of nightclubs, cafes and ambulant trovador-style musicians, followed by employment in two of the most influential bands of the era. The **Conjunto Matamoros** took him to Mexico City, where he joined the big band of **Pérez Prado**, then acquiring fame as the mambo king by applying the swing and attack of big jazz bands' brass sections to mambo style. Moré was immediately at home in this setting and his tall, mobile figure, rendered even more striking by extravagant zoot suits and his trademark white Stetson and cane, became familiar to Mexican TV and film audiences. Moré's great strength was the versatility of his powerful, agile voice – he excelled at son, mambo and guarachas, but also at slower boleros (although he recognised his vibrant rhythmic voice was best in a dynamic context – "*Fílin* doesn't really suit me," he once commented on the light romantic style of the 1950s).

On his return to Havana, Moré decided to apply Prado's soundscape to a band of his own, interpreting a wider and richer repertoire. Moré's **Banda Gigante** made its debut on August 3, 1957 on the top show of *Radio CMQ* and was an immediate hit. The band began to play virtually every night in the big dancehalls, with audiences stop-

ping their dancing to stand and watch the show in admiration. For the next ten years, until Moré's death from cirrhosis of the liver in 1963, the Banda Gigante was untouchable as Havana's hottest and most celebrated group. Moré's funeral was a State affair and his memory is still revered almost forty years later – institutions are still named after him and a weekly Cuban TV programme is devoted to his heritage.

⊙ **Beny Moré from Semilla del Son**   BMG, Spain

The Wild Man's volume from the excellent Spanish son series, featuring many classics – "Maracaibo Oriental", "Tresero de Manigua", "Francisco Guayabal", etc – recorded with a variety of bands – his own Banda Gigante, plus the Orquestas of Pérez Prado, Ernesto Duarte and Rafael de la Paz. A good (but untranslated) sleeve note and some nice vintage photos add to a worthwhile package.

⊙ **The Best of Beny Moré**   Sony, UK

A late entry in the compilation stakes from the *This Is Cuba* sub-section of the *World Up* series rushed out by Sony UK to cash in belatedly on the Cuba boom. No details on the origins of the tracks, save that they were licensed from Egrem, and badly translated sleeve notes. Nonetheless, it's an accessible, well-mastered set.

⊙ **La Colección Cubana: Beny Moré**   Nascente, UK

Budget UK compilation licensed from Egrem's proxy company in Canada and once again lacking information on the origins of the tracks. Undistinguished presentation, but the selection and sound are good on this well-priced and accessible disc.

Eliades Ochoa & Cuarteto Patria

The **Cuarteto Patria** was founded in Santiago in 1939 by a singer named **Maria Emilia García**, and spent the first four decades of its existence playing canciones and boleros in eastern Cuba without

recording or travelling even to Havana. This situation changed soon after 1978, when the guitarist and singer **Eliades Ochoa** took over its leadership and expanded the repertoire to include the deep traditional sones montunos, guajiras and guarachas he excelled at. In order to do this, he added bongos to the line-up of two guitars, double bass and chorus voices.

Ochoa was born in 1946 to a family of small farmers: his later nickname "guajiro" and trademark cowboy hat and boots affirmed his country origins. He taught himself guitar and began playing on the streets and in the bars of Santiago by the age of eleven. By the early 1960s, he had

Eliades Ochoa and his trademark hat

graduated to local radio and regular work with the **Quinteto de la Trova** and the **Septeto Típico Oriental** in the newly opened Casa de la Trova. He was asked to join the Cuarteto Patria to replace the guitarist Rigoberto Echevarría, "Maduro", who was retiring. Under his leadership, the Cuarteto began to win prizes, receive bookings in Havana and to record. In the late 1980s, Ochoa invited the elderly semi-retired trovador **Compay Segundo** to perform with Patria, and many of Segundo's songs joined Ochoa's own compositions in the group's repertoire. Segundo's appearance with the Cuarteto in Washington was one of the first steps towards the international rediscovery of the old singer. As one of the central figures of the Ry Cooder **Buena Vista Social Club** cast, Ochoa received great rewards in terms of both prestige and royalty payments from the Buena Vista success and started the new millennium at the height of his career.

⊙ A Una Coqueta   Corason, Mexico

Recorded between 1986 and 1993 with a changing cast, including the last of the original Cuarteto members, Francisco Cobas, and Benito Suárez – later a member of the newly famous Compay Segundo's new Muchachos. Featuring a good many Segundo-composed songs and items such as "El Cuarto de Tula", that Ochoa was later to introduce to the Buena Vista repertoire.

⊙ The Lion Is Loose!   Corason, Mexico

The 1995 sequel to the above, including two new members – percussionist Roberto Torres (not the Miami musician of the same name) and bass-player, William Calderon – with Ochoa's brother Humberto still on second guitar. Includes Segundo's "Saradonga", "Huellas del Pasado" and "Sabroso".

⊙ Sublime Ilusión   Virgin, Spain

First full-scale international release, with the now-famous Ochoa's name on the cover dwarfing that of the Cuarteto, and including (on

a few tracks) guest stars of dubious value – Cooder (father and son), Charlie Musselwhite on harmonica, David Hidalgo of Los Lobos on guitar. The rest of the album is superb, with Ochoa's mellow but compelling voice and stinging eight-string guitar on terrific form.

Ignacio Piñeiro y el Sexteto/Septeto Nacional

One of the most famous and influential of all Cuban musicians, **Piñeiro** was a prolific composer, and a highly inventive one with over three hundred compositions to his name, in a range of genres including not only son, son montuno, rumba, guaracha, conga and danzón, but hybrids of all sorts from Afro-son and guaguancó-son to tango-conga and canción-son. Piñeiro was born in Havana in 1888 and initiated into music in children's choirs. He worked as a cigar-maker, a mason and a docker while studying African percussion and song, and then joined a guaguancó group, **Timbre de Oro**, before being hired by the star Maria Teresa Vera as a bass player. When he founded his sextet, which almost immediately became a septet, he was successful at once, finding a residency on the radio station CMCJ. When George Gershwin visited Cuba in 1932, he worked with Piñeiro, eventually using themes from the Cuban's *Echale Salsita* in his *Cuban Overture*. Piñeiro's group did much to popularize Cuban son abroad in the 1930s, playing with tremendous success at the Ibero-American Exhibition, in effect the World Fair, of Seville in 1926 and its Chicago equivalent in 1933. In 1934, Piñeiro left the Septeto, which was led at first by Herrera and then dissolved for almost twenty years until Piñeiro and the Septeto came together for a performance on the TV programme *Musica de Ayer y Hoy (Music from*

Yesterday and Today). The Septeto continued to play with Piñeiro until his death in 1969, supporting Castro's government by playing at military bases and in return garlanded with honours.

⊙ Ignacio Piñeiro and his Septeto Nacional	Tumbao, Spain

Recorded in Havana in 1928, with Abelardo Barroso singing and Lázaro Herrera on trumpet, this is a well-designed and annotated slice of Cuban history.

⊙ Clásicos del Son	Sono Cuba/Musisoft, France

A collection licensed from the vaults of Egrem by the longstanding French tropical label, originally Sonodisc. Poorly annotated but a good selection, packed with foretastes of phrases and songs later to become famous – "Ruñidera", a subsequent Elio Revé favourite, "No Jueges con los Santos", as performed by Celia Cruz.

Arsenio Rodriguez

No figure in Cuban music is surrounded by such mystery, and mystique, as the blind tres player and bandleader **Arsenio Rodriguez**, who came to be known as "El Ciego Maravilloso" (the Blind Wonder) and whose influence is such that tres players today still describe themselves stylistically as "Arseneros". Disagreement surrounds his birth date – between 1911 and 1915 – his real name, variously given as Ignacio Loyola Rodriguez and Ignacio Arsenio Travesio Scull, and the cause of his blindness in early childhood – either an "hereditary illness" or a mule-kick. What is undisputed is that the deep Afro syncopation of his music was due in part to his Congolese slave ancestry, and that he was recognized as a genius early in life, when he began playing a tres made for him by a local carpenter, firstly in the entertainment places of his home town of Guira de Macurijes, near Matanzas, and then around the beaches of Marianao, when he came to Havana.

After playing professionally in the **Sexteto Boston** and the **Orquesta Habana,** Rodriguez began to prepare his own conjunto, which was soon to give birth to the first mambos. The mambo, according to Rodriguez, was based on a Congolese rhythm which he had always known as the *diablo*, and which had also been referred to by his fellow musicians as the *chambelona*, mixed with the trumpet passages Rodriguez pioneered with the aid of **Felix Chapottín**. Through the 1940s Rodriguez' group –

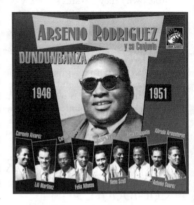

increasingly playing his own soulful minor key compositions, and featuring virtuoso instrumentalists such as the pianist "Lili" Martinez and his successor Ruben Gonzalez – was extremely popular in Havana. In 1947 Rodriguez went to the United States for an operation which he hoped would restore his sight, but which failed to do so. Much of the rest of his life was spent in either Los Angeles or New York, where his performances were cult successes among musicians – his influence on the generation of New York musicians who created salsa was tremendous – but not commercially viable. Rodriguez passed the final years of his life in poverty and died almost forgotten in Los Angeles.

⊙ **Dundunbanza**   Tumbao, Spain

A good collection, recorded in Cuba, with the usual excellent booklet, archive photos and essay (in Spanish only). Items such as

"No Me Llores Mas" and "Dundunbanza" (featuring the great "Lilí" Martínez on piano) demonstrate in their searingly melancholic attack why they are still so avidly covered by modern son connoisseurs such as Sierra Maestra.

⊙ **Chano Pozo and Arsenio Rodriguez:**   Tumbao, Spain
Legendary Sessions

An interesting selection, containing two tracks recorded in New York in 1947 with the great conga player Pozo's conjunto and Marcelino Guerra "Rapindey" on vocals, four with the Machito orchestra, featuring Tito Rodriguez as singer, and nine with Rodriguez' own conjuntos in Havana and Cuba between 1948 and 1953. In these different settings, the full exciting syncopated effect of Rodriguez' tres playing is demonstrated very clearly.

Compay Segundo & Los Compadres

One of the most remarkable musical biographies of the century from any nation belongs to Francisco Repilado, known professionally as **Compay Segundo**. The stage name originates from his role during the 1950s as half of the successful duo **Los Compadres** (The Friends, or Companions), the slang diminutive of *compadre* being "compay". The vocal duties of Los Compadres were shared between Lorenzo Hierrezuelo, who sang first (*primera*) voice, and Repilado, whose deep tones provided the harmony second (*segunda*) voice.

Francisco Repilado was born in 1907 in Siboney, Oriente, and moved with his parents to Santiago. He learnt clarinet, which he played in the Municipal Band of Santiago, but was also acquainted with the early Oriental son pioneers – he remembers Sindo Garay, for example. Throughout the 1930s, Repilado worked in Santiago and Havana, switching to guitar, as well as the seven-string guitar variant

Compay Segundo and his armónico

he had invented and named an *armónico*: as guitarist he worked with **Quinteto Cuban Stars**, then led by Ñico Saquito, and the **Cuarteto Hatuey**, before reverting to the clarinet for a decade in the conjunto of **Miguel Matamoros**. In 1942 Repilado renewed an old relationship with **Lorenzo Hierrezuelo**, another Santiago singer and guitarist also born in 1907, who had worked in the Cuarteto Hatuey and in a successful partnership with Maria Teresa Vera.

Los Compadres had considerable success, the two voices and distinctive blend of guitars backing a repertoire of simple catchy songs – mainly sones and boleros – written by the two men. In 1955, however, the partnership broke up: Compay Segundo went off to

perform solo with a backing group he called his **Muchachos** (Boys), while Hierrezuelo drafted in his brother Reinaldo to continue Los Compadres. Lorenzo died in 1995, at which point Reinaldo joined with the other members of a new ensemble which named itself the **Vieja Trova Santiaguera**.

By the 1970s, Compay Segundo had abandoned music-making to work in the H. Uppmann cigar factory, before eventually retiring. In the mid-1980s, the Santiago guajira singer, **Eliades Ochoa**, adopted Segundo's repertoire and then began to invite the old star as guest performer at Cuarteto Patria concerts. In 1994, Spain rediscovered Segundo when he appeared at the series of concerts in Seville pairing old soneros with flamenco stars. In 1996 he was invited to join the **Buena Vista Social Club** recordings (see p.315), and two years later he was an international star, playing to packed houses in the major concert halls of Paris, London, Tokyo and New York, meeting the Pope, composing busily for new albums and relishing the whole experience.

Antología	Dro East West, Spain

A selection of 34 of his greatest hits recorded in Madrid in 1995, produced by the rock star and son aficionado Santiago Auseron. Simple, powerful and beautifully recorded, much the best recording of Segundo's late years and one of his best ever.

Calle Salud	Dro East West, Spain

The old boy's big 1999 production, named after the street he'd just moved out of to a nasty new apartment, and recorded in Havana's plush new Abdala studio, Segundo's favourite studio near Malaga (he loves the trays of snacks and the paellas) and Paris, with an augmented band including the three Havana clarinettists taken on to such good effect in concerts, and star guests such as, bizarrely, Charles Aznavour. Fun and worth having, but Segundo's wavering voice is very apparent, and none of the tracks approaches his Antología work.

Sexteto/Septeto Habanero

The earliest popularizers of son as a national genre began as a sextet in 1920, became a septet with the addition of a trumpet, and then an octet with an extra singer/percussionist. Although no original members now survive, continuity has been maintained by overlapping generations of recruitment. **Manuel Furé**, leader for forty years, joined in 1952 and maintained style and repertoire through peaks and troughs of popularity. In the 1950s, the Septeto was rediscovered by the station *Radio Salas* and given its own slot. A decade later, after a temporary transmutation into the Conjunto Típico Habanero, it was reconstituted by Furé at the request of the Ministry of Culture and remained so until the 1990s, when the international interest in traditional son gave it new impetus and a large new market.

⊙ Las Raíces del Son	Tumbao, Spain

Early recordings made in Havana between 1925 and 1931, featuring the sextet, as yet without trumpet, but with the golden larynx of Abelardo Barroso on board, prior to his transfer to Ignacio Piñeiro's rival outfit. Includes their great hit "Tres Lindas Cubanas" and a version of "Mamá Inés", the early son ancestor by Eliseo Grenet.

⊙ Grabaciones Completas 1925-31
Tumbao, Spain

A 4-CD box set of more of the same period, also containing a book on the Roots of Son by the guitarist and composer Senén Suárez.

⊙ 75 Años Despues
Corason, Mexico

The eight-man Septet, recorded in 1995, led by Manuel Furé, who had taken over in 1961 three years after the death of Gerardo Martinez. Includes a new "Tres Lindas Cubanas". Good sleeve notes by Eduardo Lleranas, label proprietor and notable musicologist.

⊙ Orgullo de los Soneros
Lusafrica, France

Recorded in 1998 and led by German Pedro Ibanez, the group's singer and guitarist since 1964. Still in excellent form, with a set of guarachas, sones and boleros, half-traditional, half-written by Ibañez, and including a new version of "Mamá Inés".

Sonora Matancera

Another long established band, the **Sonora Matancera** were tremendously influential in the Latin world: one still hears Matancera songs performed by countless small-time entertainers everywhere from Aruba to Venezuela. Vintage Matancera records include Colombian

merecumbés and Mexican boleros – testimony to their constant travelling. In later years their fame was boosted by association with the singer they'd once employed, the great **Celia Cruz**.

The group was started in 1924 in the city of Matanzas, by a tresero and guitarist named **Valentín Cané**, and only arrived at its final name after periods as the Sexteto Soprano, the Sexteto Sonora Matancera and the Estudiantina Matancera. In 1926, the singer and guitarist **Rogelio Martinez**, formerly a member of Antonio María Romeus' charanga, joined: seventy years later he was still the group's leader and sole surviving original member. Throughout the 1940s and 1950s, the Matancera – featuring a succession of star vocalists, notably the Puerto Rican diva **Myrta Silva** – was in constant demand for Cuban radio and dancehall work. In 1960, by now with Celia Cruz as singer, the Matancera was one of the first groups to seek exile when they decided to go to the US permanently following a tour of Mexico (see p.183). After Cruz's departure, the band continued to play professionally and tour internationally – they were in London in 1994 – but without ever regaining their mid-century fame.

⊙ **Live on the radio 1952–58**   Harlequin, UK

An interesting selection, recorded mainly in the studios of *Radio Progreso*, of pre-Celia Cruz tracks, featuring singers from the great Puerto Rican star Daniel Santos – who did so much to add to the Matancera's pan-Latin fame – to Reinaldo Hierrezuelo of Los Compadres.

⊙ **From Cuba to New York**   Charly, UK

Twenty tracks recorded by New York label SEECO in the 1950s, with vocals by Santos, Vicentico Valdes, Laito Sureda, who was to join the revived soneros boom in the 1990s, Bobby Capo, and three numbers by the young Celia Cruz.

Trio Matamoros

The magic of **Trio Matamoros** was created by a remarkable convergence of voices, complementary guitar skills and song-writing talent in three individuals. **Miguel Matamoros** was a natural musician, born in Santiago in 1894, who worked as a carpenter, painter and chauffeur while singing in a trio, the Oriental, in his spare time. He met **Rafael Cueto** by chance when he needed a substitute guitarist for an engagement in the Teatro Albisu in Havana, and shortly afterwards the singer **Siro Rodríguez** joined in a performance at Miguel Matamoros' saint's day party in 1925. The combination of Matamoros' and Cueto's intricate guitar tumbaos and the three voic-

Miguel Matamoros   Rafael Cueto   Siro Rodríguez

es was instantly successful, and the trio also proved themselves to be extraordinarily inventive and melodious song-writers. Within months, a talent scout for RCA had invited the trio to New Jersey to record. Their first 78 single, "Olvido", backed by "El Que Siembra Su Maiz" (both still Cuban classics), was an instant hit and heralded the beginning of a hugely successful international career that lasted into the 1960s. Matamoros died in 1971, Rodríguez in 1981 and Cueto in 1991, but their songs are still performed by hundreds of groups throughout the Latin world.

⊙ **Trio Matamoros**   Harlequin, UK

A collection of 21 classic songs recorded by RCA between 1928 and the 1950s in Camden, New Jersey, New York and Havana, featuring Matamoros, Cueto and Rodríguez operating variously as Trio, Cuarteto, Septeto and even Orquesta Matamoros. Opening with the ultra-famous "Son de la Loma" and including sones, guarachas, boleros, guarachas and examples of the *capricho*, a variant of the old Spanish-style *canción Cubana*.

⊙ **Trio Matamoros**   BMG, Spain

Another good collection, licensed from Egrem by the Spanish rock star Cubanologist Santiago Auseron for his excellent *Seeds of Son* series. Undated, sounding clearer and therefore probably later than the Harlequin record, it contains two interesting congas: one of them, "Las Carnavales de Oriente", which on the Spanish record is an authentically clattering, Chinese cornet-adorned percussion exercise, is rendered as a suave son on the Harlequin disc, demonstrating yet again Matamoros' remarkable versatility.

Vieja Trova Santiaguera

Although it was the aged cast of Buena Vista Social Club who achieved greatest world stardom, the five senior citizens of the group they called **Vieja Trova**, in ironic opposition to the term *Nueva Trova*, from Santiago had the idea first. The notion of forming a touring group of retired musicians from the early part of the century arose among interviewees of a documentary on son made by a Basque TV director in Santiago in the early 1990s. **Reinaldo Hierrezuelo**, born in 1926 (aka Rey Caney), had been part of the Cuarteto Patria, Los Compadres and the Sonora Matancera amongst other groups; **Amado Machado** and **Reinaldo Creagh**, both carpenters before musicians, had been members of the early son group Estudiantina Invasora, as had **Aristoteles Limonta**, whose non-musical jobs had

included stonemasonry and acting as a blind person's guide. **Pancho Cobas**, another mason, was a longstanding member of the Cuarteto Patria, who had retired when Eliades Ochoa took over.

Old trovadores still going strong

Shortly after their formation, the Vieja Trova became one of the first beneficiaries of the Spanish rediscovery of their old colony's musical history: a tour of Spain in 1994 attracted much attention from the press, from audiences, and from record companies. Within five years, the group had a steady international career with its repertoire of old sones, guarachas and boleros, and four respectably selling CDs. By 1999, Machado and Cobas had left, replaced by **Ricardo Ortiz Verdecia** (voice, maracas and güiro) and **Manuel Galban**, the former guitarist of the doo-wop band Los Zafiros.

⊙ **Vieja Trova Santiaguera**   Nubenegra, Spain

The group's debut recording, at a combined age of four hundred plus years, made by the pioneering Madrid label boss Manuel Dominguez. It opens with a nice version of Matamoros' "El Tren" (The Train), with voice-klaxon and maraca-rendered steam hissing, and continues through an assortment of old boleros, sones and guarachas. Their age shows, though, and young Cubans would have been bewildered (if they could have heard the CD).

⊙ **La Manigua**   Virgin, Spain

A 1999 recording, masterminded by the Tropicana's musical director, Demetrio Muñiz, and sounding stronger and fuller than their (by now) three earlier records. Nonetheless, essentially a duplicate of previous work.

4

The Cuban Diaspora: I

While it was vocal **son**, rough, vital and lower class, which lay at the heart of the Cuban sound, the first steps in Cuban music's journey around the world were taken by **danzón**, an older and far more genteel instrumental form. From the beginning, the line-ups were derived from military bands, with a brass-heavy sound which included cornet, trombone and euphonium as well as clarinets, violins, double bass, güiro and timpani. By the early years of the century the **danzón orquesta** was standard at upper-class dances, and when US recording companies began travelling to Cuba with portable cylinder recording equipment, their releases of early **danzones** began to feed a fashion for Cuban music back home.

The large, unwieldy orquestas were soon threatened by smaller, lighter (and therefore cheaper) son sextets (see p.56) which in turn gradually gave way to a new format, the **charangas**, also known as **charangas francesas**. These were essentially danzón orquestas without the brass, and with a flute supplementing the violin, bass,

güiro and timbales. In 1911, this line-up was augmented by piano when the composer, pianist and bandleader **Antonio María Romeu** formed his first band in Havana, where he had arrived from his home town of Jibacoa to work as a café pianist. Romeu's orquesta became extremely popular, and Romeu himself a prolific composer. His five hundred or more danzones (danzón compositions) include the ultra-famous "Tres Lindas Cubanas" (Compay Segundo's present-day show-opener), and he also set dozens of other themes, even arias from Rossini's *Barber of Seville*. Romeu died in 1955, at which time his orquesta, now expanded into an **Orquesta Gigante** and employing new star singers such as Barbarito Diez, was still one of the most important in Havana, and a fixture of Radio Progreso's live output.

At the end of the 1920s, a new variant of the danzón known as the **danzonete** arrived on the scene, developed by one of the original members of the orquesta of Miguel Failde, creator of the danzón.

Danzón in Mexico

One of the most enthusiastic converts to danzón was **Mexico**, particularly in the towns of Merida in the Yucatan, and Veracruz, further up the Gulf. Both were even closer to Havana than New Orleans, and they consumed danzón avidly. The orquesta of **Tomás Ponce** moved to Mexico in 1916, remaining there until Ponce's death in 1972, and Mexico City and Veracruz remain great centres for old-style danzón to this day. **Veracruz**, in particular, has a spectacular weekly open air dance in the Zocalo, the main square, and a daily live danzón radio show, in which the old brass and timpani line-up of the band could have been taken directly from 1918 Havana.

Aniceto Diaz was a composer, flautist and saxophonist who had remained in his home town of Matanzas where, in 1929, he first played a new piece entitled "Rompiendo La Rutina" (Breaking the Routine) which had a slight injection of son influence and one vital innovation: a vocal line. The danzonete soon created its first star, the singer **Paulina Alvarez**, an amateur from Cienfuegos with a striking, bell-like voice. She was taken up by Diaz and eventually achieved such fame with the band of Antonio María Romeu (and later her own orquesta) that she became known as the "Empress of the Danzonete".

Although eclipsed by newer forms, the danzón itself didn't die out, remaining in the repertoires of many Cuban bands. It later provided the base for another new dance craze, the **mambo**, and, in the hands of great old performers such as **Israel "Cachao" Lopez**, became the subject of exciting new recordings at the end of the century. But first it was the turn of other styles to capture the international limelight.

Rumba

The chief style in the new wave was son – although outside Cuba it was soon to be known as **rumba** – and the most influential individual song was in fact based on a pregón, a song version of a Havana street-vendor's cry. The origin of the US craze for rumba can be found in one song, "**El Manisero**" (The Peanut Vendor), which was written one afternoon in 1928 by a Havana-born composer, pianist and theatre musician named **Moisés Simons**. Simons later recalled that he had heard a passing hawker crying out "*Maní! Maní!*" (Peanuts! Peanuts!), and immediately scribbled the song on a paper napkin. Like many pregones, the lyrics of "El Manisero" contain a

risqué double-entendre – the vendor advises housewives and young girls not to go to sleep without having first swallowed some of his hot, tasty nuts.

Moisés Simons' new song was first taken up and recorded in Cuba by **Rita Montaner**, at that time in mid-ascent to the height of her fame as a singer and all-round celebrity. Although Montaner made a number of successful appearances in New York in the late 1920s, including "El Manisero" and other Moisés Simons' songs in her repertoire, it

Rita Montaner

was another artist whose espousal of the Peanut Vendor led to the song's breakthrough, and that of Cuban music generally, in the US.

In April 1930, **Modesto "Don" Azpiazu**, whose orchestra had been one of the principal attractions at Havana's Casino Nacional for half a dozen years, was booked to play the Palace Theatre on **Broadway**. He took with him the young singer, **Antonio Machín**, who had been such a success in Havana, and in New York hired as one of his dancers an elegant, green-eyed, seventeen-year-old Havana girl, then studying typing in the city, named **Alicia Parlá**. Azpiazu's orchestra took to the stage in white ruffled shirts and red peasant neckerchiefs, and equipped with a range of Cuban percussion: this was the first full and authentic Cuban band to have played a major New York theatre, though the US had flirted with

Latin American music before. The tango boom was already a decade old, assorted habanera, bolero and Mexican corrido shadings had been used as exotic colouring by Tin Pan Alley tunesmiths, and individual Cuban musicians had worked or recorded in New York during the 1920s. Nonetheless, the Don Azpiazu orchestra performance was novel and a big success. Among the elements most commented on were Alicia Parlá's sexy and exotic dancing – the columnist Walter Winchell described Parlá as a "lovely Havana torso flipper" – and the band's third number, "El Manisero".

TUMBAO

Azpiazu and his parrot percussionist

A few months later, the Don Azpiazu band unveiled a new staging at the RKO Coliseum theatre, hamming it up with cocktail shakers filled with lead shot as maracas, and Machín making his entrance pushing a stand marked "Peanuts". In November, RCA Victor released a recording of **The Peanut Vendor** with more unusual touches – improvisation by one of

two trumpets – and a hit was born. Amid a breaking wave of enthusiasm for Cuban music, the Azpiazu orchestra began a tour of the United States, while a clutch of new **pseudo-Cuban bands** began to jump on the wagon – Azpiazu commented that "within a week there existed a Havana Royal Orchestra, a Havana Novelty Orchestra and a Havana God Knows What".

In the US, the fashion for Cuban music started by the Peanut Vendor grew and matured throughout the next three decades. Its initial stage was the so-called "**rumba**" craze (also frequently spelt "rhumba", and in either case a misnomer, as almost none of the music played was rumba, in the proper sense of Afro-Cuban percussion, but invariably son, guaracha, danzón or bolero). Why the word "rumba" was adopted is unclear, although the term rumba was also used in Cuba to describe a fast son played by trova performers between acts in Havana variety theatres.

Whatever its provenance, the rumba tag identified a genuine boom in Cuban music, and in its wake a whole range of Brazilian, Argentinian and Mexican-derived songs, of varying degrees of authenticity. The great fame of the Mexican folk theme **La Cucaracha** (The Cockroach) dates from this time, and a number of important Cuban composers and performers also benefited. **Ernesto Lecuona**, Cuba's most brilliant classical pianist and composer, found songs of his such as "Siboney" and "Para Vigo Me Voy" taken up and popularized (and in the latter case translated as "Say Si Si"). Lecuona also supplemented his classical concert career with an immensely successful popular band, **Lecuona's Cuban Boys**. At the other end of the scale, Don Azpiazu's brother, who ran a band under the name **Don Antobal**, issued a succession of recordings including an attempted Peanut Vendor follow-up called "The Ice Cream Man".

Paris: Cuba's Mariannes

The Cuban craze lost no time spreading to Europe, and Paris, spectacularly, was its first port of call. In 1928 the Cuban singer Rita Montaner divorced her husband and sailed for Paris, where she was quickly hired by the Palace theatre. The show was to be backed by the Marquita Sisters, billed as possessing the "prettiest wit and legs", and Les Willy Girls, who wielded "tropical sunshades under the Paris sky"; it was a huge success. On the playlist was Eliseo Grenet's tango-conga "¡Ay! Mamá Inés" – which Montaner had introduced in Havana in full black make-up and wearing a nineteenth-century slave outfit – and the sultry Ernesto Lecuona canción "Siboney"; both were destined to become world favourites.

The Don Azpiazu band had brought its show to Paris via Monte Carlo, where the Prince of Wales had become a fan of "rumba". On Bastille Day, 1932, Alicia Parlá opened the

Downtown: the Waldorf Astoria set

As Cuban music moved into the mainstream of US entertainment, one bandleader above all was astute enough to rise to the top of the commercial market. In 1927, Xavier Cugat formed an orchestra in Los Angeles to play Spanish and Latin American dance music. With a series of shrewd and publicity-friendly moves – including hiring a team of young male tango instructors called "the gigolos" to teach women in the audience to dance – he quickly established the music's popularity on the West Coast.

In 1930, with the Don Azpiazu orchestra wowing New York, the great Waldorf Astoria Hotel hired Cugat's orchestra as resident band at its Starlight Roof ballroom, and for the next twenty years,

Azpiazu show at **La Plantation** nightclub on the Champs Elysées, descending an on-stage stairway in a long ruffled batá de cola train to tumultuous applause. The following day, the papers dubbed her the "**Marianne of Cuba**", after the French Republic's mythical figurehead, and this became her nickname – as well as the brand name of a range of perfumes and soaps launched within months to cash in on the Cuban craze.

The Don Azpiazu band's Paris triumph was also its swan-song, however, as half its members stayed in France, helping establish Paris as a serious centre for Cuban music – a status it has never relinquished. Many Cuban musicians played in the basement "dancing" of the great Montparnasse brasserie, **La Coupole**, which retained Latin American entertainers right up to its sale and modernization in 1988. After a six-year pause, it became the setting for weekly salsa dances featuring a new generation of Cuban immigrant musicians (see Chapter 8).

Cugat was the top Latin style bandleader in the US. Although his music was diluted and modified for non-Latin audiences – many serious Afro-Cuban enthusiasts then, as now, held him in contempt – Cugat was a serious musician, and his band provided employment for many others. Not least of these was **Miguelito Valdés**, a dynamic Havana-born singer and percussionist who had come up through the **Sexteto Occidente** of Maria Teresa Vera and the **Orquesta Casino de la Playa**. His subsequent US fame rested on introducing the **conga** rhythm and dance to American stages, and making the first recording of the Margarita Lecuona hit song "Babalú", which resulted in Valdés acquiring the nickname **Mr Babalú**.

The same combination – Cugat, conga, and Babalú – was responsible for the success of the other great popularizer of Cuban music for middle America, **Desi Arnaz**. Arnaz was an upper-class young Cuban, the son of the Mayor of Santiago, who had emigrated to Miami and set up as a guitarist and singer. Trying to find a style of music simple enough for his non-Latin musicians and audiences to relate to, but still remaining distinctly Latin, Arnaz had the idea of using a simplified version of the conga Carnival dance from his home city. It worked like a dream, particularly once audiences had knocked back a few drinks. Moving to New York, Arnaz was hired briefly by Xavier Cugat, singing for the band before the arrival of **Miguelito Valdés**. Thereafter he left music for a career as husband of Lucille Ball and co-star of her weekly "I Love Lucy" TV show, making him the second (and more famous) Mr Babalú, and America's favourite Cuban.

Uptown: El Barrio

While Cugat and Arnaz entertained the Waldorf Astoria set and penetrated Hollywood, other Cuban musicians retained a more authentic approach. Still others made contacts in the worlds of Anglo band music and jazz. But beyond the downtown world of smart hotels and Broadway theatres, a new scene was emerging in the Latin district of **El Barrio**, East Harlem. By the 1930s, when a great influx of Puerto Rican immigrants had arrived, East Harlem had its own radio show, on WABC, and a number of theatres featuring Latin bands, among them the San José and the Campoamor. At these venues, big bands led by the flautist **Alberto Socarras** and the classically trained violinist **Alberto Iznaga** played authentic Latin music including boleros, danzones and *sones*, as well as Puerto Rican styles such as the plena. Meanwhile, quartets like the Cuarteto Caney, the Cuarteto Victoria and the new Cuarteto of Antonio Machín played son and bolero.

The 1930s saw the arrival in this milieu of two men who would create some of the most important advances in mid-twentieth-century Latin music, **Mario Bauzá** and Frank Grillo. Bauzá was a brilliant Havana-born wind and brass musician who had first visited New York in 1926 as a clarinettist with the Romeu band. He returned in 1930 to gig prolifically with both Latin and non-Latin bands, including the Machín Quartet – which he got into by promising Antonio Machín

Machito (right) brandishing his maracas

he would learn trumpet in two weeks – and the jazz orchestras of Chick Webb and Cab Calloway.

In 1937, Bauzá was joined in New York by fellow Habanero, Frank Grillo, whose sister Estella Bauzá had just married. Grillo, or **"Machito"** as he was universally known, was a percussionist, gifted bandleader and arranger, and a first-class sonero. He found work in the new Orquesta Siboney just formed by Alberto Iznaga, and began to make plans for his own band. In 1940, with members of the Siboney, he set up the nucleus of what shortly became **Machito and his Afro-Cubans**. A year later, Mario Bauzá joined as first trumpet and musical director. Within a year, the Machito band had backed Miguelito Valdés on recordings and settled into a successful three-year residency at La Conga club on Broadway.

The Afro-Cubans' powerful and influential brass section – three saxophones and two trumpets – was recruited from among both Latin and non-Latin jazz bandsmen, the power and swing of the New York jazz bands being transferred to a Cuban context. The Afro-Cubans also moved freely between **black and white audiences**, reinvigorating the more genteel world of the Waldorf with a hot, uptown flavour. The band's links with jazz were to prove even more influential when the **Cu-bop** era arrived, as it very soon did.

Mambo

In 1948, Machito's band, by now nicknamed **"The Cadillac of Latin Bands"**, moved to a new venue, a dilapidated dancehall on 52nd Street and Broadway, taken over by a promoter named Federico Pagani and renamed the **Palladium**. Within three years the Palladium had become the most famous Latin nightclub in the US, attracting celebrities such as Eartha Kitt and Marlon Brando, who famously

jammed with the band on congas. In 1952, the Palladium launched a new initiative, its "all-mambo policy", because by this time the world was in the grip of the successor to the "rumba" craze, mambo mania.

Almost the only thing anyone agrees about the mambo is that it originated in Havana at the end of the 1930s. The word itself may have come from a variety of African musical genres, possibly as a shout of encouragement or approval to mark the montuno of a son. Some hold Arsenio Rodriguez responsible for mambo's creation – the great tres player used the term interchangeably with the word *diablo*. According to Israel "Cachao" López, however, he and his brother Orestes used the word mambo, which was Lucumí for "story", to describe the speeded-up, syncopated passages of improvization they began to insert into danzones. Pérez Prado, on the other hand, would later claim that he had heard the word used to describe the political manoeuvring during the Machado (pre-Batista) dictatorship, and had decided to adopt it for its catchiness. When asked about Prado's claim to be inventor of the mambo, Cachao remarked placidly that Prado knew perfectly well it was the Lopez brothers who created the rhythm, but they were all friends and nobody minded.

Whatever the origins of the word, it is certain that the Lopez brothers introduced the concept to the Havana band Antonio Arcaño y sus Maravillas. In 1938 Orestes' composition "Mambo" became the first official mambo in Arcaño's repertoire, although at first Arcaño referred to the innovation as simply *ritmo nuevo* (new rhythm). At any rate, heavier, faster, more syncopated and featuring pronounced conga percussion, it became wildly popular.

But mambo's world success was achieved by a short, plain, but dynamic bandleader from Matanzas. Years later, Beny Moré would improvise the lines "Quién inventó el mambo que me provoca? Un

chaparrito con cara de foca" (Who invented the mambo that excites me? A little guy with the face of a seal). The little guy in question was Damaso Pérez Prado, known professionally as **Pérez Prado**. He rearranged Arcaño's flute-and-strings ritmo nuevo for a blaring, big band brass section, added his trademark "Uh!" cry at the pause and climax of the chorus, invented new steps for a dance, and, after a number of unsuccessful attempts in the late 1940s, broke through to massive success with hits such as "Mambo No. 5" and "Mambo No. 8".

MICHAEL OCHS ARCHIVES

Pérez Prado hits the bongos

By 1951, Prado was touring the US to huge success among non-Latin audiences on the West Coast. He was less popular in New York, where the downtown **Xavier Cugat** crowd found his brass attack a little too brash, and the uptowners accustomed to the authenticity and brilliance of **Machito** regarded his arrangements as simplistic. The mambo flourished, though, especially as played by Machito and by the other two great Latin bands of the Palladium era, those led by the Puerto Ricans **Tito Rodriguez** and **Tito Puente**.

Afro-Cuban jazz

The 1940s and 50s saw another important genre grow, with Havana and New York as its twin centres: **Afro-Cuban jazz**. In **New York**, the process was simply one of fusion between jazz and Cuban music, and had been happening since the serious influx of Cubans began in the late 1920s. **Alberto Socarras** had played throughout the 1930s with black jazz outfits, including the Benny Carter and Sam Wooding Orchestras, while his band had appeared at the Apollo with Bessie Smith, and at the Cotton Club with Duke Ellington and Cab Calloway. **Mario Bauzá** had been an early link with **Dizzy Gillespie** when the two men had worked together in the trumpet section of Cab Calloway's band. In 1931, according to Cuban musicologist Cristóbal Díaz Ayala, the **Hermanos Castro** made the first specific fusion record, a version of "St Louis Blues" adorned with brass and percussion from son, and quotes from "El Manisero". A decade later, things began to coalesce with the advent of **Cu-bop**, a meeting of the new improvisation-led jazz style of bop and a number of outstanding Latin jazz experiments.

As good as tanga

According to the American writer, Max Salazar, the true marriage of jazz and Cuban rhythm was celebrated in La Conga in May 1943, when Bauzá put together a piano tumbao from a tune called "El Botellero" (The Bottle-maker) with a staggered series of reed and bass parts, topped with an alto sax improvisation. **Dizzy Gillespie**, who was listening, asked what this extraordinary number was and somebody remarked it was as good as tanga, a slang term for marijuana; "tanga" thus became the title. **Machito** continued to be a key figure, while from the non-Latin side, the most active players

were Gillespie and the West Coast bandleader **Stan Kenton**. In 1947, having added the bongo player Jack Constanza, **Mr Bongo**, to his band, Kenton recorded a new version of "The Peanut

Vendor", with members of Machito's band on percussion. The same year, Dizzy Gillespie asked Mario Bauzá to help in "Cubanizing" his percussion section. Bauzá introduced Gillespie to a newly arrived conga-player from Havana named **Luciano**

Mongo Santamaría

"Chano" Pozo; the result was a year-long collaboration which culminated in the jointly composed **"Afro-Cuban Suite"**, the forerunner of a succession of Latin Jazz suites by a variety of bands in the following decade.

Other partnerships between virtuoso Cuban percussionists and American jazz bands blossomed. **Mongo Santamaría** arrived in 1950 and, after periods in the ranks of Perez Prado's and Tito Puente's bands, joined **George Shearing**. Four years later, **Carlos "Patato" Valdés** left the Conjunto Casino to work with Machito, then Tito Puente, before crossing over to Herbie Mann.

Descarga: Cuban jam

In Cuba, meanwhile, another jazz-linked trend was gathering pace: the **descarga**, or Cuban jam sessions. One of the first such sessions, much along the lines of those pioneered by Bauzá and Machito, and subsequently taken up by Tito Puente's Piccadilly Boys, was organized by **Norman Granz**, a visiting American jazz impresario. Granz hired a number of Havana players, including the pianist Bebo Valdés, to record a 45-rpm single entitled "Con Poco Coco" in 1952. In 1956, another session with Valdés, organized as a sort of studio party for which the musicians were paid twenty dollars each, produced a track named "Descarga Caliente", which gave its name to the genre and earned a million dollars in sales.

Other highlights of the descarga were those set up by the sophisticated international arranger and composer, **Chico O'Farrill**. It was "Cachao" López, however, who brought the descarga back to its deep Cuban roots, with a series of recordings beginning with "Cuban Jam Sessions In Miniature" which were both successful and tremendously influential. Cachao was to re-record some of this work in the 1990s for Emilio and Gloria Estefan's record company in Miami.

The Cuban jam sessions of the 1950s were crucial in the beginnings of **New York salsa**, which was soon to follow. Among the most enthusiastic descarga organizers of the 1960s was pianist **Charlie Palmieri**, who regarded his Alegre All Stars sessions as just the instrumental side of one field of music-making; the vocal version of this field, as performed by the Fania All Stars, was early **salsa**.

Chachacha

But before the arrival of salsa, one more Cuban dance craze had to play itself out, the **chachacha**. Like mambo, chachacha emerged

from the danzón heritage of the charangas. It was a Havana violinist named **Enrique Jorrín**, who worked for the **Orquesta America** charanga, who came up with the new rhythm. Jorrín observed that the fast and complex mambo was too difficult for many dancers and proceeded to simplify it, inserting a catchy one-two-three accent on the fourth beat of the bar. The phrase "cha-cha-cha!" probably originated in an imitation of the triple shuffle of dancers' soles on the floor as they moved to the beat.

Jorrín's song "La Engañadora" (The Enchantress) was the first chachacha hit for the Orquesta America, and soon other bands, of which the most successful was the **Orquesta Aragón**, were specializing in the new rhythm, which lent itself perfectly to the light but rhythmic swing of a violin section under the swooping lead of a flute. The chachacha swept the US in 1954, eagerly adopted by Anglo audiences terrified into immobility by the Afro-Cuban complexities of the mambo. Simplified at times to the point of caricature, and played by provincial nightclub bands without any of the authentic charanga finesse of the Cuban original, the chachacha was, however, fair game for extinction on the grounds of naffness when the Rock & Roll years arrived. It was, nonetheless, another important stepping stone to the salsa years.

Bringing it back home: 50 Years of Cuban Music

By the end of the 1950s, Cuban musicians had reason for considerable self-satisfaction with their half-century's work, having transformed the folk music of a small colonial island in the Caribbean into an international cultural and commercial commodity. In 1957, the government of President Fulgencio Batista woke up to the possibili-

ties for prestige and decided to organize the **50 Años de Musica Cubana** festival.

A Cubana airliner was chartered to fly in dozens of musicians from New York, including Mario Bauzá, the entire Machito orchestra, Arsenio Rodriguez, Chino Pozo (cousin of the murdered Chano) and Alberto Socarras. Antonio Machín was invited from Spain, Miguelito Valdés from Mexico. Waiting in Havana to perform were stars-to-be such as Beny Moré, Rolando Laserie and the Sonora Matancera with their new singer Celia Cruz. Even the great American ballad star, Nat King Cole, was in town, looking for Bebo Valdés to orchestrate an album of Latin songs he wanted to make. There were non-stop award ceremonies, concerts, jam sessions and parties. As Machito later said, "it was a glorious day for Cuba."

At the same time, it was a nervous one. Batista's government was terminally unpopular, and in Mexico, **Fidel Castro**'s revolutionaries were planning their return. Fidelista exiles in New York threatened to blow up the plane and the musicians with it. The face of Cuban music-making, like all things Cuban, was about to change dramatically.

Artists

Antonio Arcaño

The man whose band created the mambo was born in Havana in 1911, and lived and studied in Guanabacoa and Regla, where he learnt cornet and clarinet in the Regla brass band, before turning to flute and joining **Las Maravillas del Siglo**, the band of the top

singer Fernando Collazo. In 1937 he created his own orchestra, in enlarged **charanga** format, which he named **Arcaño y sus Maravillas**, because, the saying went, its eighteen musicians comprised "an ace on each instrument and a marvel all together." This band was further enlarged in 1944, with a sixteen-piece violin section, whereupon it became known as the **Orquesta Radiofónica de Arcaño**, and played daily with great popular success on Radio Mil Diez. A committed Socialist, Arcaño contributed both financial and moral support to the Party before the Revolution. During this time his band held at bay the advancing fashion for son sextets and septets with its impeccable and complex **danzones**, which included danzón-arranged pieces of Tchaikovsky or Gershwin to add tone to the proceedings.

In the early 1940s, Arcaño began to vary his danzón repertoire with what he called simply *el nuevo ritmo* (the new rhythm), which was in fact the progenitor of the **mambo**, a speeded-up improvisatory passage invented by the brothers **Israel and Orestes López**, who played bass and cello in the Maravillas. Arcaño maintained his success up to the Revolution, after which he gave up performance for teaching. In 1966 he became an administrator in the Seminario de Musíca Popular, and taught flute in the evenings. In the 1970s, he returned to the studios of Egrem to re-record some of his band's old material. He died in Havana in 1994.

⊙ **Danzón Mambo**   Tumbao, Spain

A good collection of recordings from 1944–51, opening with Orestes López's composition "Mambo", probably the first song to claim affiliation to the new genre. Orestes Lopez composed hundreds of mambos for Arcaño, who completed the sound with his flute flourishes.

⊙ **El Melao**   Musica del Sol, Spain

Sixteen slightly later tracks, less treble-dominated in recorded tone. Mainly features danzones, but also another Orestes López mambo, entitled (presumably without too much brain-wracking) "Goza Mi Mambo" (Enjoy My Mambo).

Mario Bauzá

Although at the end of his life **Mario Bauzá** came to be recognized as a major figure in his own right, he spent much of his career in the shadow of his colleague and friend **Machito**, his genius known to other musicians, but not the general public. Bauzá was born in the Cayo Hueso barrio of Havana in 1911, studied music from childhood and by his mid teens was first clarinet in the new, but short-lived, **Orquesta Sinfónica** of Havana. During this time he met Machito – then a budding young singer and percussionist – and his sister Graciela. In 1926 he went to New York with the orchestra of **Antonio María Romeu**, where he fell in love with the Harlem jazz scene. Three years later, as soon as he obtained a passport, Bauzá gave up his jobs in Havana and bought a ticket on the SS Oriente for New York. Travelling on the same ship was the **Don Azpiazu Orchestra**, heading for the series of engagements which would shortly make them, the song "El Manisero", and Cuban music generally, famous across the United States.

In New York, Bauzá immersed himself in both the burgeoning Latin scene and jazz. He talked his way into the Cuarteto of Azpiazu's star vocalist, **Antonio Machín**, by promising to learn to play trumpet within a fortnight, obtaining an instrument from a pawnshop and playing scales non-stop. He also learnt saxophone and played in the jazz bands of Noble Sissle, Chick Webb and finally Cab Calloway, where he met **Dizzy Gillespie**.

In 1936, Bauzá revisited Havana to restart his relationships with Estella Grillo, whom he married, and Frank Grillo, who asked him to

look into the possibilities of starting their own band in New York. Two years later, Grillo was becoming known as "Machito", and in 1941 Bauzá joined Machito's Afro-Cubans as musical director. He began redesigning the band, using the absences of musicians on wartime national service to replace them with jazz-trained players. His influence was crucial, writing hits such as "Tanga", the first Latin jazz number, and "Mambo Inn".

Bauzá left the Afro-Cubans in 1975, dissatisfied with the band's reduction in personnel. His 1977 solo record, **La Botánica**, went unremarked, but a follow-up in 1986, **Afro Cuban Jazz**, with musicians of the stature of **Paquito D'Rivera**, **Ray Santos**, **Carlos "Patato" Valdés** and **José Fajardo**, was a great success. This paved the way for a trio of highly praised albums made for the German company Messidor in the early 1990s, **The Legendary Mambo King**, **My Time Is Now**, and **944 Columbus**. Bauzá died of cancer in 1993, weeks after completing the last record, having spent the last year of his incessantly hard-working life feted as a giant of Cuban music.

⊙ **Afro Cuban Jazz**   Caimán, US

Produced by the Argentinian pianist Jorge Dalto after almost a decade's absence from the recording studio by Bauzá, this album set the tone of his late personal success. Features his classic tracks (including "Mambo Inn") and a constellation of top guest musicians, with Graciela in better voice than ever.

⊙ **The Legendary Mambo King**   Messidor, Germany

The first and most praised of Bauzá's collaborations with the German label's proprietor, enthusiast Götz Wörner, features a new five-movement suite arrangement of "Tanga" by the eminent Chico O'Farrill. Graciela is joined by another great oldster, Rudy Calzado, who takes what would have been Machito's vocal lead, and by a top-flight, 24-strong band of musicians.

Cachao

Israel "Cachao" López was born in 1918, the youngest child of a father and mother who both played and taught bass. (Israel's sister, **Coralia**, was later to compose danzones which Cachao would record, while his nephew **Orlando** became an eminent bass virtuoso and member of the cast of **Buena Vista Social Club**.) López learnt piano and bongos and accompanied silent movies before taking up bass himself. At 13 Israel, Orestes and their father were all members of the **Orquesta Filharmónica de la Habana** – Cachao was paid in tram tickets until the orchestra began to attract wealthy sponsors. Always in the company of Orestes, a hard-drinking, womanising virtuoso in whose musical company the modest, abstemious Israel seems to have felt slightly overshadowed, López began to play in conjuntos, joining **Arcaño y sus Maravillas**.

According to Cachao, the two López brothers came up with the concept and name "mambo" while with Arcaño, as a variation of the

slower danzones and boleros which were the staples of his repertoire. In the 1950s Cachao was central to another new movement in Cuban music, the descarga, when he began to assemble small groups of musicians at the Havana Panart studio between 4am and 9am, after their shows, to record jam sessions. Chief participants were Orestes Lopez, Guillermo Barretto, Tata Güines, El Negro Vivar, Generoso Giménez, Gustavo Tamayo, Yeyito Iglesias and Niño Rivera: a lengthy series of successful albums, including the celebrated **Cuban Jam Sessions in Miniature**, resulted.

ANDREW LEPLEY/REDFERNS

The inimitable Cachao López

In 1962, Cachao left Cuba by ship, choking back tears as he watched the Malecón recede into the distance. The Revolution was a glory at first, he said, but then the regime hardened and became unbearable. Cachao spent two years in clubs in Alicante and Madrid, where the visiting

Perez Prado hired him to fill in on bass, before arriving in New York where he worked steadily, recording, organizing further descargas. In 1970 he moved to Las Vegas, where he worked for eight years in hotel shows including the one at Caesar's Palace, where he backed Paul Anka and Sammy Davis Jr. An inveterate gambler, Cachao lost all his money at the Vegas tables and arrived in Miami in 1978 broke, ready to start again from scratch at the age of sixty.

Cachao spent over a decade in Florida obscurity, before his fame was revived by the Estefans and their friend, the Cuban-American actor Andy García. Cachao had played bass on **Gloria Estefan**'s hit album **Mi Tierra**, and in 1993, at the suggestion of García, Cachao undertook the first of three highly successful albums of **Master Sessions**, re-recording a selection of classic material, including danzones by all three members of his generation of the López family, with an all-star cast. By the end of the 1990s, the Cachao song-title and slogan "Como Mi Ritmo No Hay Dos" (There's No Other Rhythm Like Mine) was acknowledged as truth by millions of international Latin fans.

⊙ **La Leyenda, Volumes 1 & 2**   Kubaney, US

Two sets of lovely danzones recorded in 1957 in the studios of Havana's Radio Progreso. Includes the original "Buena Vista Social Club" and others written by the Lopez's for social institutions such as the Sociedad Antonio Maceo and Isora Club. A small but sprightly violin section and a flute take the lead melody while Cachao's bass busies itself in both fingered and bowed manner, demonstrating his remarkable range. The opening track of Volume 1, "Canta Contrabajo" (Sing, Double Bass), is a jewel-like demonstration of his discreet virtuosity.

⊙ **Master Sessions, Volumes 1 & 2**   Epic/Sony, US

The Andy García/Emilio Estefan recordings which rescued Cachao from relative obscurity, featuring superb musicianship and beautiful arrangements. Volume 1 opens with a champagne

cocktail of a duet between Cachao's bass and Paquito D'Rivera's clarinet on Lecuona's danza "Al Fin Te Ví" (Finally I Saw You), while Volume 2 closes with a Corona-smoke of a santería chant led by Cachao's singing bass posing as Akpwon. Sleeve-notes by both Cristóbal Díaz Ayala and Guillermo Cabrera Infante confirm these records as unmissable.

Xavier Cugat

Born in Gerona in Spain in 1900, **Xavier Cugat** was taken to Havana by his family at the age of three, where he embarked on the first stages of a classic Cuban early-starter's musical career, studying violin from age six onwards at the Peyrellade Conservatory, working as a teenager as a theatre entertainer (in a trio including Moisés Simóns, composer of "El Manisero", on piano) and joining the **Orquesta Sinfónica** of Havana as violinist. By this stage Cugat was also showing talent as an amateur cartoonist, and when the great Italian operatic tenor **Enrico Caruso** performed in Havana, a combination of Cugat's role in the accompanying orchestra and an entertaining caricature he drew and presented to Caruso led the two to become friends.

It was Caruso who suggested Cugat came to New York, offering to introduce him in musical circles. Once there, Cugat studied further, succeeding in performing once at Carnegie Hall, but he came to the conclusion he would never achieve world class status as a classical violinist and abandoned music, moving to Los Angeles. He first worked as an antiques salesman, then fell back on his other major talent – he prospered as showbiz caricaturist on the *Los Angeles Times*.

Cugat returned to music via composing film scores and decided to set up a Latin band starring his new wife **Carmen Castillo** to play nightclubs in the Hollywood area. His timing was perfect: the public

response was rapid and enthusiastic, and by 1932, with the rumba wave rolling out across the nation, Cugat's orchestra was starring at the Ambassador Hotel in Los Angeles and the **Waldorf Astoria** in New York, where his eye for a good-looking girl led him to hire the young Rita Hayworth.

By the mid 1930s, Cugat's slick, polished act, simplified and embellished with pretty dancers, had made him the most successful of the Latin bandleaders with a non-Latin public. "Americans knew nothing about Latin music – so they had to be given music more for the eyes than the ears", he once said. In the dynamic, conga-straddling act of his top vocalist **Miguelito Valdés**, however, Cugat managed to deliver popular spectacle combined with real quality. Cugat's appearances on the NBC *Let's Dance* programme led to his being christened "the rumba-tango king" and his numerous Hollywood film appearances spread his fame even further. His favourite among several dozen films was *You Were Never Lovelier*, in which Rita Hayworth, by now a star, shared the lead with Fred Astaire, whom Cugat claimed to have introduced to Cuban music. Immensely popular until the 1960s' rock years, Cugat spent the final

part of his life retired in a luxurious house in Barcelona, where he died in 1990.

⊙ **Xavier Cugat with Dinah Shore**   Harlequin, UK

A great collectors' disc, illustrating the full penetration of Cuban music into mainstream America in the early 1940s. A mixture of Cuban boleros and "rumbas", international hits – "When The Swallows Come Back To Capistrano" – and period curiosities sung by Shore, Miguelito Valdés and Lina Ronay. Plus a terrific reproduction of a Cugat drawing from the Puerto Rican collection of Cristóbal Díaz Ayala.

⊙ **Rumba, Rumbero**   Tumbao, Spain

Superb collection from the period 1937 to 1943, mainly featuring the voice of Miguelito Valdés, with a good 1940s' caricature of the maestro's faintly Walter Matthau-like features reproduced on the cover.

José Fajardo

The man who ignited the **charanga** fashion in New York in the 1960s was born in Pinar del Rio in 1919 and studied **flute** with his father. His musical career was delayed by military service and a period spent in the police force in Havana, after which he joined the bands of **Antonio María Romeu** and then **Arcaño y sus Maravillas**.

José Fajardo formed his own charanga, **Fajardo y sus Estrellas**, in 1949, and set about building a major reputation for his own fast, agile flute lead, the swing of his six-strong violin section and the smart outfits and presentation of the band, which quickly became the great rival of **Orquesta Aragón**, the brand leaders. By the mid 1950s, Fajardo was in such demand among the booming cabarets of Marianao that he ran three sets of Estrellas simultaneously, dashing from one to another in the evenings to play at least once in person at each.

In 1958, the Fajardo band played with great success at the **Waldorf Astoria** in New York, and two years later, after a tour of Japan and the US, José Fajardo decided not to return to Cuba, where he faced political charges. Taking up the new **pachanga** rhythm, which he rendered as a faster, choppier chachacha, Fajardo ran a very successful band throughout the 1960s, based variously in New York, Miami and Puerto Rico. By the 1990s, Fajardo was living in New York, playing occasionally with a variety of old colleagues at clubs such as SOBs – he even turned up in London in 1998 in the cast of the ex-Fania pianist **Larry Harlow's** Latin Legends band.

⊙ **Super Hits – Fajardo y su Charanga**   Kubaney, US

A totally un-annotated record but one containing some fascinating and enjoyable music, not least a selection of exceedingly funky boogaloos, including a "Batman Boogaloo" with an excellent if anonymous singer, and Fajardo's song-thrush-on-amphetamines flute embellishments.

⊙ **Leyendas: Mister Pachanga and his Orchestra**   Sony Tropical, US

A good set of chachachas and pachangas, including a novel version of "Son de la Loma" recorded in the mid 1960s with the singer Roberto Ledesma, then at the beginning of his career.

Ernesto Lecuona

Child prodigy, prolific composer and international ambassador for Cuban culture, **Ernesto Lecuona** became his country's most eminent twentieth-century musician by virtue of his ability to excel in both classical and popular music. Born in 1895 in Guanabacoa, he was taught piano as a young child by his sister Ernestina, who also went on to achieve fame as a pianist and composer. Aged six, the young

Lecuona's photograph appeared in the Havana paper *El Figaro* as a marvel of precocious piano talent; at twelve he was earning pocket money as a silent movie accompanist in the Parisién Cinema; and a year later his first composition, a two-step called "Cuba y America", was published.

Lecuona rapidly made a name composing first danzas and then zarzuelas, the Spanish light operas popular in Spain and Cuba until the 1960s. In works such as *El Cafetal* (The Coffee Estate) and *El Batey* (The Cane-cutters' Shack), Lecuona demonstrated a remarkable flair for combining classical Spanish-derived structures with Cuban colouring – Lecuona was one of the earliest users of the term Afro-Cuban as applied to music. He also became known for orchestral suites such as his 1919 *Andalucia*, containing the celebrated danza "**Malagueña**" – which was to be recorded over the century by everyone from Placido Domingo to James Last – and languid boleros such as "**Siboney**", which Rita Montaner performed around the world.

Lecuona was among the first Cubans to perform with great success in the European centres of Paris and Madrid – he remained a huge star in Spain all his life – as well as in the Americas. In the US he was known both as a virtuoso concert pianist – the *Los Angeles Times* called him Gershwin's best interpreter and compared him to a Cuban Chopin – and as a dance-band leader: the **Lecuona Cuban Boys** were one of the top bands of the "rumba" era. At the time of the Revolution, Lecuona was touring abroad, but returned to give concerts in aid of the victims of the fighting, before leaving again for Spain, in search of a cure for the lung ailment that was sapping his strength. He died in 1963 while visiting the birthplace of his grandparents in Tenerife.

⊙ **El Cafetal**   Montilla, Spain

A re-issue of a vintage recording of one of Lecuona's most famous
zarzuelas, a sort of upstairs-downstairs story of the betrothal and
marriage problems of the masters and slaves on an early
nineteenth-century coffee plantation. Contains some beautiful arias
and much historical interest.

⊙ **Cuban Originals: Ernesto Lecuona**   RCA/BMG, US

A collection of Lecuona's most famous pieces, rendered on piano by
the maestro himself. Begins with the immortal "Malagueña".

⊙ **Lecuona Cuban Boys, Vols. 1, 2 and 3**   Harlequin, UK

All the great hits of the 1930s and 40s compiled into three
excellent CDs, with the usual exemplary sleeve notes produced by
this label.

Antonio Machín

The singer who introduced "**El Manisero**" to New York and thence
the world was born in the port of Sagua, probably in 1911, to a poor
black mother and a Galician immigrant father. One of sixteen children, he sang as a child in church, but worked as a building labourer
on leaving school after realizing that being black would bar him from
the operatic career he coveted. He later recalled watching silent
movies in an open-air cinema from the fourth floor of a hotel site, and
attributed his early fascination with showbusiness partly to this experience.

He began singing after moving to Havana to find work, and his
naturally fine voice was noted by an established older guitarist,
Miguel Zaballa. The pair started work as a duo playing outside sea-
front food stands, before moving up to cafés and finally visiting radio
studios looking for casual spots. Before long Machín's talent was

noticed by **Don Azpiazu**, who hired him as solo singer for his orchestra at the Casino Nacional. Machín was still only sixteen, and the first black musician to be given work in the Casino.

In 1930, Machín's role in the Azpiazu orchestra's great New York success enabled him to set up his own successful quartet, with an old friend and colleague, **Daniel Sanchez**, singing second voice. After several years of American stardom, Machín began a meandering and equally popular tour of Europe, ending up in Paris leading his band at the nightclub, La Coupole.

In 1939, with the outbreak of war making French travel difficult, Machín got on a train to Barcelona, without any plans or preparation, and started anew in Spain. After a year playing provincial theatres and Barcelona "taxi-girl" dance joints for a few pesetas, Machín offered to sing free in a Madrid club, La Conga, in the hope of moving upwards. The idea worked: he was hired as vocalist by a top Madrid night-club band, **Los Miuras de Sobré**, with whom he gained enough contacts and sufficient reputation to go solo in 1942. An

Antonio Machín, Spain's favourite Cuban

increasingly successful career in the country's top venues was crowned by a series of hits, notably "Angelitos Negros" (Little Black Angels), performed in a style tailored intelligently to the Spanish market – suave, polished boleros with cleaned-up lyrics (this was the Franco era). By the 1960s, Machín was a huge star in Spain, known as "the most Spanish of Cuban singers and the most Cuban of Spanish singers." He died in 1977, and his grave near Seville was one of the first places of pilgrimage of the veteran Compay Segundo when he came to Spain at the beginning of his own, late, rise to fame in 1994.

⊙ **Antonio Machín, El Manisero**   Tumbao, Spain

Recordings from 1929 and 1930, with the orchestras of Don Azpiazu and Antonio María Romeu, and Machín's own Sextet, beginning with the Azpiazu version of the Peanut Vendor.

⊙ **Cuarteto Machín 1935–35**   Harlequin, UK

An excellent selection of Machín's quartet work, extending the risqué double-entendre pregón repertoire typified by "El Manisero" with "El Viandero", in which the comestible for sale is a long, thick, tasty yucca.

⊙ **Los Boleros de Machín**   Divucsa, Spain

A triple CD collection of the romantic boleros which made Machín famous in Spain, with nary a tumescent vegetable to be seen.

Machito and the Afro-Cubans

The director of the the the **Afro-Cubans**, the group which just may have swung more tightly and brilliantly than any Cuban band ever, was born **Francisco Raúl Grillo** in the Marianao beach district of Havana in 1909. He spent his early years gigging as a percussionist and singer in an assortment of Havana bands, including the **Sexteto Occidente** and the **Sexteto Nacional**, and then New York-based groups, among them the orchestras of **Noro Morales** and **Xavier Cugat**, to whom he was introduced by his brother-in-law, Mario Bauzá. In 1940, after a couple of failed attempts, "Frank" Grillo, known to the public as "Machito", succeeded in putting together his first group, composed largely of members of the Orquesta Siboney, with whom he had been playing at the new Club Cuba in Manhattan.

The following year Machito invited **Mario Bauzá** on board as trumpeter and musical director. Bauzá brought a strong jazz sensibility – he had been playing with Dizzy Gillespie in Cab Calloway's orchestra – and began to reorganize the brass and percussion sections to inject greater depth and power. With Machito leading the band from front-of-stage, facing the audience and wielding his trademark maracas, and Bauzá in tight control in the back row, the Afro-Cubans were an immediate success.

Early vocalists with the Afro-Cubans were **Miguelito Valdés**, followed by **Graciela**, Machito's sister, who provided the slow, sultry boleros Machito himself never wanted to sing – he described himself as having a drunkard's voice – and also spicy guarachas. In 1946, the final key element of the Afro-Cubans' sound arrived, in the form of the pianist and arranger **René Hernandez**. For ten years, the Afro-Cubans' brilliant rhythmic foundation, composed of Hernandez,

Bobby Rodriguez on bass, Luis Miranda on congas, José Mangual on bongos and Ubaldo Nieto on timbales, underpinned an incendiary brass section which gave the band of that era the sound, to quote the jazz writer Nat Chediak, of gods. Gods, furthermore, endowed with great arrangers of the stature of **Chico O'Farrill**, **José Madera** and **Roy Santos**, with a cast of band members including Virgilio Martí, Cachete Maldonado, Andy Gonzalez, Nicky Marrero, Tito Puente, Carlos "Patato" Valdés and Adalberto Santiago, to name only a few ex-Machito members of the Latin aristocracy of New York.

Machito's collaborations with jazzmen included work with Dizzy Gillespie, Zoot Sims, Charlie Parker, Buddy Rich, Dexter Gordon and Herbie Mann, and made him one of the key developers of **Afro-Cuban jazz**. But Machito's band had passed its prime by the 1970s, when Machito's son Mario Grillo took over the musical direction. Mario Bauzá left and the group was reduced to an octet. Nonetheless, the Afro-Cubans were still successful, winning a Grammy Award in 1982 for the record **Machito and his Salsa Big Band**. Machito was in the middle of one of his many successful seasons at Ronnie Scott's in London in 1984 when he was found dead in his hotel room, the victim of a cerebral haemorrhage.

⊙ **Machito and his Afro-Cubans**   Harlequin, UK

A fascinating collection of 22 early Machito tracks, five from a live broadcast from Birdland in 1950, complete with introductions by the disc-jockey Symphony Sid, and containing a sizzling short version of Mario Bauzá's famous "Tanga", with great solos by Bauzá and Zoot Sims. The other tracks are from "transcription discs", specially recorded as-live pieces for radio. The album is commentated by a learned but colourful sleeve note.

Rita Montaner

"**Rita de Cuba**", as la Montaner became known, was born in 1900 to a middle class family in the black suburb of Guanabacoa. Her father, a doctor, was white, and her mother of mixed race, and her career continually oscillated between the poles of Afro-Cuban music and European opera and theatres, making her, as the researcher Jordi Pujol puts it, a composite of "black Rita" and "white Rita". The "white" strand of her personality dominated her early life: she studied musical theory, piano and singing at the Peyrellade Conservatory, married a law student, had two children and began to give recitals of operatic arias in Havana theatres, her mellow, attractive voice gathering much praise.

During the early 1920s she gave numerous amateur performances of works by the key Cuban composers Lecuona, Roig, Anckermann and Roldán, but while on holiday in New York she was discovered by the **Schubert Follies**, with whom she undertook, to her husband's displeasure, a tour of the US. On her return to Havana, she plunged into the worlds of both the concert hall and music-hall, achieving fame with her version of the new Eliseo Grenet song "¡Ay Mamá Inés!" and Lecuona's celebrated Creole capriccio, "Siboney".

In 1928, Montaner abandoned her society-wife role and espoused artistic bohemia, divorcing her husband and heading for **Paris** with the actor Paco Lara, her lover, where she was a brilliant success. In 1931 she was back in New York, this time in Al Jolson's company in the show *The Wonder Bar*, and soon followed up with seasons in Paris and in Mexico, where she began her artistic association with the great Havana pianist and singer **Bola de Nieve**.

In the mid 1940s, Montaner's radio work made her a household name throughout Cuba and she developed the role of a mischievous

gossip in shows such as *Mejor Que Me Calle* (Better I Kept Quiet) and *La Chismosa* (The Gossip) – Ramon Grau, then Cuban President, is supposed to have listened to Montaner's show to find out the word on the street. When televi-
sion became widespread, Montaner's similar shows *Rita & Willy* and *Rita and Cucho* were similarly popular. Throughout the 1950s, Montaner kept the many sides of her career going, combining television and radio with popu-
lar music. She played *La Calle* at the Montmartre Cabaret with **Beny Moré**,

whose theatre debut she arranged, and sang with the **Conjunto Matamoros**. She didn't leave serious music behind, either, starring in the Havana debut of Giancarlo Menotti's opera *The Medium*. She was appearing in a Cuban version of Noel Coward's *Hay Fever* in 1957 when she began to display symptoms of the cancer of the larynx which killed her the following year. Her funeral procession to the Colón Cemetery was attended by thousands of mourners.

⊙ **Rita de Cuba**   Tumbao, Spain

A selection of classics recorded between 1928 and 1941, backed by three important orchestras or one of Montaner's long-term pianists, Rafael Betancourt and Nilo Mendendez (they play in duet on three tracks). Montaner's high operatic voice opens with a stately,

swaying version of "El Manisero", and over the next 22 tracks she performs the gamut of guarachas, pregones, tango-congas ("¡Ay Mamá Inés!", plus three more), canciones from Grenet and Lecuona which sound almost like tropical Puccini arias, and even the "guaracha musulmana" (Muslim guaracha) called "Ali Baba".

Chico O'Farrill

Arturo "Chico" O'Farrill was born in 1921, the son of a well-off attorney of Irish origin, and spent his early years on the family estate in Havana's Vedado district. He attended an American military academy in Georgia and then law school in Havana, but dropped out to play the trumpet, joining the big band of **Armando Romeu**. After unsuccessful experiments with forming Cuban jazz groups in Havana, some years ahead of his time, he moved to New York in the late 1940s, where he worked as an arranger. O'Farrill's breakthrough occurred when he managed to sell "Undercurrent Blues" to **Benny Goodman**, who was so impressed he hired the young Cuban as arranger throughout 1949.

The Goodman connection provided an introduction to **Stan Kenton**, one of the most Latinophile of bandleaders, for whom he arranged the album **Cuban Episode**, before writing his celebrated "Afro-Cuban Suite" for the **Machito** band, with **Charlie Parker** as soloist. By the early 1950s, O'Farrill was able to form his own orchestra, touring the US: in Los Angeles' Sombrero Club he met the Mexican singer **Lupita Valerio**, who shortly afterward became his wife, muse and business partner.

In the mid 1950s, O'Farrill returned to Havana where he became one of the leading lights of the new fashion for records of Cuban descargas pioneered by **Cachao López**. O'Farrill's Vedado villa terrace became the setting for after-hours jam sessions which, transferred to vinyl by

the Gema, RCA and Columbia companies, became major sellers. In 1957, O'Farrill headed for the showbiz Mecca of Mexico before returning to New York and spending a decade and a half providing musical settings for a range of artists from Count Basie to Ringo Starr, supplementing his income by writing TV jingles.

Never a prolific recording artist in his own right, O'Farrill experienced the Cuban maestro rediscovery syndrome in 1995, with the recording of his first album in thirty years, the critical success **Pure Emotion**, followed by a series of concerts including a celebrated Lincoln Center date in New York with Wynton Marsalis, and a European tour with a new band directed by his son, the pianist Arturito O'Farrill.

⊙ Heart of a Legend   Milestone, US

Superb 1999 production by the Chico O'Farrill Afro-Cuban Jazz Big Band, bringing together a score of the most eminent Afro-Cuban jazz men alive, including Cachao, Chocolate, Patato, plus Juan Pablo Torres, Arturo Sandoval and Paquito D'Rivera. Tracks range from the famous "Locos de la Habana", rich in Cachao bass and Torres trombone, to a wonderfully earthy son-based "La Verde Campiña", adorned with great solos by D'Rivera and the young violinist Ilmar Gavilán, plus a blues sung by Nat King Cole's brother Freddy. Classy sleeve-notes, with a long piece by the novelist Oscar Hijuelos.

Orquesta America & Enrique Jorrín

The **Orquesta America** began life in Havana in 1942 as a charanga, founded by the bandleader **Niñon Mondejar**, and playing a standard repertoire of **danzones**. In 1946 Mondejar hired a twenty-year-old violinist and budding composer from Pinar del Río named **Enrique Jorrín**, who had served his musical apprenticeship in the orquesta of **Antonio Arcaño**. According to the music historian Dora Ileana Torres, Arcaño had observed in Jorrín's danzones something a bit Gallego – Spanish, not quite kosher – around the final movement, and this difference manifested itself fully in 1949, when Jorrín wrote a tune called "La Engañadora" (The Enchantress) about a *chica* who hung around the corner of Prado and Neptuno streets in Havana. "La Engañadora" was not only a catchy song, but it employed to the full a new rhythm, simple and regular, with a strong one-two-three (**chachacha**) at the end of each bar, as Jorrín had observed the difficulty many dancers had with the complex, syncopated mambo, the most recent development of the danzón.

It was not until 1953, when it appeared on the B-side of an Orquesta America record entitled "Silver Star" that "La Engañadora" was officially described as a "mambo chachacha", but the dance was already sweeping Cuba. It soon spread to **Mexico**, where both the Orquesta America and Jorrín (who in 1954 formed his own orquesta) travelled to show **Pérez Prado** who were the real chachacha bosses. From there they moved on to the US, where the huge middle-of-the-road success of the chachacha eventually drove a new generation of listeners away from Latin music into the arms of rock. Jorrín died in Havana in 1987, and the Orquesta America continues, nowadays under the direction of the bass guitarist **Jorge Machado**.

⊙ Mano a Mano, Orquesta America y Orquesta Aragón   Egrem, Cuba

Hand to hand – very much as in "combat" – features a dozen great chachacha hits by the rival top bands arranged in pairs. America's "Silver Star" is followed by Aragón's "El Bodeguero"; America's "La Engañadora" by Aragón's "El Paso de Encarnación", and so on.

⊙ Las Leyendas de la Musica Cubana   Tumi, UK

A praise-worthy if flawed four-CD set, with a twenty-page booklet by the eminent Cuban musicologist Helio Orovio. Features recordings from the recently re-formed Orquesta America, divided into sections according to genre – bolero, chachacha, danzón and guaracha-son.

⊙ Exitos de la Orquesta Enrique Jorrín   Orfeon, US

Just what the title says – a collection of big chachacha hits from Jorrín's own band, recorded in Mexico in the late 1950s.

Orquesta Aragón

The band which did as much as any Cuban group to reinforce musical ties with mother Africa was created in 1939 in the colonial town of Cienfuegos by **Orestes Aragón**, a dental technician by day and bass-player by night. Aragón's socialist principles – he was a fervent Party member – dictated the band should be run on co-operative lines, with equally shared payments, In 1948, Aragón had to retire through illness, and the violinist **Rafael Lay**, who had been hired as a thirteen-year-old prodigy, took over as director, a job which he held until his death in a road accident in 1982, whereupon his son **Rafaelito Lay**, also a violinist, took over. By 1950, the Orquesta Aragón was outgrowing its **Cienfuegos** constituency, playing the Guantánamo Carnival and tentative dates in Havana social clubs,

although Havana bands at first tried to freeze them out, a move partly frustrated by support from Beny Moré, who was also born in the province of Cienfuegos.

Aragón's fame rose with their espousal of the new **chachacha** style. Rafael Lay went to see its inventor, Enrique Jorrín, who allowed him complete access to the **Orquesta America** scores, which Lay proceeded to copy out. In 1954, Aragón's "El Aqua del Clavelito", recorded by RCA Victor, was a hit first at Santiago Carnival, then

YOURI LENQUETTE

throughout the island. The same year, Aragón recruited an important new member, the flautist **Richard Egües**, whose virtuosity made him one of the most influential players in Latin America. Egües, christened Eduardo, was also a highly effective composer, contributing the first international hit "El Bodeguero" to Aragón's repertoire.

The Cuban Revolution found Aragón at the height of their success, and their existing political sympathies made them close co-operators with the Castro regime, and highly favoured State artists. In the 1960s they toured Europe and the Soviet Bloc, adapting a string of pop and rock hits including Tom Jones's "Delilah". In the 1970s they toured the Socialist-leaning States of Central and West Africa, where their influence did much to nurture a taste for Cuban music. The 1980s and early 1990s saw the band struggling for survival, but in 1997 Aragón signed to the record company Lusafrica, beginning a new international career on the World Music circuit.

⊙ **Cuban Originals: Orquesta Aragón**   RCA/BMG, US

Eleven classic tracks, beginning with "El Bodeguero", the tale of chachacha dancing in the aisles of the corner grocers which was taken up as a world hit by Nat King Cole. Shows off the sizzling flute, violin and percussion form that made Aragón the band for whom the number one spot of the Cuban hit parade was said to be reserved.

⊙ **La Charanga Eterna**   Lusafrica, France

Aragón's 60th anniversary album, recorded mainly at Havana's new Abdala studio, with star guests recorded separately in Puerto Rico (the veteran *salsero* Cheo Feliciano), Caracas (the old Aragón animateur Felo Bacallao) or Paris (the Congolese Papa Wemba). Thirteen old favourites, from Lecuona's "Siboney" to Arsenio Rodriguez's "Bruca Manigua", described interestingly as a "chá-congo."

Chano Pozo

Luciano Pozo y Gonzalez, **"Chano Pozo"**, played a seminal role in the creation of Latin jazz, but was almost equally famous for his violent and premature death. He was born in Havana in 1915, the half-brother of the famous trumpeter **Felíx Chapottín**, and took up conga-playing, singing and song-writing at an early age; he was also an enthusiastic parader, dressed in top hat and tails, with the Havana carnival *comparsa* Los Dandys. By the time he went to New York in 1946, he had considerable experience in Havana cabarets, notably the Sans Souci, where he attracted great attention in the show Congo Pantera, and his songs "Blen, Blen, Blen", "Nagüe", "Manteca" and others had been performed by artists such as Miguelito Valdés, Machito and Rita Montaner.

In New York, Pozo re-established contact with his cousin, the *bongosero* **Francisco "Chino" Pozo**, and began to work with Machito and Arsenio Rodriguez, among others. Pozo's introduction to the jazz world came via **Mario Bauzá**, who introduced him to **Dizzy Gillespie**, with whom he played and recorded the earliest examples of Cu-bop and toured extensively. Pozo and Gillespie shared a taste for marijuana, *manteca* (butter) as it was called in barrio slang, and it was an argument over a bent deal which led to Pozo's death in 1948. Sold a number of joints which turned out to be made of oregano rather than grass, Pozo confronted the vendor in a Harlem bar, El Río, and was shot dead.

⊙ **Legendary Sessions:**   Tumbao, Spain
Chano Pozo & Arsenio Rodriguez

Only six tracks on this album of US recordings feature Pozo (on congas and vocal) but they give a great taste of Pozo's catchy songs and his brilliant congo playing. Pozo is helped out by a "Conjunto

for Pozo" including eminent friends such as Machito, Tito
Rodriguez, Arsenio Rodriguez and Marcelino Guerra.

Pérez Prado

A stocky, elegantly dressed bandleader and pianist, **Dámaso Pérez
"Seal Face" Prado**'s popularising talent made him one of Cuba's
most internationally famous musicians. Prado was born to poor parents in Matanzas in 1916. He and his brother Pantaleón, who later
followed in his footsteps as a mambo orchestrator, studied piano at a
private music school, and by the age of sixteen Prado had put
together his own dance band, playing successfully in his home
region. Moving to Havana, he found work in the cabarets, where he
played in the orchestra of **Paulina Alvarez**, the "Empress of
Danzonete". His orchestrating skills were noted by the local manager
of the major US music publisher Peer, who hired him as house
arranger, and this position gained him entrée to the top-ranking
Orquesta Casino de la Playa, whose star vocalist Orlando
"Cascarita" Guerra had been impressed with his work.

   With the Casino de la Playa, Prado began employing a rhythmic
block chord approach to piano interludes – and using the word
mambo increasingly. In 1949, having failed to persuade Peer's manager to let him set up his own band, Prado moved to Mexico and
found a residency at the 1-2-3 Club in Mexico City, where he immediately prospered. Prado set up a new orchestra heavily influenced
by the US jazz big bands, with a powerful brass section of four saxophones, five trumpets and a trombone, plus a percussion squad
strengthened by double congas and timbales. This proved to be a
formidable dance machine, possessed of a succession of star trumpeters such as **Chilo Morán**, heirs of the strong Mexican military

brass tradition. For his sound, Prado began composing simple but dynamic "mambos" and applied his adaptable new orchestration to a repertoire of Cuban and Mexican standards. Prado became a fixture of Mexico City nightlife, and before long was writing mambos for a stream of films – appearing in eleven of them himself.

At the same time, Prado began to record for RCA Victor, at first in Mexico, where he produced his hits "Mambo No. 5", followed by the massively successful "Que Rico El Mambo" and "Mambo No. 8". In the early 1950s, Prado hired Beny Moré as singer and reigned supreme over Mexican dance music while the mambo boom played out its course, wowing New Yorkers – and being condemned by the church in Peru for immorality. When the **chachacha** burst out of Havana, Prado applied himself to the new rhythm, producing another massive hit, "Cerezo Rosa", which became a chart-topper in the US under the name "Cherry Blossom Pink & Apple Blossom White".

By this time Prado had moved to the US, having been expelled from Mexico over a dispute about back contributions to the powerful Musicians' Union. He eventually returned in 1964, by which time he had taken his music into cinema in the US (*Chachacha Boom* in 1956) and Italy (Fellini's *La Dolce Vita* in 1960, which featured Prado's catchy number "Patricia"). He attempted, without much success, to launch another new rhythm, the dengue, and finally died in Mexico City in 1989, shortly before the world boom in Cuban music.

⊙ **Cuban Originals: Perez Prado**   RCA/BMG, US

An essential compilation of Prado's original RCA recordings, including the big hits "Mambo No. 5", "Mambo No. 8", "Que Rico El Mambo" and "Cerezo Rosa", as well as numbers such as Prado's "Lupita", which was revived in the 1990s by the Colombian Fruko, mambo-ized Mexican rancheras ("Cucuru cu Paloma") and boleros

(Agustín Lara's "Maria Bonita" and "Granada"), even a zany Flight of the Bumble Bee, the bee impersonated by a drunkenly warbling trumpet and Prado's "Unh" sounding as if he's just been stung.

⊙ Mambos by Beny Moré   Tumbao, Spain

Moré started his real fame in Mexico as Prince of the Mambo (to Prado's King thereof) and this set of 1948–50 Mexican recordings shows the Prado band on cracking form, from the opening mambo "Babaratiri" (later to become the Guinness snail-race TV commercial soundtrack) to the closing guaracha "Será La Negra".

⊙ Dengue-Reggae   Orfeon, US

A late-period curiosity, on the cover of which the maestro displays his new goatee, and containing a quartet of the latest dengues, plus a boogaloo and a leavening of mambo.

Mongo Santamaría

One of the most visible and influential conga players in the world, **Ramón "Mongo" Santamaría** taught himself to play. Born in 1922 in

the Havana rumba district of Jesús María, Santamaría learnt sacred **santería** percussion in his youth, and worked as a postman while finding a place in the Tropicana house orchestra. In 1948 he travelled to Mexico with **Pérez Prado**'s band and from there to New York, where he began to work with **Tito Puente**

before making his solo debut album **Changó (Drums and Chants)**. In 1958 he left Puente's band to work with Cal Tjader; it's said that Puente then had to cut the trickier numbers from his repertoire as his percussion section was incapable of playing them without Santamaría's conga expertise.

After a brief return to Havana in 1960, when he recorded with **Carlos Embale**, **Merceditas Valdés** and **Niño Rivera**, Santamaría entered more deeply into the US jazz world. In the early 1960s he formed his group **La Sabrosa**, which began to work with guest musicians such as the young **Chick Corea** and **Herbie Hancock**. Santamaría became one of the most prolific Cuban players in the US, performing with his own group (which featured as arrangers and star soloists the trumpeter Marty Sheller and the tenor saxophonist Hubert Laws), arranging for La Lupe, guesting with the Fania All Stars and Dizzy Gillespie, and producing a steady flow of live and studio albums.

⊙ Mongo Santamaría's Greatest Hits	Sony/World Up, UK

A new compilation of the 1960s Latin funk/jazz/boogaloo era, including the hits "We Got Latin Soul", "Dock of the Bay" and "Mongo's Boogaloo". Also included is Herbie Hancock's tune "Watermelon Man", which became a huge crossover hit in 1962 and Santamaría's signature tune.

5
Bolero

O f all the misunderstood Cuban musical genres, **bolero** has the largest burden to dispel. The Cuban bolero, sultry, often despairing and unashamedly romantic, links the earliest of *trovadores* with millennial pop idols such as **Luis Miguel**, and the kitsch aesthetic of **Pedro Almodóvar** films with the purity of 1940s' Socialist revolutionaries. The bolero's European influences include French romances, Italian operatic arias and Neapolitan song (Cuban bolero is quite separate from both the rustic Andalusian folk dance and Ravel's ultra-famous piece by the same name), but just like son, it was the fusion of such influences with **African percussion** which gave rise to the totally new form.

The first boleros were created in Santiago in the latter part of the nineteenth century by the early *trovadores* (see p.152), the singer-songwriters of that period. According to the bolero expert Rosendo Ruiz, son of the bolero songwriter of the same name, the districts of **El Tivoli** and **Los Hoyos** were particular haunts of popular *trovadores*, and among their styles was a song form combining the flamenco multi-finger strumming known as *rasgueado*, an instrumental introduction on guitar known as a *pasacalle*, and a repeated five-note rhythmic phrase, the *cinquillo*, which was the mark of the early boleros.

The *trovadores* were often connected with **revolutionary politics**, and from its outset the bolero took on the same associations, even though lyrically the genre always concerned itself with love. This irony was reinforced in the 1940s and 1950s, when a new generation of bolero-impelled romantic singers grew up in the ambit of the Socialist Party and its radio station Radio Mil Diez. In the late nineteenth century, however, the revolutionary political aim was independence from Spain, and some of Cuba's most prominent independence theorists and activists, men such as Antonio Maceo and Guillermo Moncada, mingled socially with the *trovadores*.

It was one of the most politically connected of the *trovadores*, **Pepe Sanchez**, who wrote what is universally acknowledged as the first bolero. The lyrics of his "Tristezas" (Sadness) are still archetypes of the genre in their themes of love, loss and betrayal: "luck is my enemy – my passion can never bear fruit – the kiss you one day gave me, I keep in my heart".

After Cuban independence, the bolero was transported to **Havana** in the repertoires of the *trovadores*, who began to move to the capital, as well as in the intermission acts of circuses and theatre troupes. The form began to evolve, becoming less bound by the *cinquillo* trademark, which was sometimes relegated to a theme played by an accompanying instrument. Bolero composers began to use the texts of poets, leading to a greater lyrical sophistication. A series of hugely popular songs appeared, spreading throughout the island and even internationally, including **Eusebio Delfín**'s "Y Tu Que Has Hecho" (And What Have You Done) – known to every Cuban as *en el tronco de un arbol* (on the trunk of a tree) after the first line of its lyric – and a series of songs to women, "Mercedes", "Santa Cecilia" and "Longina" (the last is still played by Compay Segundo). A decade later, "Quiereme Mucho" (Love Me Lots), the first move into

romantic song-writing by the eminent composer and orchestra direc-tor **Gonzalo Roig**, outgrew its huge Cuban success and began to enter the repertoire of American singers, translated as "Yours".

Dance band boleros

The 1920s and 1930s saw the bolero branch out in two major direc-tions. One was a lyrical, piano-accompanied style, the other a hot, exciting development which came from the newly established son trios and septets, who added the montuno chorus of a son, creating the hybrid **bolero-son** which quickly became a dancehall favourite. As so often before, it was a musician from the east of Cuba, a veter-an of both trova and son, who was most famously responsible: **Miguel Matamoros**'s "Lagrimas Negras" (Black Tears) established itself as the classic of the genre and opened the way for ever greater variation in the years to come.

By the 1940s, artists such as **Arsenio Rodriguez**, **Beny Moré** and the **Sonora Matancera** were performing boleros, and hybrids were created as the genre was adapted to successive new vogues. As mambo exploded across the world of Latin American music, blaring mambo brass sections were attached to bolero arrangements, creat-ing **bolero-mambos**. Among them were numbers subsequently to become standards, such as "Quizás, Quizás" (Perhaps, Perhaps) and "Acercate Mas" (Come Closer) by **Osvaldo Farrés**, an industrial designer and amateur songwriter from Havana whose songs were translated and used in several Hollywood films of the 1950s. The pianist, author and songwriter **Bobby Collazo**'s "La Ultima Noche" – "you left me the night as my memory of your betrayal...Ay! " – was equally classic. When the **chachacha** rhythm appeared in the 1950s, it was not long before its leading innovator, the Orquesta America, began to adapt popular boleros to a chachacha rhythm, and then,

with the rival Orquesta Aragón in hot pursuit, to write custom fusion numbers which became known as **bolero-chas**.

Throughout the 1950s, the bolero boomed in its dance band form, and the greatest star of Cuban music at that time was also its greatest interpreter. If **Beny Moré** was unrivalled as a sonero, he was also an ace at the dynamic, soulful rendition of a bolero. He had learnt the craft of music in the conjunto of **Miguel Matamoros**, and during his early years in Havana playing cafés and bordellos had taken every chance he could get to go to the nightclubs of the Marianao beach district, where among others he listened to **Panchito Riset**, one of the top early bolero-son singers. And it was no coincidence that Moré had the first truly fertile years of his major career in Mexico, with both Matamoros and the mambo bandleader **Pérez Prado**,

Bolero in Mexico

The bolero, like other Cuban musical styles, spread to **Mexico** via the Yucatan peninsula, which contained large numbers of both Spanish colonialists, and later, exiled Cuban independence activists. At the end of the nineteenth century, before Mexico possessed modern roads, residents of the town of Merida could more easily reach Havana than Mexico City: indeed, wealthy Merida landowners would send their laundry over to Havana on the ferry. The first boleros were brought to Yucatan by Cuban musicians travelling with theatre companies, though they were soon followed by the *trovador* **Alberto Villalón**, in 1908. Twenty years later, the Mexican bolero-writing tradition had given rise to the national hit "Nunca", written by **Guty Cárdena**, which successfully made the return journey to Cuba, covered by the great Orquesta America.

because by this time Mexico was a bolero centre of equal importance to Cuba, as both consumer and producer.

Bolero ballads

The **piano** entered Cuba widely in the 1930s, partly as an accompanying instrument for between-reels entertainment in cinemas, and partly as a salon instrument for bourgeois houses. It became the instrument of preference for a range of songwriters from serious orchestral composers such as **Gonzalo Roig** and **Ernesto Lecuona** (whose work included a number of fine boleros, most notably the famous "Siboney") to jazz-influenced innovators such as **Bola de Nieve** and a number of outstanding female writer-performers, led by **Isolina Carrilla**, creator of the perennial "Dos Gardenias".

The piano won its way to the heart of Cuban music, however, in an alternative strand of Cuban bolero which grew up around piano accompaniment in the 1930s and 40s. The style's chief star was **Agustín Lara**, a singer and Mexican matinee idol renowned throughout the Spanish-speaking world. A sort of rough-voiced Latin Cole Porter, his style was inventive and idiosyncratic, yet rooted firmly in the piano bolero tradition.

By the end of the 1950s, the golden age of the bolero, the genre covered a range including the refined and ever more studied pieces of these artists, and the popular dance versions of the star orquestas, big bands and conjuntos. There were also extravagant nightclub boleristas, including the remarkable **Freddy**, as described in the novels *Tres Tristes Tigres* and *Ella Cantaba Boleros* by **Guillermo Cabrera Infante**.

At the lower end of the artistic scale, the 1950s' bolero market had also become saturated with formulaic productions in which the classic bolero themes – loss, betrayal, love and hate – had turned into

melodramatic cliché. This market was an extension of the 1940s' boom in **boleros de victrola**, songs created by the hundred for the early jukeboxes. Many of these could be found in Havana's burgeoning red light nightspots, the bolero in its earliest days having been seized upon as the perfect dance for erotic encounters (like the tango and danzón, dancing couples held each other close). The seedy and melodramatic connotations of bolero were eventually to drive it out of fashion, although **Agustín Lara**, who had worked as a bordello entertainer in his youth, once commented that "anyone who is romantic also has a fine sense of what is *cursi* (in bad taste) and not to reject it is a mark of intelligence. If I can only translate my emotions by using the baroque language of bad taste, then I'm not ashamed to do so".

Fílin

In any event, before the bolero strand of romantic song was temporarily eclipsed by fashion, it underwent another transmutation, with the creation of a new variation known as feeling which soon became Hispanicized as **fílin**. Fílin came into existence as a reaction against both the excessive orchestration and melodrama of the bolero, indeed of romantic song generally, and its commercialism. The new songs had simple guitar accompaniments and aimed to express direct, honest emotions, hence "feelings". (The word was also used as an expression of approval for outstanding jazz solos.) "When I perform my song "Novia Mía" (My Girl), commented one of the new genre's founders, **José Antonio Méndez**, "I don't perform it thinking of a record company, but simply as if I were speaking to my girl". **Cesar Portillo de la Luz**, another founder of the movement, spoke of the cloying sentimentality of romantic song and the desire to create a style and language that would be lyrical, but relate to the everyday reality of young people.

Musically, fílin drew on the traditions of trova and bolero, but also on North American jazz, blues and romantic and film music. The founders of the genre were avid listeners to American music broadcast on the radio, and also cultivated visiting black American marines in the Havana docks to obtain Ella Fitzgerald and Billie Holiday records. The earliest stirrings of fílin date to the end of the 1930s, although the style didn't develop fully until the 1940s and only achieved wide dissemination later still, on the advent of the Revolution. The founders of fílin belonged to a group of friends who used to meet around Central Havana to talk, listen to music, play and compose together, sometimes in Maceo Park, often in the house of one of their number, **Angel Díaz**, the son of the old trova star Tirso Diaz.

A notable characteristic of the fílin movement was its involvement in revolutionary opposition **politics**. Many of the fílin artists were members of the Socialist Party, and their early careers were helped by the Party's radio station, Mil Diez, the so-called "broadcaster of the people", which aimed to support authentic, non-commercial music. The young **Lázaro Peña**, working as union representative in a textile factory, used to visit Mil Diez to hand over donations collected among the workforce, as did the *fílinista* **Tania Castellanos**, who when not composing was a steelworker and union activist. After the Revolution, the new regime repaid the fílin writers – under Castro, Méndez and Castellanos were made successive Presidents of the Cuban Society of Musical Authors. Although the lyrical preoccupation of fílin continued to be romantic, politics made the rare intrusion, with, for example, **Tania Castellanos**'s "Por Angela" (For Angela) – an ode to the Black Power activist, Angela Davis – or **Cesar Portillo de la Luz**'s "La Hora de Todos" (The Hour of Everyone), with its march-theme and references to the struggle of the North Vietnamese.

Twilight Years

The maturity of fílin coincided with the downturn in fortunes of its parent, the bolero. In the 1960s the advent of the British-led rock revolution cast a pall over tropical music generally. The chachacha and the bolero were regarded as old hat by a new generation, and a spate of Latin rock cover groups arrived on the scene. For romantic music, the new consumers looked instead to the **balada**, a Hispanicized version of the Anglo-American slow ballad, and boleros shrank to an afterthought in the repertoire of those artists who didn't discard them altogether. Among those few were the Puerto Rican singer-guitarist **José Feliciano** and Cuban doo-wop stylists **Los Zafiros**.

Through the 1960s and 1970s, the bolero subsisted in the **cabarets**, and in certain die-hard Havana nightspots such as the **Rincon del Fílin** (the Fílin Corner), in the rooftop nightclub of the Saint John Hotel, the **Pico Blanco**, and in the **Gato Tuerto** (the One-Eyed Cat) near the Hotel Nacional. It also existed robustly outside Cuba, in unfashionable low class enclaves. In **Mexico**, mixed with local ranchera songs, it enthralled tequila and beer drinkers in cantinas, purveyed by singers such as the wonderful peroxide diva, **Paquita la del Barrio**. In the **Dominican Republic**, where it had transmuted into the **bachata** – early Santiago romantic boleros had been known alternatively as *bachatas* – it continued to entertain the patrons of the little *colmado* bar-stores and the prostitutes who often frequented them. In **Spain**, where the great Cuban singer Antonio Machín had first made boleros popular in the 1930s and 1940s, it was adopted by the gypsy community, becoming, in the hands of stars such as Moncho, **"El Gitano del Bolero"**, the **bolero moruno**.

Comeback

When a new generation of Spaniards rediscovered salsa and other tropical dance musics in the 1980s, the film director **Pedro Almodóvar** fell under the camp retro spell of old *boleristas* such as the Mexican **Chavela Vargas**, using their music in films such as *High Heels*. In Mexico, the young pop star **Luis Miguel**, realizing that a successful album of retro classics could not only capture a new youth market but also appeal to nostalgic older generations, began to record his series of **Romances** albums with the songs of Lara and other classic *boleristas*. His success was such that when the great Spanish operatic tenor **Placido Domingo** decided to record his own album of boleros in 1996 he went to Miguel's producer and arranger, the Argentinian-born Bebu Silvetti. By the end of the 1990s, everyone from Julio Iglesias to the Spanish rock singer Luz Cusal was recording boleros.

Back in Cuba, bolero was also bouncing back. In 1986, the **Boleros de Oro** festival was founded in Havana and soon established itself as one of the island's most important music events. By 1998, the festival was able to boast that it had attracted the first Japanese bolero singers, one professional working under the name Yoshiro, and several more amateurs, all of whom attracted favourable comment for their perfect Spanish diction. At the same time, a number of the big 1980s' and 1990s' star popular groups and singers, notably **NG La Banda**, **Paulito y Su Elite** and **Bamboleo**, began once more to include boleros in their acts.

Finally, the Buena Vista phenomenon in 1997 turned out to favour the bolero as much as the son, which had up to this time been the chief beneficiary of interest on the part of World Music audiences. Both **Ibrahim Ferrer** and **Compay Segundo**, major stars of the first

wave of Buena Vista hit albums, were accomplished *boleristas* and brought songs such as "Dos Gardenias" to a new multi-million-strong world audience. The artist to whom it fell to set the seal on this mass breakthrough was **Omara Portuondo**. From the 1960s to the 1980s,

Julio Etchart

Omara, the fiancée of filin

Omara had forged a steady career as one of Cuba's most popular all-rounders, though her international success was limited to tours of Communist ally states and guest appearances at European Socialist events such as the French Fête de l'Humanité. Portuondo never abandoned her bolero and fílin repertoire, and was recording a new album in the genre, **La Novia del Fílin**, in the Egrem recording facility in Havana when Ry Cooder and the Buena Vista musicians were putting together their first album in an adjacent studio. Invited to duet with Compay Segundo on the old Maria Teresa Vera classic, "Viente Años", Omara became one of the greatest individual success stories of the Buena Vista series.

Artists

Elena Burke

Had it not been for Omara Portuondo's leap to world stardom with the Buena Vista Social Club group, **Elena Burke** would have gone down in history as the major female success of the fílin movement, her status and popularity equalling Portuondo's over many decades. Burke was born Romana Burgues in Havana in 1928 and, like so many young Cuban entertainers, began singing among friends, before moving into amateur radio shows in the early 1940s.

By 1942 Burke had broadcast on Mil Diez, and thus entered the *fílinista* circle. In 1947, she was hired by the choreographer Roderico Neyra, the famous "Rodney" of the Tropicana's heyday, to be a

singing member of the celebrated song-and-dance troupe, the **Mulatas da Fuega** (Fiery Mulatas). With the Mulatas she supported Josephine Baker during the American star's shows at the Teatro Encanto.

In the 1950s, Burke worked with several of the small vocal groups popular at the time, beginning with a trio, **Las Cancioneras**, before proceeding to the well-known quartet of the prolific bolero writer **Orlando de la Rosa**, and finally providing much of the impetus behind the formation of the seminal **Cuarteto d'Aida**, directed by Aida Diestro, with Omara and Haydee Portuondo, and Moraima Secada. The success of Las d'Aida made the careers of all of the individual members, and in 1958 Burke went solo, appearing in shows and on television accompanied either by the guitarist

Froilán Amézaga or by pianists, including **Frank Dominguez** and **Enriqueta Almanza**. Although an interpreter primarily of traditional boleros, ballads and the fílin repertoire, Burke also benefited in the 1960s from modern new material written by the young **Juan Formell**, the dynamo behind Los Van Van. She continues to be one of Cuba's best-known artists, though relatively little-known outside, while her daughter **Malena Burke** carves her own niche in Miami exile with a similar range of material.

| ⊙ Elena Burke En Persona | Egrem, Cuba/Virgin, Spain |

A good 1995 album recorded in Havana with Enriqueta Almanza on piano, Burke's current guitarist Felipe Valdés, the ubiquitous Tata Güines on congas and Junio Isel on bongos, showing Burke still to be in good voice. The Spanish-licensed record has a much better booklet, as one might expect.

| ⊙ Elena Burke En Compania | Egrem, Cuba |

Interesting if patchily recorded set of collaborations with a great range of Cuban artists, from Omara Portuondo and Moraima Secada to the Orquestas Aragón and Jorrín.

| ⊙ La Reina del Feeling | Orfeon, US |

Sixteen classic boleros and ballads recorded in Mexico around the early 1970s.

Francisco Céspedes

Francisco Céspedes is the latest in a long tradition of Cuban singers to use Mexico as a springboard for careers as international romantic stars. Céspedes was born in the early 1960s in Santa Clara, the final resting place of Che Guevara. He embarked upon and abandoned medical studies before moving to Havana and frequenting musical circles in the early 1980s. He was attracted to jazz – he met Arturo Sandoval at informal weekend jam sessions at a friend's house – as well as the classic bolero, trova and fílin of the 1940s and 1950s.

Céspedes' deep, powerful, smoky voice gradually found him work, usually singing fílin songs, accompanied by his guitar, or guesting with the **Orquesta Cubana de Musíca Moderna** and a small group led by **Pucho López**, with whom he obtained his first trips abroad, to Spain at the beginning of the 1990s, and then to Mexico, where he

decided to stay. Based in Mexico City, Céspedes began to work his way into the show-business mainstream, busking or playing small bars and clubs. His songs, which he was now writing prolifically,

combined the simple, unmannered but emotional spirit of Cuban 1940s' and 1950s' romantic music with current fashions in Latin American ballads.

In 1992 came his first breakthrough, when the romantic idol **Luis Miguel** recorded Céspedes' "Pensar En Ti" (To Think Of You). Céspedes was talent-spotted by the major label, Warner, and during a year-

long residency at the club El Candelero attracted major Spanish artists such as Miguel Bosé, Alejandro Saenz and Joan Manuel Serrat. In 1997, Céspedes' first Warner album, **Vida Loca**, came out. The title song was a hit and the album sold over 1,500,000 copies.

⊙ Vida Loca   WEA, Mexico

A slight touch of international Latin ballad blandness is tempered by Céspedes' superb voice and his gift for finding a tune which suits it perfectly.

⊙ Dónde Está La Vida   WEA, Mexico

More of the same, beginning with the title track, which, like "Señora" from the first album, achieved the feat of hitching itself to a mass-audience Mexican soap, *La Casa En La Playa* (The House on the Beach), thereby assuring its success.

Frank Emilio Flynn

Although as a founder-member **Frank Emilio Flynn** is forever associated with the **fílin movement**, a major part of his work is in the jazz field, and he has contributed in distinguished fashion to the world of danzón. In fact, as he told the magazine Salsa Cubana, he considers himself "a pianist without a style of my own," aiming rather to play "everything in its style."

Flynn was born to an American father of Irish origin and a Cuban mother in Havana in 1921. He lost his sight due to illness as a teenager and thereafter learnt through an acutely developed musical ear and Braille. Flynn's first love was the **danzón**, which he learnt by listening to the **Antonio María Romeu** orquesta on the radio, before he came to know the Romeus personally. Flynn got to know other influential musicians, playing with **Ignacio Piñeiro** on Radio CMBG, and in 1946 achieving his breakthrough into regular work on Radio Mil Diez thanks to the support of Miguel Matamoros.

Through Radio Mil Diez, Flynn met the fílinista group, and was soon working with **José Antonio Méndez**, **Omara Portuondo** and the Loquibambia group. In 1959 he was the leading light, with the percussionist Guillermo Barretto, of the new **Quinteto Instrumental de Música Cubana**, which subsequently transmuted first into the **Orquesta Cubana de Música Moderna** and then **Los Amigos**, the whole ensemble of groups being one of the key institutions of post-Revolution avant garde music creation. During this period Flynn created important pieces such as the descarga "Gandinga, Mondonga y Sandunga" and the "Scheherezada Cha-Cha-Cha", the latter for the social club of that name.

Although Flynn continued to play sporadically at home and at international jazz festivals throughout the 1970s and 1980s, his pro-

CRISTINA PIZA

file was low, a state of affairs remedied in the 1990s with new international interest in his work. He recorded three albums for the French label Milan, co-starred in the major Cuban show, *Noche Tropical*, in Japan, and, at the invitation of Wynton Marsalis, played New York's Lincoln Center with "Cachaíto" Lopez and Tata Güines, two old colleagues from the Modern Music Orchestra, and Ñico Rojas, the long-neglected fílin founder-member.

⊙ **Barbarísimo**   Milan Latino, France

Flynn's return to the Latin jazz centre-stage, recorded in 1996 with a new generation of top musicians, notably Miguel "Anga" Diaz on

congas, Changuito on timbales, Carlos del Puerto on bass and Orlando "Maraca" Valle on flute. Cracking new versions of "Gandinga, Mondonga y Sandunga" and the "Scheherezada Cha-Cha-Cha", plus suave jazz versions of "Buena Vista Social Club" and Mario Bauzá's "Mambo Inn".

Freddy

Of all the stars of Cuban song, none is more spectacularly colourful than the remarkable **Fredesvinda García**, aka **Freddy** (also often spelt Fredy), which is no doubt why the novelist Guillermo Cabrera Infante chose her as the inspiration for his character La Estrella, the "black whale" of a nightclub entertainer with the rich oily voice and the gigantic thighs. She was apparently no less inspirational for the film director Pedro Almodóvar, who sought out an old copy of the rare cult record on his first visit to Cuba.

Freddy was born in 1930 to a poor family in Camagüey province and moved to Havana at the age of twelve to work as a housemaid. She eventually found a job cleaning the house of **Aida Diestro**, the pianist and director of the **Cuarteto d'Aida**, who invited her to a rehearsal and helped introduce her to show-business circles. Freddy was already making a name for herself in any event, as a fixture and occasional performer in the bars and clubs of Vedado, where she would unleash her smooth, deep, masculine voice on a torch song, often unaccompanied, in the small hours after the shows had finished. Freddy's capacity for consuming, as well as performing, in bars ensured her weight remained colossal and her appearance as exotic as her sound.

In 1960, Freddy was abruptly discovered and hired by the director of the casino of the Hotel Capri, where her act became a sell-out. The Havana label Puchito, in its last months as a private entity,

recorded her lone album, with orchestration by the lawyer-pianist-arranger **Humberto Suárez**. The following year, Freddy realized her outré image was not in keeping with revolutionary ideals and headed for Puerto Rico, where she died of a heart attack at age 31, her stardom extinguished as rapidly as it had risen.

⊙ La Voz del Sentimiento   Melodie, France

On the only album she ever made, Freddy's remarkable voice – like foie gras steeped in Armagnac – is backed by terrific orchestrations rich in swathes of violin or Hammond organ and studded with blasts of brass. The dozen songs range from Gershwin's "The Man I Love" (the version which inspired Omara Portuondo, who knew and admired Freddy) to Agustín Lara's "Noche de Ronda", and make the average *fílinista* sound like Val Doonican. The album is also available as Ella Cantaba Boleros on the Spanish label, Música del Sol.

José Antonio Méndez

José Antonio Méndez, one of the two great stars of guitar-backed fílin (along with Cesar Portillo de la Luz), was born in the Los Piños suburb of Havana in 1927, and took up guitar and singing while studying to be an agronomist. Quite independently of the other fílin initiators, he listened to the same American music and evolved a sim-

ilar style. Felix Contreras reports a conversation with Ñico Rojas, one of the first members of the Diaz house fílin group, in which Rojas describes visiting a friend's home in Los Piños to borrow a book on hydromechanics. Noticing a guitar in the room, he began to play, whereupon his host remarked on his unusual style, extraordinarily like that of another friend of his who lived nearby. Rojas asked to meet this friend. It turned out to be José Antonio Méndez, who did indeed play in the new style. "That's fílin", Rojas told Méndez, and immediately took him to meet the group.

Méndez was soon organizing the group **Loquibambia**, performing on Radio Mil Diez. Among his earliest compositions was "La Gloria Eres Tu" (You Are The Glory), written in 1947, which proceeded to become a huge hit and ultimately one of the most famous Cuban songs ever. Even so, the first fílin creators were perceived as uncommercial, partly because of their Socialist affiliations, and many struggled to get by. As a result, Méndez moved to **Mexico** suddenly in 1949 where he enjoyed great success. After the Revolution, he returned to Cuba, where he enjoyed considerable prestige. He was knocked down and killed by a bus in the street in 1989, days after a concert in his honour at the Teatro America in Havana. Cristóbal Díaz Ayala, who was in Mexico City at the time, recounts that the public mourning was extensive, with Méndez's music played throughout the city all night when the news of his death broke.

⊙ Sentimiento   Bis, Cuba

All Méndez's great hits, including of course "La Gloria", on a recent re-compilation by the more accessible of Cuba's state record labels.

Cesar Portillo de la Luz

The son of a cigar-roller, born in Havana in 1922, **Cesar Portillo de la Luz** taught himself guitar, singing the traditional trova songs he loved as an amateur. Throughout his early life he supported himself as a housepainter, all the time listening avidly to North American jazz on the radio and nurturing his song-writing ambition. His introduction to fílin occurred while playing at a friend's house, when the *trovador* **Angel Díaz** appeared at an open window. They found they were neighbours, whereupon Díaz invited the young man round to the famous **Callejón de Hammel** house to meet and play with the members of the nascent fílin movement.

By 1946, Portillo de la Luz was finding professional singing engagements, particularly on Radio Mil Diez, where he obtained a weekly programme slot, *Canciones del Mañana* (Songs of the Morning). His first serious composition, "Ave de Paso" (Bird of Passage), written to a transitory girlfriend, established his tone with its soft, jazz-influenced melody and simple romantic lyric. In 1950, he published "Contigo en la Distancia", which began its path to international fame when it was performed and recorded in Mexico by the top singer Andy Russell. So novel and overpoweringly romantic was "Contigo", said Portillo de la Luz, that the song was accused of influencing the birth rate. Its success, and possibly the Mexican population boost, was repeated by other great romantic numbers such as "Tu, Mi Delirio" (You, My Madness) and "Noche Cubana" (Cuban Night).

From the late 1950s onwards Portillo de la Luz led a quintet which played at top Havana cabarets like the **Gato Tuerto**, but after the Revolution his song-writing developed a new non-romantic, propagandist strand, with items such as "O Valeroso Vietnam" (Oh Brave Vietnam). Nevertheless, in 1999, when the Gato Tuerto reopened to

cater for the new tourist boom, Portillo de la Luz was one of its first regular performers.

⊙ Un Momento con Portillo de la Luz   Artex, Cuba

A rare example of a recording of the maestro. Hard to find, however, as it was issued by the now defunct Artex label.

Omara Portuondo

Omara Portuondo was born in 1930 in Central Havana's **Calle Salud**, the street later made famous by fellow resident Compay Segundo. She was the child of a mixed-race marriage, still a rarity in those days, her father a black baseball player and her mother of upper-class Spanish extraction. Omara recalled her parents never went out together or acknowledged each other in the street, so afraid were they of the opprobrium of white society.

The young Omara entered show-business aged fifteen as a dancer at the Tropicana and, in spite of her shyness, began to mix with the group of young would-be singers and songwriters who comprised the nascent filin movement. The *filinistas* were all enthusiasts of American jazz, particularly Ella Fitzgerald, Sarah Vaughan and Benny Goodman, and Omara's first music-making consisted of jazz duets she sang with her sister Haydee at these gatherings, the pair being dubbed **Las Tailumitas**. The two girls shortly became members of the **Loquibambia Quartet**, a vocal group put together by Frank Emilio Flynn, and performed on the Socialist Radio Mil Diez. It was at this early stage of her career that Omara acquired her nickname **la novia del filin** – the fiancée of filin – from a Mil Diez presenter's announcement.

In the filin circle, Omara met **Elena Burke**, who got her a stand-in role with the Orlando de la Rosa quartet's Mexico tour. Omara later recalled that she had learnt a lot from Burke, especially how to make

do with just two stage dresses by constantly changing their appearance with small adornments. In 1952, Omara and Haydee joined the musical director and pianist Aida Diestro and the singer Moraima Secada in a new vocal group, the **Cuarteto Las d'Aida**, which achieved great success with its

sophisticated mixture of American vocal jazz and Afro-Cuban elements, and the vivacious, dynamic staging of the four singers. Las d'Aida backed **Nat King Cole** at the Tropicana, recorded an album for RCA Victor, and toured internationally. The group was playing in Miami in 1961 when news of the rupture of relations between Cuba and the US broke; they flew back immediately to Cuba. Haydee left for exile soon afterwards and never returned, but Omara stayed, and became a fixture of the new socialist arts establishment.

In 1967 Omara went solo, taking the opportunity offered by the scarcity of singers, so many having fled Cuba, and by the 1970s Omara was one of Cuba's best known artists. She spent the next 25 years working steadily as a headline act at the Tropicana, touring the Communist world and making a succession of indifferent Egrem LPs, mainly in the bolero/fílin mode, finally being awarded a VIP apartment in a new concrete block overlooking the Malecón in Havana.

In 1995, the Spanish rediscovery of Cuban music reached Omara, tentatively at first. She spent several months earning a pittance play-

ing Seville nightclubs, but recorded two well-received albums with the Madrid label, Nubenegra. Back in Havana, she resumed her weekly show in the Café Cantante in Havana. In 1996, she was invited by Egrem to record a new album, entitled **La Novia del Fílin**, and she was in the middle of this when the Buena Vista Social Club producer **Juan de Marcos Gonzalez**, in an adjacent studio, asked her to duet with Compay Segundo. Three years later, she was one of the stars of the biggest selling Cuban recording project of the century and had recorded a new solo album, **Omara Portuondo**, which was also a major international hit.

⊙ La Colección Cubana: Omara Portuondo   Nascente, UK

A good collection of sixteen songs from seven albums originally issued between 1967 and 1996, interspersing the more familiar romantic material with lively *sones*. High points include four tracks from the 1996 **La Novia del Fílin**, with Portuondo in good voice, accompanied by subtle and soulful guitar and flute.

⊙ Palabras   Nubenegra, Spain

A smooth and well-produced collection of Cuban and Spanish songs recorded in Spain in 1997. Omara is accompanied by lilting Spanish guitar and accordion, with occasional brass and percussion.

⊙ Desafíos   Nubenegra, Spain

The second Spanish album from 1997, a duet with the fluid piano of the great Chucho Valdés, on a collection of Cuban standards.

⊙ Omara Portuondo   World Circuit, UK

Omara's post-Buena Vista album, beautifully orchestrated by Demetrio Muñiz, director of the Tropicana orquesta, with large and lush string and brass sections. Features a rich selection of pre-1960s' Cuban classics with Ruben Gonzalez on piano and Cachaíto López on bass.

6

Trova

ike so much Cuban music, the story of **trova** begins in the east, where Santiago, the old capital of Oriente, played its usual important role. Up to the late nineteenth century, what was referred to as **canción** (urban song) was based on a mixture of whatever was predominant in Europe – opera arias, Neapolitan songs and French romances – with some input from the burgeoning music of Mexico and the new states of Venezuela and Colombia.

The development of distinctive **Cuban canción** coincided with the growth in numbers of the itinerant singer-songwriters, at that time referred to as *cantadores*, who later became universally known as **trovadores**, and their music as **trova**. Like the troubadours of medieval France, they travelled the countryside, accompanying their songs on stringed instruments, usually guitars. But unlike the old troubadours, the *trovadores* of Oriente were not educated and aristocratic, but poor and self-taught. Often they worked at humble jobs and sang in their spare time or in the evenings in bars or in the street. Even when they achieved fame as performers or songwriters, financial success rarely followed.

Long regarded as the first truly Cuban song is "La Bayamesa" (The Girl from Bayamo), which became the national anthem some fifty years after it was composed, in 1851. The local poet and indepen-

dence leader, **Carlos Manuel de Céspedes**, originally wrote the song with friends as a serenade for a girlfriend, but it charmed a very much larger audience than its intended one. The song spread throughout eastern Cuba, later becoming a favourite of the **mambí guerrillas** fighting the Spanish in the Sierra Maestra. These men already had a crop of patriotic songs at their disposal – "La Guerrilla", "Cuba Para los Cubanos", "La Caída de Guacamayo" and many others – but "La Bayamesa" joined the ranks of these battle hymns anyway. Something about the music, a languidness and an unusual use of feminine word endings in rhyme, impressed listeners as strongly Creole, quite different from the European-modelled songs which were previously the norm. Today, the cobbled square at the heart of old Bayamo is named **Plaza del Himno** – Anthem Square.

The early stars

The greatest of the early *cantadores*, however, was an exception. **José "Pepe" Sanchéz** was born to humble but not impoverished parents in Santiago in 1856. His social acquaintance was remarkable for a person of mixed race at that period, including Santiago high society, senior figures in the arts world and the top revolutionary leaders. His pleasant baritone voice and fluid (self-taught) guitar technique may have helped his advancement in society, but his greatest gift was his extraordinarily inventive and original feel for composition, which enabled him to transcend the formulaic European-based norms of his time, making his songs radically "Cuban". As well as "Tristezas", the first Cuban **bolero** (see p.130), Sanchéz bequeathed numerous classics, notably the trilogy of "Rosa" songs.

Sanchéz was also crucial as a propagator. He taught guitar to a number of the major names of the next generation of trova, including

three out of the four *trovadores* who became known in the early decades of the twentieth century as "the four great names of trova" – **Rosendo Ruiz, Alberto Villalón, Manuel Corona**, and the greatest of them all, **Gumersindo "Sindo" Garay**.

Sindo Garay gave Cuba its second famous musical Bayamesa while visiting a friend in the town; sitting on a veranda musing on the history of the town, he wrote a new song called "La Bayamesa". From its first performance in the Ciné-Teatro Bayamo it was a hit, and subsequently became one of the most famous of the hundreds of songs written by Garay during his 101 years. It was in part this extreme longevity, coupled with a gift for prolific composing, which led to Garay's importance, but he was also a fine guitarist, a charismatic performer, and a polished singer of the duet harmonies he was instrumental in popularizing. It was due to Garay and his contemporaries that the *primo* (first) and *segundo* (second) voices were introduced.

Taking it to Havana

Sindo Garay was also a vital element in taking the trova style **from Oriente to Havana**. By the beginning of the twentieth century, the war of independence had crippled Cuba economically, and a great stream of impoverished agricultural workers, labourers and artisans made its way to Havana. Garay and his circle of friends and co-*trovadores* were among the ranks. In Havana, the *trovadores* practised their art in the flourishing **variety theatres**, and as interval acts in the new cinemas and in cafés. The performers fraternized socially and maintained the tradition of meeting in the evenings to talk and play, always trying out new compositions on the group. From these meetings grew up the characteristic trova practice of writing "responses" to each other's songs, follow-up compositions which

answered, commented on or extended the story of the song responded to.

The *trovadores* almost always worked at menial jobs in addition to performing. Of Garay's three fellow trova grandees, only **Alberto Villalón**, the author of classics such as "Boda Negra", "Esta Muy Lejos" and "Me Da Miedo Quererte", was comfortably off, as the son of a proprietor of coffee plantations. **Rosendo Ruiz**, author of "Falso Juramento" and "La Reja", worked as a tailor though, like Pepe Sanchéz, his art enabled him to circulate in the salons of Santiago's white plutocracy. **Manuel Corona**, author of "Longina", "Mercedes", "Una Mirada" and "La Habanera", and the most accomplished of the response-song writers, worked as a cigar-roller and died in extreme poverty in 1950.

When trova made its next step, from the popular theatres of Havana to the capital's **high society**, it did so largely because of another atypical trovador. **Eusebio Delfín**, a modestly-born man from Cienfuegos, studied accounting and worked his way up to the position of Director of the Banco Commercial de Cuba, all the time practising the guitar-backed singing and composing he had studied as a young man. Delfín moved into exalted social circles when he married Amalia, the granddaughter of Facundo Bacardí, the founder of the great Santiago rum dynasty. Due to Delfín's efforts the **guitar**, hitherto regarded as a lower-class Bohemian instrument, gained acceptance as a salon instrument in high society. More importantly still, Delfín also extended the instrument's stylistic range from strummed playing to a finger-picked arpeggio technique, and his polished songwriting left classics of trova and bolero such as "Y Tu Que Has Hecho?" and "La Guinda".

With trova established as a part of the musical landscape of Havana, the stage was set for the arrival of the final great star (and

the first female one) of its early phase. **Maria Teresa Vera**, the daughter of a Spanish father and a freed slave mother, duly arrived from her home town of Guanajay in the early years of the century, found work in a china shop, and began to study and work with **Manuel Corona**. Her natural, graceful voice, gift for ornamentation and improvisation and excellent guitar style soon found her work, first in Havana theatres, then among the first artists to be recorded

Maria Teresa Vera and Rafael Zequeira

by the newly installed Victor Gramophone Company. By the 1920s, she was playing in New York, and with her newly formed **Sexteto Occidente** (of which the bass player was Ignacio Piñeiro), incorporating the latest style, **son**, into her repertoire.

Throughout the 1930s and 1940s, trova continued to diversify, overlapping the fields of bolero and son. The great new *trovadores*, notably **Miguel Matamoros**, included *sones*, *guarachas* and boleros in their repertoire, and freely mixed the styles together. By the 1940s, the style known as **fílin**, a derivation of both the bolero and trova, was capturing the attention of the most important guitarist-songwriters, and it was to form a bridge to the next major development, **nueva trova**.

Revolutionary songs: nueva trova

The **1959 Revolution** was, on the whole, favourable to trova and many *trovadores* were committed to the Revolution. Indeed Cuba possessed a long history of anti-government trova, from **Eliseo Grenet**'s "Lamento Cubano" (which led to the author's expulsion from the country under the Machado dictatorship) to **Rosendo Ruiz**'s "Redención", written shortly after the Russian Revolution in 1919 and regarded as one of the earliest socialist songs in the Americas. More recent *trovadores*, and virtually all of the fílinistas, were **Socialists** and – worse still in the music business – uncommercial, quite unlike the lucrative trade in mambo, bolero and chachacha.

Although the **Castro regime** was not against dance music in itself, it was inimical to the American-controlled companies which dominated the market. Numerous fílinistas backed the new regime (see Chapter 5) and were officially rewarded. In addition, new singer-songwriters began to write specifically in praise of the Revolution and its heroes. One of the first appointees to the newly created National

Council of Culture in 1959 was the singer **Carlos Puebla**, whose most famous song was to become "Hasta Siempre, Comandante", a rapturous ode to **Che Guevara**, written on the Argentinian guerrilla-doctor's departure for revolutionary struggle in Bolivia. In 1962, Puebla became the entertain-er in residence at the old Hemingway-trail bar and restaurant, the **Bodeguita del Medio**, long a trova haunt. At this time, half a dozen years before his death, the wizened figure of Sindo Garay would still appear in the Bodeguita from time to time to play a song or two.

In 1967, the first stirrings of **nueva trova** (new trova) manifested themselves, and once again Bayamo was involved. A young man from the town, **Pablo Milanés**, was prominent among partic-ipants in a festival of

OSVALDO SALAS

El Che, icon of the Revolution

protest song organized by the **Casa de las Americas**, a Havana cultural institution. Milanés had started his musical career writing and playing fílin-influenced songs with local groups and he, like many young musicians, was increasingly interested in the range of politically engaged, usually left-wing song movements appearing internationally in the wake of Bob Dylan, Joan Baez and Pete Seeger. Outside Cuba, the same movement, known as **nuevo canción**, involved artists as diverse as Violeta Parra and Victor Jara in Chile, Mercedes Sosa and Atahualpa Yupanqui in Argentina, and Chico Buarque and Caetano Veloso in Brazil. The innovations introduced by Milanés and his fellow nueva trova artists added a politicized lyrical approach to an eclectic musical one, bringing shades of jazz, Brazilian and north American music to their melodies.

Though Cuban **"protest song"** attacked the policies of foreign countries, notably the US, rather than those of Cuba, nueva trova's lyrics were elliptical and poetic, far removed from a simplistic party line, and hence at first encountered official scepticism. The nueva trova movement was a largely amateur one, with students and workers of all categories competing on equal terms with professional musicians.

In 1969, the Cuban **Institute of Art and Cinema** decided to create a special unit to accommodate, and perhaps contain, the burgeoning nueva trova musicians. Directed by **Leo Brouwer**, Cuba's top classical guitarist, its aim was the creative transformation of traditionally-based music. Apart from Milanés, the **Grupo de Experimentación Sonora** (Experimental Sound Group), as it was baptized, consisted of Leonardo Acosta, the saxophonist and musicologist, Sergio Vitier, guitarist, Eduardo Ramos, bassist, Pablo Menendez, an American-born guitarist, Emiliano Salvador on piano, and the three most important singer-guitarists of the nueva trova movement, Noel Nicola, Sara

González and Silvio Rodríguez. Both the latter artists rapidly achieved individual popularity. **Sara González** began to write a stream of critically acclaimed songs, among them "La Victoria", celebrating the rout of the Bay of Pigs invasion. **Silvio Rodríguez,** who had started his writing career publishing poetry in *El Caimán Barbudo*, the cultural magazine of the Young Communists, began to produce songs such as "Mariposas", "El Barquero", "La Canción de la Trova", "Ojalá", and "Unicornio", which placed him in the forefront of the Latin American **nueva canción** (new song) movement.

By the end of the 1970s, Rodríguez and Milanés had begun to tour internationally to great acclaim and in Spain Rodríguez's first two albums became best sellers, while Milanés' prolific song-writing – his "Yolanda" became an international standard – and equally prolific film scores earned him large sums of money. Both Rodríguez and Milanés consequently achieved high status in the Cuban establishment, Milanés becoming a Deputy in the Cuban Assembly and Rodríguez opening the first and biggest semi-private recording facility in Havana (see p.285).

The new generation: novísima trova

As the nueva trova generation settled into the new establishment, other artists followed in their wake, and their relationship with the State was not always as cordial. Xiomara Laugart, Anabel López, Alberto Tosca and Donato Poveda achieved rapid acceptance on radio and television, and **Gerardo Alfonso** found a ready public market for his songs "Son los sueños todavía" (They're Still Dreams), another paean to Che Guevara, and "Sábanas Blancas" (White Sheets), which became the theme tune to the weekly TV programme on Havana life, *Andar La Habana*. But **Pedro-Luis Ferrer**, a highly

talented and iconoclastic songwriter, had his career frozen for his mildly satirical lyrics and tactless public remarks, while **Santiago Feliu**, a long-haired and bearded New Age minstrel, found it impossible to get radio and television play, in spite of attracting large crowds to his performances.

By the early 1990s, the latest heirs of the trova tradition were overlapping with an alternative scene in which Havana's rockers, still regarded with deep suspicion, formed a prominent part. In 1993, the musician Alberto Faya, a founder-member of the 1972 **Movimiento de la Nueva Trova**, wrote in the journal of the Casa de las Americas of the "obscuring" of nueva trova by an "ambivalent" language which was leading to deviation from the revolutionary message, coupled with an involvement in "so-called contemporary Western music, particularly rock" – a description which fitted the biggest star of what became called **novísima trova** (the newest trova) like a glove.

Carlos Varela, a solo singer-guitarist, had begun his career auspiciously, with help from Silvio Rodríguez and Pablo Milanés, but as his songs' criticisms of the state became less veiled, and his music turned more towards rock, he too experienced difficulty in translating his great public popularity into media attention. By the late 1990s, however, while open dissidence was still out of the question in a Cuban singer's work, the changing economic climate, and the resultant relatively free international recording options open to stars like Varela, meant there was room for even mildly insubordinate artists. At the same time, the rise of the small alternative home studio meant that young artists such as Fernando Becquer and Samuel Aguila were leading the way for a new wave of amateurs – Luis Alberto Barbaría, Pepe del Valle, Andy Villalón – the *trovadores* of the future.

The House of Trova

While nueva trova developed in millennial Cuba, another institution at the opposite end of the spectrum also flourished. By the 1980s, many of Cuba's towns possessed **Casas de la Trova** (trova houses), state-subsidized performance spaces, usually in old houses with patios where **traditional trova and son** were performed by both amateur and professional artists. The first of these, and the most famous, was the Casa de la Trova of Santiago, on the Calle Heredia, just off the central square, which by the late 1990s was a place of pilgrimage for music tourists from around the world.

Santiago's Casa de la Trova opened in 1968, the formal continuation of a tradition which had started decades earlier in the café next door, where amateur singers would congregate after work. It has since established itself as a key institution in the preservation of the repertoire of the Santiago *trovadores*, which includes a considerable element of eastern son. Around two dozen acts – soloists, quartets, quintets and full bands – are based in the Santiago Casa, playing daily from 10am, starting with the oldest artists, and finishing in the early hours of the morning, often with dancing. A queue of young musicians waits to take the place of retiring senior members, thus maintaining the traditional styles and arrangements. Prominent performers at the Calle Heredia have included **Eliades Ochoa** and the **Cuarteto Patria**, the **Septeto Típico Oriental** and a remarkable pair of sisters, the **Duo Hermanas Ferrín**, whose repertoire includes not only familiar sones and guajiras, but also items such as the Manuel Corona bolero "Madre Mia" rendered as an Italian operatic duet – a rare echo of the bel canto influence on Cuban song.

Artists

Bola de Nieve

One of Cuba's most unusual and distinctive artists, **Ignacio Villa** was given his stage nickname **"Snowball"** (an allusion to both his colour and physical stature which, not surprisingly, he disliked intensely) by the singing star Rita Montaner when he worked with her as accompanist at the Seville Biltmore Hotel in Mexico City in 1933. Like Montaner, he was born in the suburb of Guanabacoa, in 1911, where he studied piano at the Conservatorio Mateu and began the profession of music-making, like so many young pianists, as an accompanist for silent movies. His virtuosity at the piano was recognized by another Guanabacoa-born musician, the great composer and bandleader **Ernesto Lecuona**, who used to leave the young pianist to direct his orchestra during his absences.

Bola de Nieve
LAS GRANDES CANCIONES DEL GENIAL ARTISTA CUBANO

Bola de Nieve developed his remarkable singing style because he had to. "I would have liked to be an opera singer", he once said, "but I've got the voice of a fruit seller, so I had to resign myself to selling fruit on stage, seated at a piano". This modest

description belies one of the most polished and theatrical singing styles in Cuban music, much influenced by and compared to French **chanson**. "I am the song I sing", was Bola de Nieve's dictum, and he invested each number with tremendous expressiveness. As he began to perform internationally, his repertoire included songs in English, French, Italian, Portuguese and even Catalan, all equally polished. In the 1940s and 1950s he toured the US in the company of Rita Montaner and American stars such as Lena Horne and Paul Robeson, and was still working when he died of a heart attack at Mexico City airport in 1971, on his way to the next stage of yet another Latin American tour.

⊙ **Bola de Nieve**   Nuevos Medios, Spain

An Egrem-licensed compilation, adorned with a foreword by Camilo José Cela, grand old man of Spanish literature, who recalls a long night drinking and talking at the Tropicana in 1965 with the artist he describes as a "delicate and elemental spirit". Thirty-two songs in the maestro's best crooning, whispering, chuckling *chansonnier* vocal style, all accompanied by sparkling piano, ranging from the Eliseo Grenet classics "¡Ay Mamá Inés!" and "Drume Negrita" to "Be Careful, It's My Heart".

Pedro-Luis Ferrer

A legendary name among Cuban opposition singer-songwriters, **Pedro Luis Ferrer** was born in the small town of Yanguaji in the province of Las Villas in 1953, and left school as early as he could, finding formal education intolerably boring. He taught himself guitar and tres, and moved to Havana, where, in 1969, he began to associate with musicians such as Carlos Alfonso, leader of the progressive band **Síntesis**. After a short period in a similar fusion group, **Los Dada**, he began to work as a solo singer-songwriter. His original,

melodic compositions attracted public attention, as did his distinctive nasal delivery, and for a decade his success grew, with three LPs, and a tour of Europe in 1974.

At the same time, Ferrer's lyrics were attracting official attention. Some songs, like "La Desnudez de Mario Ague" (The Nakedness of Mario Ague), with its insane protagonist bathing naked in a river

by moonlight, were noted for their general unorthodoxy; others for critical references. "Inseminación Artificial" mocks one of the experimental cattle-breeding projects beloved of Castro himself. In 1985, according to unconfirmed reports, Ferrer overstepped the limits when, on a tour of Peru, he referred to Celia Cruz as "Cuba's greatest singer" in an interview. On his return, he was interrogated by the

police and was denied either an exit visa or official performance space in Cuba for almost ten years.

In 1994, with the thaw in State control, Ferrer began to be rehabilitated, singing at the Artists' Union for an award ceremony – he used the occasion, apparently, to embarrass the authorities by referring to the exodus of the Cuban *balseros* (raft refugees) as a "political manipulation". The same year he received permission to visit Miami for a six month singing engagement. In 1999 his first record for fourteen years was published by an American company, after which he again played New York and Miami dates, accompanied by an eight-piece band including his daughter Lena as singer and percussionist.

⊙ **Pedro Luis Ferrer**   Havana Caliente, US

Ferrer's triumphant return to a central position in the international range of Cuban music shows him to be above all a composer of catchy, melodic, non-generic songs, a little in the mould of Juan-Luis Guerra. Quirky, swaying toe-tappers such as "Como Me Gusta Hablar Español" (I Love Talking Spanish) and "Inseminación Artificial" abound, but the best tracks are pop-rumba combinations of Ferrer's melodic voice backed by chorus and Afro-Cuban percussion: "La Tarde Se Ha Puesto Triste" (The Afternoon's Become Sad) is a fine poetic example.

Juan-Carlos Formell

Neither a member of the nueva trova school, which he despises, nor a pure dance stylist in the mould of his father, **Juan Formell**, founder of **Los Van Van** (with whom his relationship has not always been warm), **Juan-Carlos Formell** is a leading figure among a new breed of Cuban singer-songwriters who draw on the earliest traditions of trova and son.

DITA SULLIVAN

Formell was born in 1964 in Havana and brought up by his grandmother, who would tell him stories of life back in Oriente. His grandfather, **Francisco Formell**, the conductor and arranger for Ernesto Lecuona, died when he was an infant, and, as his father apparently didn't encourage him in a musical career, he went his own way, teaching himself guitar and then studying bass. He began writing songs in his teens, and, after military service, found work as a solo artist, playing in the Habana Libre Hotel.

According to Formell, his lyrics were regarded as unsatisfactorily ambiguous by the authorities, and his personal life contained undesirable unorthodoxy: he was a devotee of yoga, and, worse, the Baha'i faith. In 1993, after a series of bass-playing jobs, he joined the popular conjunto **Rumbavana** for a tour of Mexico, and jumped ship in Chiapas. Busking his way north to the border, he entered the US

as a wetback, crossing the Rio Grande, and after being arrested and bailed out, he took a bus to the East Coast.

For the following six years, Juan-Carlos worked in **New York**, first busking, then playing small clubs with a band of recent fellow exiles. A residency at the Zinc Bar in Greenwich Village attracted favourable comment, as did a season at Café Nostalgia in Miami, and in 1999 he made his first record. Formell remains vehemently critical of the Castro regime and the musical styles close to it, regarding nueva trova as a mere copy of American protest music.

⊙ **Songs From a Little Blue House**   Wicklow/BMG, US

A collection of thirteen songs conceived as a sequence. The album is infused with water imagery throughout, from the opening instrumental "Agua Dulce" (Sweet Water), which invokes the *orisha* Ochún, to the closing one, redolent of yearning for his eventual return to Cuba "after the nightmare". Formell's gentle, simple voice, acoustic guitar and touches of relaxed bass, percussion and discreet brass clothe the attractive songs, which also draw heavily on animal and flower-filled childhood memories – of which the most powerful is the little house of the title, Formell's grandmother's old home in Oriente.

Sindo Garay

A name of great lustre in Cuban music, and a prototype for the remarkable Cuban trait of longevity among musicians, **Sindo Garay** was performing right up to his death, appearing in the Bodeguita del Medio in 1966, at 101 years of age, to strum the magisterial opening chords of the introduction to his great standard, "La Bayamesa". His idiosyncratic appearance – spotted bow-tie, weathered Oriental-featured face, omnipresent cigarette and youthful grey quiff – led Lorca to refer to him as "the great Pharaoh of Cuba".

Gumersindo "Sindo" Garay was born in 1867 in Santiago to a poor family. He received little schooling, and taught himself to read, it is said, by looking at street-signs and posters and asking passers-by to tell him what they said. Although he received some musical tuition from the proto-trovador **Pepe Sanchéz**, he was largely self-taught. He wrote his first song at age ten, "Quiereme Trigueña" (Love Me, Mulatta). Garay supported himself throughout his early years working as a clown and trapeze artist in a circus, and, like many early *trovadores*, he moved in independentist circles, in his case acting as a messenger for the **mambí freedom-fighters** – an account discovered by the French writer Francois-Xavier Gomez has him swimming across Santiago Bay to deliver a dispatch. Later, Garay named all of his children after the pre-Hispanic Siboney Indians of Cuba – his sons **Guarionex** and **Guarina** became his accompanists.

Garay's success was due in part to his charismatic performance and prolific composing, but also the freshness and inventiveness he brought to trova; his minor key second voice parts were totally new and set a model for decades to come. In 1928, Garay accompanied Rita Montaner for her successful performances in Paris, and throughout the first half of the century he was a feature of all of the important Havana radio stations. He remains, alongside Maria Teresa Vera, the greatest of the old trova artists.

⊙ **La Perla Marina, Canciones y Boleros de Sindo Garay**   Bis, Cuba

Fourteen of the maestro's classics, recorded in the 1930s, including the great "La Bayamesa", "Guarina", dedicated to his son and accompanist, "Tardes grises" (Grey Afternoons), "Ojos de Sirena" (Siren Eyes) and "Germania", which he wrote, according to the musicologist Cristóbal Díaz Ayala, after listening to Wagner.

Gema y Pavel

Born in Havana in 1965, **Gema Corredera** had studied guitar and musicology at Havana's Escuela Nacional de Arte. **Pavel Urzika** was brought to Cuba by his parents from the Ukraine months after his birth in 1964, and took up guitar on leaving university. Neither attempted to join the ranks of officially employed State musicians, but began working in semi-official theatre.

In 1990 they met and soon began to perform together, two years later joining the **Teatro Estudio de Cuba**, a small theatre company invited to a festival in Cádiz. They stayed on when their colleagues returned, busking and playing in bars, then making their way to Santander where a cousin of Pavel had held out hopes of a recording opening. This never materialized, and their *trovador* wanderings recommenced, a pair of ambulant tropical hippies with long hair, berets and guitars. In 1994 they were noticed playing in a Madrid bar by the proprietor of a prominent Spanish world music label, Nubenegra, and taken up as recording artists, producers and A&R consultants for Nubenegra's operation in Havana. A European tour, dates in Miami, and two CDs followed, along with the production of a multi-artist tribute record to Maria Teresa Vera, and a collection of recordings by young amateur

nueva trova singers from Havana. Gema and Pavel returned to Havana in 2000, where they parted company.

⊙ **Cosa de Broma**   Nubenegra, Spain

A 1991 collection demonstrating Gema y Pavel's clear relation to the 1940s' fílin style they aimed to update. Gema's mellow voice blends with her partner's guitar, augmented variously by bass, piano, guitars and assorted brass. The repertoire ranges from classic old boleros – "Longina", "Noche de Ronda" – to Pavel-arranged versions of Los Zafiros's "Caminadora" and Lennon & McCartney's "Girl". The eclectic treatment is clearly influenced by jazz and Brazilian music.

Pablo Milanés

When the nueva trova movement bloomed in the late 1960s and early 1970s, **Pablo Milanés** received a head start. Most of the other artists working in the new form were young, amateur and unknown, attracted to fashionable folk and protest music, while Milanés had an established name and career. He was also a proficient guitarist, and the new movement had adopted the **guitar** – portable, demotic, self-sufficient – as its main vehicle. Ironically, Milanés' later career demonstrated him to be the *trovador* most inclined to work with other instrumentalists, but at the beginning he was, like his peers, a singer-guitarist.

Born in Bayamo in 1943, he studied classical technique at the Amadeo Roldán Conservatory in Havana, but aged sixteen joined a vocal group, **El Cuarteto del Rey**, which included blues and negro spirituals in its repertoire. He rapidly identified with the aesthetic of the fílin movement and began to compose songs in that style. His earliest song to attract serious attention was "Mis 22 Años" (My 22 Years), in 1965. Soon major names of fílin such as Omara Portuondo

began to adopt his work, but by that time, Milanés had formed his second group, **Los Bucaneros**, subsequently moving on to a solo career.

When the **nueva trova** movement began to coalesce in earnest after the 1967 protest song festival at Havana's **Casa de las Americas**, Milanés' work was not initially well received by the Government. Elliptical, poetic and undogmatic, his songs gave no appearance of enthusiasm for a rigid Communist party line, and he spent some time on obligatory work camps in the countryside. This period of disfavour did not last long, however, and within a decade Milanés had become a central part of the revolutionary movement, singing to huge crowds on the 1st of May as warm-up act for Castro's speeches, and finally becoming a Deputy in the Cuban Assembly.

From his early fílin days, reinforced by his time with the **Experimental Sound Group** of ICIAC, Milanés retained a taste for instrumental richness, and he has consistently performed with small groups of

bass, keyboards and sometimes a saxophone or a cello. He was an early proponent of the inclusion of **son** in nueva trova and also brought in influences from Latin America, notably **Brazil**. Milanés has been, in fact, a key link between Cuba and Brazil, which were estranged just as thoroughly as Cuba and the US through the years of Brazilian military rule.

By the early 1990s, Milanés' prolific composing – songs, film and television scores – and his international touring had earned him enough money and prestige to be able to set up, with government approval, a private cultural foundation and record label in Havana. The **Pablo Milanés Foundation**, before it closed amid controversy (see Chapter 8), had opened an office in Spain. Although health problems interrupted his work during the 1990s, he continues to be an active member of the Cuban musical elite.

⊙ **Serie Millennium 21 – Pablo Milanés**　　　　　　Universal, US

A good-value double-CD set (in a series which, tellingly, also includes Abba and Richard Clayderman), kicking off proceedings with the wistful Simon & Garfunkel-esque "Yolanda", a song covered internationally on a massive scale. The 21 tracks include a dozen songs by Milanés (not all of them his most famous compositions), and a selection of standards of bolero and fílin such as "Tu Mi Delirio", in a bossa nova-tinted rendition, and "Noche de Ronda". The selection of arrangements is characteristic, varying from simple guitar or piano accompaniment to lush orchestrations redolent of George Martin's work with the Beatles.

Carlos Puebla

From the first year of Castro's seizure of power, the singer and guitarist **Carlos Puebla** cast himself as the griot of the Revolution, writing an unstoppable stream of simple but melodic songs telling the

stories of the deeds and personalities of the new regime. Born in Manzanillo in 1917, Puebla only founded his quartet, **Los Tradicionales**, in 1953. After the Revolution, the group took up residency in the afternoons and evenings at the **Bodeguita del Medio**. Musically, the Tradicionales' most famous style was gentle distinctive country son, with strong guitar lines and beautiful melancholy harmony choruses.

Some of Puebla's finest songs were addressed to **Che Guevara**: "Que Pare El Son" (Stop The Son) and, above all, "Hasta Siempre Comandante", treated him as a heroic, almost saintly figure. The latter was used to great effect on the soundtrack of the Costas-Gavras film about the Pinochet coup in Chile, *State of Siege*; with its hymn-like chorus – "here the profound transparency of your divine presence is clear, Comandante Che Guevara" – it rarely fails to stir up the revolutionary spirit. But Puebla's vast output (he wrote as many as a thousand songs) also included lighter numbers, rib-ticklers such as the "Son de la Alfabetización" and "La OEA es cosa de risa" (The Organization of American States is a Laughing Stock). He died in 1989.

⊙ **La Bodeguita del Medio**   Milestone/Riverside, US

A live 1957 recording from the Bodeguita del Medio, before Puebla had become a fixture, with the Tradicionales as a trio. The disc has an authentic period feel, including a selection of pre-Revolutionary *sones*, *guarachas* and boleros.

⊙ **De Cuba Traigo Un Cantar**   Egrem, Cuba

A collection of Puebla's patriotic commentaries on the state of the country, a sort of musical version of *Granma*, the Party newspaper. "Son de la Alfabetización", "Comités de Defensa" (on the citizens' defence/surveillance group, a number which had them rolling in the aisles at the Bodeguita), "Todo por la Reforma Agraria" (All for

Agrarian Reform, a dance-floor smash) and "David y Goliat" (guess who was who).

Silvio Rodríguez

Born in the small town of San Antonio de los Baños in 1946, **Silvio Rodríguez** grew up rejecting the world of chachacha and mambo, attracted instead to the simplicity and directness displayed by Bob Dylan and the Beatles. "We rejected artists' outdated habits, their way of dressing and performing. We objected to that mythical being who appears and disappears like magic on the television screen amidst colourful light. We wanted to clarify that we should compose socially committed songs and that we shared the same struggle and the same ideology. It wasn't only a new way of creating, but a new way of being."

Four years after the Revolution, Rodríguez was drafted into the army, where he spent four years. By this time he was reading Byron and Poe and composing his first songs, mainly romantic, but beginning to tackle contemporary **political themes**, although not Cuban ones: "¿Por Que?" attacked racial discrimination in the United States, "La Leyenda del Aguila" (The Legend of the Eagle) was a protest against US involvement in the Vietnam War. Not long after demobilisation in 1967, he made his first major stage performance at the Palacio de Bellas Artes in Havana. In the same year, Rodríguez was prominent among participants in the seminal **Encuentro de la Canción Protesta**. Although it was not until the following year that he first heard the records of Bob Dylan, South American protest song was very much an influence, as were the Beatles for their mould-breaking adventurousness. In 1970, Rodríguez was a natural for inclusion in the **Grupo de Experimentación Sonora** of ICAIC.

JULIO ETCHART

At this stage, Rodríguez's songs were regarded as advanced and problematic, unlike Pablo Milanés', which attracted universal admiration. Nonetheless, Rodríguez was regarded as the single most active artist in bringing nueva trova into the musical establishment in its early days, and he soon did become a star. At first his national popularity rested on innumerable public performances in theatres, factories, collectives and community associations, but soon the media and Egrem, the State record company, began to diffuse nueva trova. In the 1980s, Rodríguez's work grew in international popularity, and not only in regions associated politically with Cuba. Rodríguez became enormously successful in Spain, where his royalties made him one of Cuba's richest performers in a time of generally sparse

earnings for his fellow musicians. The 1990s saw Rodríguez, like Pablo Milanés, a grandee of the Cuban establishment. Like Milanés, he was a deputy in the National Assembly, permitted the rare privilege of investing his earnings in a private business, the Abdala recording studios and label (see Chapter 9).

⊙ **Cuba Classics 1: Canciones Urgentes Greatest Hits**   Luaka Bop, US

An excellent compilation on David Byrne's label, the sleeve equipped with an admiring introduction by Byrne, an interesting interview with Rodríguez, some background and full lyrics. The songs come from six classic Egrem albums recorded between 1975 (the year of his first, Días y Flores) and 1988 (the year of O Melancolía), and give a comprehensive flavour of Rodríguez' world view. Styles range from the early political rhetoric, tinged with Beatles' musical colouring, through the hippie-era imagery, damsels and unicorns of "I Dream of Serpents", culminating in the poetic introspection of "O Melancolía".

⊙ **Silvio**   Fonomusic, Spain

A major new set of songs recorded "unplugged" (backed by a sole acoustic guitar). Personal poetic preoccupations haven't made Rodríguez any less concerned with specific political issues: "Hombre" is a love song to Che Guevara, and "El Necio" (The Stubborn One), comes with a demand for the evacuation of the US Navy base at Guantánamo Bay.

Carlos Varela

Carlos Varela was born in 1964 in Centro Habana, where he still lives with his wife and his brother Victor Varela, a leading young playwright. Resolutely committed to city life in general, and in love with Havana in particular, he sees his songs as little plays with the Cuban capital as setting. Varela grew up listening to as much American rock as to *nueva trovadores* like Silvio Rodríguez and Pablo Milanés.

Although he professes great admiration for the two – he once referred to Silvio Rodríguez as God, and Pablo Milanés as Chango – he has always rejected traditional Cuban music as a model, commenting that you don't need to wear a *guayabera* (a traditional Cuban four-pocketed shirt) and smoke a cigar to display *cubanía* (Cubanness).

Varela began composing and singing, accompanying himself on acoustic guitar, in the early 1980s, helped by Milanés and Rodríguez, and by the end of the

decade his songs were attracting considerable attention. After his debut solo performance in Havana's **Instituto de Arte y Industria Cinematográfica** his popularity was such that he could regularly fill the showcase Carlos Marx Theatre. Within a decade, Varela concerts at the venue would attract queues of young people for days in advance. By this time, Varela had changed the solo singer-guitarist format, acquiring a rock group to back him, and sporting the long hair and tight black jeans of a Cuban *alternativo*, which at first would entail trouble with the police.

At the same time, Varela's lyrics came in for criticism on a variety of grounds. "Guillermo Tell", which describes William Tell as a harsh father who didn't understand his children, was interpreted as veiled criticism of the father of the nation (Castro). Other songs were attacked

for pessimism and being "unconstructive" in the face of the difficulties of the Special Period, and his songs were denied radio play. In the mid 1990s, Varela's career benefited, like that of Silvio Rodríguez, from intense Spanish interest. His album **Como Los Peces** (Like Fish) was produced and released first in Spain, with Spanish guest artists, and was only distributed officially in Cuba five years later. In 1999, Varela was one of the Cuban artists involved in the "music bridge" event, in which a party of American performers, led by Mick Fleetwood, Andy Summers and Burt Bacharach, spent a week in Havana writing and performing with Cuban counterparts. Latterly Varela has reverted to occasional solo performances, accompanied by his guitar.

⊙ **Como Los Peces**   BMG, Spain

Varela's first international album is primarily a mixture of Spanish and American MOR rock, interspersed with softer ballads backed by strummed guitar and synthesized strings or piano. The older nueva trova influence is audible on tracks like "Grettel", a gentle love poem to his wife. Cuban flavour is imparted lyrically by touches such as the quote from Miguel Matamoros's "Lagrimas Negras" in the title track, although the music could be the Eagles or Mark Knopfler. Devoid of explicit criticism of the regime, Varela's tone is nonetheless clearly disenchanted.

⊙ **Carlos Varela en Vivo**   Bis, Cuba

A live set, recorded at one of Varela's Carlos Marx Theatre extravaganzas, featuring nine extended versions of his great early hits, including "Guillermo Tell", "Soy Un Gnomo", "Cuchilla en la Acera", "Tropicollage" and "Jalisco Park".

Maria Teresa Vera

An unglamorous figure according to period photos, with a simple, untrained and at times rough voice, **Maria Teresa Vera** is nonethe-

less one of the great icons of Cuban music. Today, "Veinte Años", the song she wrote in 1935, is one of Cuba's most internationally famous, covered by everyone from septuagenarian Buena Vista star Ibrahim Ferrer to young French Cubanophile singer-songwriter Cyrius Martinez. In 1961, one of the earliest major cultural acts of the new government of Castro was the organization of a homage to Vera on the fiftieth anniversary of her first performance.

Maria Teresa Vera was born in 1895 in Guanajay, near Havana, to a poor mixed-race family. She took up guitar and singing young, and, when the family moved to Havana in search of work, began to associate with the coterie of early *trovadores* who had also recently arrived. In particular, she studied guitar with **Manuel Corona**, who accompanied her sporadically at the beginning of her career. Her distinctive voice and presence began to attract attention and in 1914 she wrote her first song, "Este vez te tocó perder", a Colombian *bambuco*; shortly afterwards she made one of the earliest Cuban records.

In 1916, Vera formed a partnership with the singer **Rafael Zequeira**, which continued until Zequeira died in 1924, by which time the duo had achieved considerable success, performing in the Apollo and on the radio in New York. Shortly after Zequeira's death, Vera formed an early son group, the **Sexteto Occidente**, with the son pioneer **Ignacio Piñeiro** as a member and continued to perform with great success until, in 1937, she entered her final musical partnership, with the younger **Lorenzo Hierrezuelo**, an Oriente-born singer-guitarist of trova family stock. Together Vera and Hierrezuelo had over two decades of great success, conquering **Mexico** gloriously in 1947.

Vera retired from performance in 1962 due to ill health, and died three years later of cerebral thrombosis. By this time a new genera-

tion of artists, the creators of **nueva trova**, had appeared, but both its leading stars, Pablo Milanés and Silvio Rodríguez, considered Maria Teresa among their most important influences.

⊙ El Legendario Dúo de la Trova Cubana   Tumbao, Spain

A definitive collection of early Vera, with Rafael Zequeira as the other half of the legendary duo. Features a selection of songs by all the founding fathers of trova, with criollas, canciones, claves, boleros, bambucos, guarachas and early rumbas, plus some curiosities, such as the 1923 "Llorando A Papa Montero", with its response song, written by Manuel Corona, "Resurrección de Papa Montero". Top quality sleeve notes by the eminent Cuban musicologist Maria Teresa Linares.

⊙ Boleros Primordiales   Nuevos Medios, Spain

A selection of recordings from the 1940s and 1950s accompanied by additional guitars, trumpet and percussion. Classics include Matamoros's "Lagrimas Negras" and Eliseo Grenet's song made famous by Vera version, "Las Perlas de Tu Boca" (Your Mouth's Pearls).

⊙ Veinte Años   Musica del Sol, Spain

An excellent mid-period compilation of all the best items not on the previous two records, including the immortal title track.

7

The Cuban Diaspora: II

The 1960s were lean years for Latin music. The scene was lacklustre enough in the US, and times were even harder for Cuban musicians at home. The failed, US-backed anti-Castro invasion at the **Bay of Pigs** in 1961 and the **Cuban Missile Crisis** the following year ended the already frosty relations between Cuba and the US, and ruptured contacts with much of Latin America at the same time. Tourism died, the theatres and shows at the casinos closed down, and all Havana nightlife ground to a halt. The new government nationalized record companies, banned musicians from private employment and obliged them to seek government permission for foreign tours: many Cuban artists with international careers chose to leave at the earliest opportunity, and some of those touring abroad simply stayed on.

The first exiles tended to be established professionals with contacts abroad. Known as the *exodo farandulero* (the showbiz exodus), the first wave included some of the top singers: Olga Guillot and Rolando Laserie joined the **Miami** community, while **La Lupe** and

Celia Cruz made their way to **New York**. At this time, Celia Cruz was the dynamic young vocalist of the veteran band La Sonora Matancera.

Rogelio Martinez, the band's leader, had arranged a residency at the Hollywood Palladium in Los Angeles; when he suggested staying on in California, the entire group agreed and they have never returned to Cuba since. For Celia Cruz and Latin music, the repercussions would be enormous.

The 1960s

The last Cuban-invented musical genre to travel abroad was the **pachanga**, a would-be successor to the chachacha. Its inventor, the bandleader **Eduardo Davidson**, fled to the US in 1961, where the style underwent a brief craze. But the scene awaiting Cuban exile musicians in the US was otherwise less than propitious. With the

advent of the rock and pop revolution which swept the world's youth in the wake of first Elvis Presley and then the Beatles, the big mambo and chachacha bands in their frilly *guarachero* sleeves or tuxedos were decidedly unfashionable. In New York City, the big Latin night-clubs hit hard times, and in 1964, when the Palladium lost its liquor licence and closed, an era ended.

Not all Anglo-American fans deserted. One of the most loyal con-stituencies was the **Jewish community**. In the "borscht belt" – the resorts in the Catskill Mountains favoured by the East Coast Jewish middle class – dozens of Cuban-style "rumba bands" carried on playing the hotel ballrooms. Some of the musicians themselves were Jewish, among them **Larry Harlow**, the son of a jazz bandleader and an opera singer, who had fallen in love with Latin music as a kid in Spanish Harlem, and then with Cuban culture generally on a visit to Havana in 1956. Harlow was shortly to play a crucial role in the cre-ation of **salsa**.

In New York, the early 1960s were the years of the home grown **charanga**. As the big bands lost their edge and their venues, a range of new bands in charanga format came forward – a violin section, a flute, piano, bass, timbales and tumbadoras, with a lead voice and male chorus. The models, and some of the bandleaders, were Cuban. The groups of José Fajardo and Mongo Santamaría were soon joined by **Pupi Legarreta**'s charanga, when the Havana-born violinist and arranger fled the Revolution. **Roberto Torres**, a singer and percussionist from Güines, arrived in New York at the same time and founded the **Orquesta Broadway**, the start of a major US career which would make him one of the most prominent anti-Castro exiles in Miami. Increasingly, however, New York's non-Cubans led the bands as a new generation of dynamic young musicians began to emerge. **Charlie Palmieri**, a classically-trained pianist born in the

Bronx to Puerto-Rican parents, worked his apprenticeship in the big bands of Xavier Cugat, Tito Puente and Tito Rodriguez, then formed his **Charanga Duboney**. As flautist and singer, he hired **Johnny Pacheco**, a young musician who had arrived in the Bronx from the Dominican Republic's merengue centre, Santiago de los Caballeros. Pacheco soon left Duboney and formed his own highly successful charanga. **Ray Barretto**, a Brooklyn conga-player of Puerto Rican parentage, formed the **Charanga Moderna**.

Boogaloo and the conjuntos

As rock, pop and soul made ever greater inroads into mainstream America's listening, the charangas wavered, and bandleaders began to look to cross-over formulae. English-language cover versions began to sprout within the repertoires of Latin entertainers. In 1963, a chance hit from **Ray Barretto**'s band ushered in a new era: "El Watusi" featured a loose, rough rhythm augmented by hand-claps, shouts and applause and a swaggering Spanglish street babble of a lyric. The story went around that Barretto's singer had left the stage briefly and some onlooker started filling in as a joke at the microphone. As Johnny Pacheco later commented, "we were all trying to record cross-over numbers for the American market and along comes this Barretto vocal talking complete nonsense and it takes off". "El Watusi" was a million-seller and ushered in the brief and entertaining era of the **boogaloo** (bugalú in its Spanish spelling), whose name gestures vaguely to boogie. The craze lasted several years and threw up a number of hits: Pete Rodriguez's "I Like It Like That", Johnny Colón's "Boogaloo Blues", the Filipino barrio punk Joe Bataan's "Subway Joe", as well as offshoots such as Richie Ray and Bobby Cruz's "Jala Jala", and Eddie Palmieri's "African Twist". The biggest star of the boogaloo era was **Joe Cuba** (another non-Cuban,

despite his stagename), who put together a neat little sextet composed of percussion, piano, bass and vibes. He came out with a string of hits, from the son-boogaloo "El Ratón", starring his new singer Cheo Feliciano, to the million-selling "Bang Bang" which marked the peak of the boogaloo phase in 1967.

By the end of the 1960s, the new styles had eclipsed the charangas. Roberto Torres's Orquesta Broadway continued through to the next charanga revival, but many of the other bandleaders changed their format. In 1967 Ray Barretto had been one of the first to abandon the violins and flute and go for a smaller, tougher line-up. Charlie Palmieri's younger brother, Eddie, had also opted for a conjunto format, with a brass section, mainly trumpets, in lieu of the strings.

As the line-ups of New York's Latin bands changed to a leaner, harder, brass-driven format, so the social context of their music increasingly dictated change. The era when Cuban music related either to palm-shaded *bohios* and cane fields or to the elegant nightlife of Havana was long gone. The first rich, white Cuban immigrants to New York may have found their way among the elite, but most of the newcomers joined the Puerto Ricans, Dominicans and other Hispanics in the poor, rough barrios of **East Harlem**, **Queens** and the **Bronx**. The new bandleaders who arose from this milieu idolized the Cuban models, particularly the rougher, rootsier conjunto style of Arsenio Rodríguez, but they also admired Puerto Rican bands, who themselves played a mixture of son and local genres such as bomba and plena.

New York Salsa

While bandleaders like **Johnny Pacheco** and **Ray Barretto** built tough new soundscapes, young artists such as the singer and trombonist **Willie Colón** and the wild young *sonero* **Hector Lavoe**

Salsa

No one knows the origin of the term salsa. The Spanish word simply means "sauce", from where it's not such a huge step to its colloquial meaning of "a bit of flavour", and thence "spiciness" or "excitement". Experts have compiled lists of references, among the earliest of which are Ignacio Piñeiro's song "Echale Salsita" and Beny Moré's on-stage exclamations. Two Venezuelan instances date from the 1960s, namely the radio programme *La Hora del Sabor, Salsa y el Bembé* (The Hour of Flavour, Sauce and Partying) and the album by Federico & His Combo Latino, **Llego La Salsa** (Salsa Has Arrived).

In any event, it is clear that the term *salsa* had been around in Latin music for a long time when the management of Fania records began actively to promote it as a simple, memorable term for a morass of relatively arcane genres. And whatever its history, the word took off with the music. By the end of the 1970s, Fania Records and its offshoot labels had become the Tamla-Motown of the new genre; typically, when the major labels began to sign Fania's stars, they were already too late to catch the salsa wave.

appeared, singing of the dangers and pleasures of barrio life in a style which mixed son and plena, boogaloo and guaguancó in a blast of raw energy. Very soon a business machine came into existence which packaged and sold this sound, and gave it a name. The machine was a company called **Fania Records**, founded in 1964 by Johnny Pacheco and an Italian American lawyer named Jerry Masucci.

Fania Records began with Masucci delivering albums to shops from the boot of his car and took off fast. Among the artists Fania

signed were many of those who were to become the grandees of salsa – Willie Colón, Hector Lavoe, Ray Barretto, Larry Harlow, Louie Ramírez, Mongo Santamaría, Louis "Perico" Ortiz, Dave Valentín, Cheo Feliciano, Ismael Miranda, Pete "El Conde" Rodríguez, Adalberto Santiago and the Panamanian Ruben Blades, who soon began a sensational partnership with Willie Colon. **Tito Puente** and **Celia Cruz** joined Fania when Masucci took over the older New York Latin labels Tico and Alegre Records. Publicity was generated by events such as the 1971 concert of the supergroup the **Fania All Stars** (filmed as *Nuestra Cosa Latina*) and Larry Harlow's Latin answer to Tommy, a rock opera named *Hommy*, about a deaf, dumb and blind boy who played mean bongo. Once again the national and international media began to talk about Latin music and this new sound called **salsa**.

Salsa continued to spread throughout the Latin world and beyond, although not to Cuba. Salsa had Cuban son at its core, and from the late 1970s onwards a recurring theme was a return to deep Cuban roots, but the mother island itself remained isolated. The US, with its huge Latin community, became the major producer of salsa, aided by its semi-colony, Puerto Rico, and important centres of salsa *afición* developed in Venezuela and Colombia. **Venezuela**, its capital Caracas flush with oil wealth, emerged as a recording and production centre and also gave the world star bands such as La Dimensión Latina, whose vocalist and bass-player, **Oscar D'León**, went on to become one of the best and most popular modern *soneros* in the world. The cities of Cali and Barranquilla in **Colombia** became salsa meccas, with huge crowds of *salseros* avid for the regular visits of the Fania All Stars or Puerto Rico's Gran Combo. Occasional concerts by Cuban *campesina* (country-style) stars also drew large audiences: Colombia became a major market for **Celina González** and

her successor **Albita Rodríguez**. Colombia also developed a range of superb salsa acts, from **Fruko y sus Tesos** and the **Latin Brothers** to **Guayacán** and **Los Nemus del Pacífico**. Again, these bands cultivated a modern, but deeply original, Cuban son base to their music. At the time, many of Cuba's bands were belatedly trying to catch up with rock and soul.

New flavours

Jerry Masucci's first retirement left New York's salsa scene open to the competition. The void was soon filled by a Puerto Rican-born New Yorker named **Ralph Mercado**, whose record company, RMM, precisely charts the trends of New York's Latin scene up to the end of the twentieth century. In the 1980s came **merengue**, the fast, galloping rhythm of the Dominican Republic. It spread like wildfire through the Latin clubs of the US, partly because of a huge influx of Dominican immigrants, partly because the music was simple and very catchy, and partly because a lot of young, hungry bands, ready to work for modest fees, appeared on the scene. Ralph Mercado set up a new division, Merengazo Records, and took a healthy slice of the action.

Salsa romantica was an adaptation of melodic love songs to a smooth, light salsa backing. The style sprang from a single album, **Noches Calientes**, created in 1984 by the Fania producer Louie Ramirez. It was a surprise smash hit and soon young *salseros* such as Lalo Rodriguez and the Puerto Rican **Eddie Santiago** were upping the ante and creating **salsa erotica**, light, frothy songs with suggestive lyrics. Rodriguez's "Ven Devorame Otra Vez" (Come, devour me once more), with its celebrated reference to moistened bed linen, was a prime example.

By the mid-1990s, salsa erotica, always held in contempt by old school salsa fans – they referred to it as *salsa monga* (limp salsa) –

had lost favour. At the same time, a range of Latin dance hybrids arrived alongside a revival of more traditional salsa. Latin hip-hop, Latin house and Latin jungle thrived in New York clubs such as the Copacabana or Mercado's own Latin Quarter: the big, glitzy main room would be full of smart twenty-something dancers swirling expertly in pairs to a fifteen-piece Puerto Rican salsa band, while a younger, more casual crowd milled about to the thudding beat of Junior Gonzalez or DLG (Dark Latin Groove) in the darker back room. Towards the end of the decade, the first members of the advance guard of Cuba's own new bands began to arrive after an absence of three decades (see Chapter 8).

Miami Salsa

While New York was the centre for Cuban-based music through the first era of salsa, its southern rival, **Miami**, became more important in the decades after the Revolution. An upstart of a city compared with grand old Havana, Miami grew gradually out of the swamps and citrus orchards of Florida at the beginning of the twentieth century. The adjacent resort of **Miami Beach**, on a long sandy island across the bay, had been developed in the 1930s, when Cuban bands had come down from New York to play the hotel ballrooms, and Desi Arnaz had actually based himself in Miami. But it was not until the 1960s that Miami's Cuban population became significant, and another fifteen years after that before Miami became a major source of Cuban-based music.

Cubans arrived in Miami in waves following the Revolution. First came the business elite, the owners of sugar mills or tobacco estates, then came the professionals and representatives of US companies, and finally the blue collar workers: agricultural labourers and

fishermen, followed by increasingly poor and desperate exiles. Some arrived in dramatic circumstances: the **Mariel boatlift**, in 1980, collected some 100,000 people, including many prisoners and officially despised homosexuals. Recent years have seen waves of *balseros* (raft-people), ragged groups clinging to inflated truck tyres and the like, fished out of the sea by the US Coastguard.

As the Cuban population of Miami grew around fifty percent, the area around Eighth Street (known as Calle Ocho) and Flagler Street transformed itself into **Little Havana**. Cuban pastry stores grew up to provide the multi-tiered cakes for the extravagant *quinces* (fifteenth birthday parties for girls), fruit stalls mixed *batida* shakes, and dozens of Cuban restaurants, often with the same names as the expropriated Havana establishments their owners had left behind, catered for the exiled population. Every year, as Calle Ocho's **carnival** grew bigger and more extravagant, the Havana carnival seemed to shrink

Little Havana souvenir art

and become more threadbare. Even Havana's last remaining luxury entertainment attraction, the **Tropicana**, acquired a Miami rival. The Cachaldora family, former owners of a chic Havana restaurant, opened a string of nightclubs in Miami, culminating in the Tropigala in the Hilton Hotel on Miami Beach – which lost no time in staffing its chorus line with defectors from the Ballet Folklórico de Cuba and rivalling the Tropicana itself in Latin kitsch.

Politically, Miami's atmosphere was, and is, vastly different from that of New York. While New York was home to exiled pro-Castro activists before the Revolution, Miami virulently opposed Castro after he came to power. You still meet elderly men in baseball caps and T-shirts with the insignia of the Brigada de Asalto 2506, the veterans of the Bay of Pigs attack, and organizations like Alpha 66, espousing commando raids within Cuba, openly run offices in Little Havana. Miami Cubans expressing pro-dialogue opinions were shot or bombed in the 1970s. Such attitudes extend to music: radio stations such as WQBA – "La Cubanísima" – and WAQI – Radio Mambí – would not dream of playing records of modern Cuban groups.

Nostalgia and modernity

The first exiled musicians to put Miami on the map were, not surprisingly, devout anti-Castroists. One of the most devout, and most influential musically, is **Roberto Torres**, the founder of the Orquesta Broadway, who moved his newly-formed label SAR Records down from New York in 1982. Torres began to issue a stream of beautifully produced albums mixing the profound nostalgia for traditional Cuban culture which is such a feature of Miami with fine modern arrangements, and employing a number of top-rate exile artists, notably Alfredo Valdés, "Chocolate" Armenteros, Papaíto, and La India de Oriente. A leading light of the charanga revival of the late 1970s, Torres

also scored an international hit with his creation, the **charanga vallenata**, which combined the swinging flute and violin charanga format with an accordion played in the rollicking vallenata style of Colombian coastal country music.

Two more stars of the charanga revival arrived in Miami in 1980. Both **Hansel Martínez** and **Raul Alfonso** had had family connections with the Batista regime and fled Cuba in 1960. In New York they founded as joint lead singers the highly successful **Charanga 76** and then left to perform as **Hansel and Raul**. Their music, while traditionally based, was melodically modern, using pop harmonies and dynamics. A third artist, **Willie Chirino**, showed an even more pronounced dichotomy between tradition and modernity in his work, combining pop and rock melody and harmony with smooth salsa instrumentation. His name is primarily associated with slick, rock-tinged salsa hits, among them anti-Castro songs like "Jinetera" (Prostitute) or "Memorandum Para Un Tirano" (Note to a Tyrant), which are relayed to Cuba, ninety miles away, by Miami's proselytizing radio stations. In 1998 he succumbed to the fashion for roots revivals and produced an album of classic Cuban songs called "Cuba Libre" (Free

Willie Chirino

Cuba), a title with a double meaning – it functioned as an advertising theme for the Bacardi corporation who were promoting what they claimed to be the centenary of the invention of rum and Coke.

In the 1970s, Bacardi's tradition of music sponsorship gave employment to **Emilio Estefan**, a musician who would become the leading Cuban entertainment entrepreneur of Miami, and one of the most successful in the world. A manager in the Bacardi corporation, Estefan founded the **Miami Latin Boys** as a sideline, but in 1974 a student called Gloria Fajardo joined the band. The Latin Boys became the **Miami Sound Machine**, Gloria and Emilio got married, and, as Gloria Estefan, the shy ex-student went on to become one of the biggest Cuban stars of all time. The Estefans' first hit records succeeded by combining Emilio's preferred Miami funk-pop with a spicing of Latin percussion. In 1985, the huge hit "Conga" revisited the traditional Santiago carnival beat which had surfaced periodically at Christmas parties since it was first made popular by Desi Arnaz.

In 1994, the Estefans formed their **Crescent Moon** group, which proceeded to have enormous success with middle-of-the-road Latin teen idols such as Jon Secada, as well as more commercially risky projects. The best of these was the pair of Master Sessions albums by the great old bassist **Israel "Cachao" López**, featuring Cachao's old repertoire of danzones and descargas, newly recorded by a top-notch cast including Paquito D'Rivera, Nestor Torres, Juanito Márquez, Alfredo Valdés Jr and many more. The albums were well publicized due to backing by the Cuban-American actor Andy García, and accomplished the feat of reintroducing one of Cuba's most eminent musicians to a large international audience after decades of obscurity. Two years later, Cachao's nephew, **Cachaíto Lopez**, another of the many virtuoso bassists of the family, was also

to be thrust into the international limelight, in his case from Havana, by his inclusion in the Buena Vista Social Club line-up.

One of the most striking beneficiaries of the 1990s' Latin boom was another Estefan protégée, a Cuban-born campesina singer named **Albita Rodríguez**, who became a cult success with Miami Beach's burgeoning jet-set – Madonna and Gianni Versace were both highly public fans. Repackaged in a white suit with a hint of lesbian chic, "Albita" was signed to Crescent Moon for her first album, **No Parece A Nada**, which sold 100,000 copies. Miami's old guard grappled with the thorny problem of whether to applaud her for defecting or disparage her unorthodox image.

Miami détente

In the mid 1990s, the de facto ban on Cuban bands from Havana playing in Miami began to crumble, but not without resistance. For decades, the official US position had been that Cuban acts could only play inside the US by special arrangement as part of an educational/cultural exchange package, the prime motive being to minimize Cubans' access to financial gain from concerts. While groups such as **Los Muñequitos de Matanzas** had played other parts of the US, Miami, dominated politically by the Cuban exiles, steadfastly refused permission for concerts by visiting Cuban artists. At the same time, a shift in Miami's music audience had taken place. A new generation of Cuban Americans, with no first hand experience of Cuba itself, included many more young people who wanted to forget the past, negotiate with Castro and leave politics out of music. And to the new non-Latin salsa fans of **South Beach**, political opinions for or against the Castro regime were a complete irrelevance.

In 1998 and 1999, a series of events pitted the new spirit of openness against the die-hards. A US-financed film about the Cuban doo-

wop group, **Los Zafiros**, who had experienced a meteoric burst of fame in the 1960s (see p.219), was a huge hit in Cuba, sparking a cult revival and earning an estimated $3 million in box office takings for the Cuban state distributors. When *Zafiros – Locura Azul* was screened in Miami, it attracted a crowd of five hundred protesters. Four months later, the anti-Castro agitators were out again, this time outside a concert by **Compay Segundo**, **Chucho Valdés** and **Omara Portuondo**. After a bomb scare, the concert was abandoned in mid performance. The biggest demonstrations of the decade, however, were reserved for the following year, when Cuba's most popular contemporary dance band, **Los Van Van**, played Miami. Los Van Van are particularly detested by the Miami hard-liners as being enthusiastic supporters of the Castro regime, mostly because their name refers to a famous speech by Castro which describes the 1969 sugar harvest target as "going, going". Although the concert took place, the two thousand spectators were outnumbered by protesters.

As these high profile battles took place, however, other Cuban acts quietly slipped into Miami without controversy. The Havana nueva trova star **Carlos Varela** guested at a small Miami Beach club, and gradually the embargo on Cubans became a thing of holes and patches, rather than an impenetrable surface.

One of the most symptomatic Miami success stories of the 1990s was a club which was first opened in 1995 on Calle Ocho by **José "Pepe" Horta**, former Cuban Cultural Attaché to UNESCO and Director of the Havana International Film Festival. Horta decorated his new nightspot with old film posters and projected films of classic Cuban entertainers. A house band played an eclectic mixture of son, bolero and other old classics. Already an object of suspicion, Horta attracted further revilement from the die-hards when he began to encourage Cuban musicians to visit the club and jam with the band.

On several occasions Café Nostalgia was picketed by baying crowds, but the club thrived and even released a successful album by the house band. With new backers and premises, Horta began 2000 with plans for a chain of Café Nostalgias, places where musicians from inside and outside Cuba could meet freely and escape the politics which had kept them divided for almost half a century.

Artists

La Lupe

Lupe Victoria Yuli Raymond is one of Cuban music's true originals though also, according to some, barking mad. She was born in poverty in Santiago in the 1930s and started her professional life as a teacher, though her spare time was spent singing in a trio called **Los Tropicales** and entering radio talent shows doing Olga Guillot impersonations. By 1959 she had given up the classroom for an act involving extravagantly oddball versions of rock'n'roll songs in a basement club in Havana named La Red (The Net). The first years of the Revolution saw **La Lupe** break through to sudden fame, discovered both by the curious Havana public and by a variety of foreign intellectuals attracted to the Cuban capital by the arrival of Castro. Pablo Picasso, Jean-Paul Sartre and the inevitable Ernest Hemingway all eulogized her wild act, for which Hemingway coined the neat phrase, "the art of frenzy".

The Havana-born writer and La Lupe compiler Pedro Rojas later recalled the mixed excitement and scandal of witnessing La Lupe's first TV appearance, with her trademark shrieks "Yiyiyi!" and "Ahí na ma!", and her hair-tearing, shoe-throwing and demented dancing. During La Lupe's brief Havana stardom she recorded two successful albums, **What the Wave Brought** and **La Lupe Is Back**, but her stage and private antics soon approximated to what was regarded as deviance in the new Cuba and she left for exile, first in Mexico, where **Mongo Santamaría** recorded a proto-salsa album with her. Moving on to New York, La Lupe's career prospered for several years: she sang with Tito Puente's band, recorded rock, boogaloo, salsa and boleros, and became a TV regular with an act which now included being carried off the stage in an oxygen mask. Susan Sontag cited her in an essay on camp, as one of the icons of the phenomenon. Things then started to go downhill. Her record label, Tico (along with Puente), concentrated their promotional effort on the newer, sleeker, less unpredictable salsera, Celia Cruz. La Lupe's personal life became chaotic, with much money spent, allegedly on santería cures and consultations. La Lupe died in 1992, impoverished and forgotten, having devoted her final musical efforts to recording hymns for the evangelical sect she had joined at the end of her life.

⊙ Trilogia	Manzana, Spain

An excellent three CD set of greatest hits, from Cuban country through sultry boleros and ballads to rock, boogaloo, salsa, Puerto Rican bomba, Beatles covers and curiosities too numerous to mention.

Celia Cruz

The star who would become variously known as the "Queen of Salsa" and the "Guarachera del Mundo" (the World's Guaracha

Singer) was born in Havana in 1924. **Celia Cruz** studied to be a teacher, but diverted into show business after winning a radio talent show singing the tango "Nostalgia". In the 1940s and 1950s, she studied music at Havana Conservatory, performed on the radio and worked in the cabaret of the Sans Souci and at the Tropicana, where she was the protégée of the establishment's most important choreographer, "Rodney" Neyra. In 1950 she took over as lead vocalist with the **Sonora Matancera** and the following year made her recording debut with the band. She began to tour abroad widely, and her first New York performance took place in 1957. A year after the Cuban revolution, Matancera left for

DAVID REDFERN

Celia, Queen of Salsa

another Mexican tour, never to return. In Mexico Cruz made a number of film appearances and worked with the Mexican band of Memo Salamanca before she married Pedro Knight, Matancera's trumpeter, who later became her manager.

In New York, Cruz began to work with **Tito Puente**'s orchestra, a relationship which would last to the end of Puente's life in 2000. She also visited Spain and renewed her friendship with the gypsy *tonadillera* **Lola Flores**, whom she had met when Flores visited Cuba

– Celia Cruz and the New York salsa stars became idols among Spanish gypsies in the 1970s and 1980s.

Cruz's fame really took off when she was adopted by salsa's founders, the **Fania** team, making her debut on the Fania label with the band of Johnny Pacheco on the album **Celia & Johnny**. A year later she appeared with the Fania All Stars at Yankee Stadium, by which time her quick-fire "Químbara" and show-stopping "Bemba Colorá" were becoming established favourites. Around this time she also acquired her trademark mid-song cry of "*azúca-a-a-r!*" (sugar!), born, she claims, of a waiter asking her if she wanted sugar in her coffee – she replied with appropriate disbelief, as a Cuban coffee is unthinkable without sugar. Throughout the heyday of salsa, Cruz appeared with all the top Fania bandleaders and wingers – Willie Colón, Ray Barretto, Papo Lucca, Pete "El Conde" Rodríguez – as well as renewing her partnership with Tito Puente, whose orchestra accompanied her through the 1980s. The 1990s saw Cruz joining the organization of Ralph Mercado, recording and touring with the band of the new salsa star Jose Alberto.

In 2000 Cruz moved to Miami, where her first Sony album was made under the directorship of **Emilio Estefan**, with guest appearances by his wife Gloria, among others. Cruz has retained a powerful antipathy to the Castro regime almost from its arrival in power, a feeling which is fully reciprocated. But whatever her politics, her immense prestige in the Latin music world remains undimmed.

⊙ **On Fire: The Essential Celia Cruz**   Manteca, UK

A good value re-licensing of material originally recorded on the SEECO label, mostly with the Sonora Matancera. Classic early Cruz, including "Quimbara".

⊙ Celia Cruz & Johnny Pacheco: Double Dynamite   Charly, UK

Features great music from Celia's early Fania period: a terrific
band playing excellent songs like "Las Divorciadas", "Siete
Potencias" and "Barin Barin".

⊙ Fania All-Stars with Celia Cruz   Sony, US

Just what the title states, opening with the live recording of
"Bemba Colorá", taken from Celia's first ever concert with the All
Stars, and closing with appropriately titled "Diosa del Ritmo"
(Goddess of Rhythm).

⊙ Azúcar Negra   RMM, US

Excellent 1993 album made in collaboration with the Estefans
introducing Celia's most recent pan-Latin mode. Recorded in New
York, Miami, Santo Domingo, Madrid and London, it includes
ballads, a bolero, some light, up-tempo Estefan numbers and a
cover of a song by Mecano, Spain's biggest pop act of the 1980s. An
interesting rather than a great album.

⊙ Mi Vida Es Cantar   RMM, US

A superb 1998 potpourri. Salsa tracks (including "Canto a
Lola Flores" and "Patica de Chivo") mix with merengue, a
flavour added by Santo Domingo's hottest *merenguero*, Kinito
Mendez.

⊙ Celia's Duets   RMM, US

Yet more star guests, constellations of them, from old stable-
mates (Willie Colon, Tito Puente and Cheo Feliciano) through
newer salsa aristocrats (Oscar D'León, Willie Chirino and La
India) to newer ventures such as a merengue with Johnny
Ventura and an essay in tropicalia with Brazilian star Caetano
Veloso. Cruz displays her high energy, virtuoso showmanship
throughout, and nowhere more so than in duet with Oscar
D'León.

Rolando Laserie

William Newton Calasanz **Rolando Laserie,** the son of a tobacco worker, was born in Santa Clara in 1923 seven decades before the town became the last resting place of Che Guevara. He arrived in Havana in 1940, and started his musical career in a group with Raúl Planas (later of Buena Vista fame), worked in Pérez Prado's band in Colombia before returning to become a percussionist with Beny Moré, and in the orchestra of Radio Progreso backing the duo Olga and Tony. His move into singing was sudden, idiosyncratic and successful. "One day he just got up and started singing, and from then on he was a singer," according to Bebo Valdés, the then leader of the radio orchestra.

Laserie's rough-edged, passionate, syncopated delivery of boleros – traditionally sung suavely and melodiously – marked him out as a completely individual talent. His first record, the bolero "Mentiras

Tuyas", astonished the song's sceptical composer by selling 30,000 copies within days of its release. Laserie rapidly acquired the sobriquet "El Guapo de la Canción" (the guapo of song), with the word "guapo" used not in its normal sense of "handsome" but in its Cuban slang meaning of daring, or street-tough, in reference to the boldness of his singing style.

Laserie's career soon took off abroad – he was particularly popular in Argentina, where he added tangos to his repertoire – and it was from Mexico that he and his wife and Bebo Valdés fled to the US, first to New York, later to join his numerous Cuban exile friends in Miami. In later life, illness prevented him from performing often; his last notable work was with Cachao Lopez, on the Master Sessions albums and in a final concert in Miami in 1996.

| ⊙ El Guapachoso | Discos Fuentes, Colombia |

| ⊙ El Guapo de la Canción, 18 Exitos | Discos Fuentes, Colombia |

Two collections of Laserie's classic late 1950s material, recorded for the Cuban GEMA label with lovely, swinging, brassy big bands directed by Ernesto Duarte and Bebo Valdés. The former includes the big hit "Mentiras Tuyas", "18 Exitos" and the jolly "El Muerto Vivo" which was taken up a decade later by the Barcelona gypsy rumba singer, Peret.

Roberto Torres

An excellent singer and successful recording artist, **Roberto Torres** is also notable as a producer of traditionally-based Cuban son montuno with a modern edge. He began his career in the town of Güines as a singer with the Orquesta Swing Casino and the Conjunto Universal, moved to New York immediately after the revolution and worked with Fajardo's orquesta and the Orquesta Broadway. He then went solo and created a family of labels, SAR, Guajiro and Neon, before relocating to Miami in the 1980s. Apart from his own prolific recordings, which include numerous homages to great Cuban stars such as Beny Moré, Torres produced albums by a nucleus of eminent Cuban émigré artists including Papaíto, trumpeter Alfredo "Chocolate" Armenteros, former bolero singer La India de Oriente, Alfredo Valdés (who sang

with the Septeto Nacional) and his piano-playing son Alfredito Valdés.

Torres' hybrid invention, the charanga vallenata – the "vallenata" part added to the flute charanga by Colombian vallenato accordionist Jesus Hernandez – gave birth to the hit song "Caballo Viejo", later modified by the **Gypsy Kings** to create the international hit "Bamboleo". Although heart bypass surgery slowed Torres down in the 1990s, he continues to be one of the most important figures of Miami's music community, and a die-hard anti-Castroist and critic of rapprochement.

⊙ **Lo Mejor de Roberto Torres, Vols. 1 & 2**   SAR, US

Two "best of" discs of the maestro's own songs and classics. They feature Cuban composers such as Miguel Matamoros, but also songs by the Puerto Rican Rafael Hernandez, "Lamento Borincano", and the Colombian Rafael Escalona, "El Testamento".

⊙ **Roberto Torres Rinde Homenaje a Beny Moré**   SAR, US

A hot, swinging brass section, steady bass, excellent tight coro and Torres in good soulful voice. Top class dance music which makes a worthy tribute to the rhythm barbarian.

⊙ **Roberto Torres y su Charanga Vallenata, Vols. 1-3**   SAR, US

Torres' historic charanga vallenata is essential for any collection and with the first two discs there is the added bonus of José

Esposito's beautiful sleeve paintings depicting typical Colombian campesina scenes. Musical highlights include "Rio Crecido", "La Parranda es Pa'amenece" and the famous "Caballo Viejo" with its unmistakable opening accordion and flute figure. All great stuff.

Willie Chirino

One of Miami's musical aristocrats, along with the Estefans, **Willie Chirino** has a road named after him – since 1995 a stretch of NW 17th Avenue has been named Willie Chirino Way. His office is cluttered with gold discs, keys to assorted cities and framed letters from the political establishment, including the inevitable note on White House paper from Ronald Reagan. Chirino began as an evening entertainer in his spare time, but began to compose prolifically during the 1970s, developing his trademark blend of light rock, salsa and a basket of other tropical genres, notably Brazilian pop and Dominican merengue (his later work has similarities with both Juan-Luis Guerra's

and Ruben Blade's). Chirino's colourful compositions treat subjects as diverse as love, dancing and the iniquities of the Castro regime, as he sees them.

⊙ Oxigeno   Sony Discos, US

A good example from the peak of Chirino's middle period, with the
first of the star guests which were to become a feature of US salsa
albums – in this case Arturo Sandoval. A classic list of songs,
including the opener, "Mister, Don't Touch The Banana", a tale of
American tourists at a santería ceremony.

⊙ South Beach   Sony Discos, US

The cover shot, showing Chirino standing in front of a pink, black
and white 1950s Studebaker on Ocean Drive, says it all. Arturo
Sandoval crops up on the guest list once more, along with new
Miami arrival Albita Rodríguez. The repertoire includes one song
by the modern Cuban son composer, Candido Fabre, and a blast of
vitriol directed at Castro, "Memorandum Para Un Tirano".

⊙ Baila Conmigo   Sony Discos, US

A 1997 classic, worth preserving for one track alone, "Bongo", a
dance-floor filler written by another young Cuban, David Alvarez,
in praise of the *binomio de chivo* (goat-skin duo).

Gloria and Emilio Estefan

In 1993, **Gloria** and **Emilio Estefan** decided to record a back-to-
roots album totally in Spanish of Cuban standards and new sones
and boleros. Typically of Emilio Estefan, the best musicians and
arrangers were called in: Cachao López on bass, Nestor Torres on
flute, Paquito Hechavarría on piano, Tito Puente guesting among a
strong percussion section, Nelson González on tres, the eminent old
guitarist and arranger of the Orquesta Riverside, Juanito Márquez,
arranging and conducting the Miami Strings and the London
Symphony Orchestra's string section. The resulting album, **Mi Tierra**,
was a resounding success – aesthetically and commercially – selling
over 3 million copies. It was also the start of a series of traditionally-

based but modern, Spanish-language records which transformed Gloria into a serious player in the tropical music stakes as well as the pop charts.

Two years later, **Mi Tierra** was followed by **Abriendo Puertas**. This time the geographic scope was widened to include not only Cuban styles, but styles from Colombia – vallenato accordion and the old Pacific coast African currulao rhythm – and Dominican merengue. The album was presented at a lavish international launch at the chic Delano Hotel in South Beach, attended by executives for Sears and Roebuck who were sponsoring the latest Gloria Estefan tour.

Five years and two Gloria Estefan English pop albums passed before the third of the roots trilogy, **Alma Caribeña**. The theme was again pan-Caribbean, the mood ranged from upbeat salsa to softer pop-styled boleros and bachatas, and the team included Ruben Blade's brother Robert as arranger and song-writer, a prominent role in the musical direction for the Miami Sound Machine founder Hernan "Teddy" Mulet, and guests ranging from Jose Feliciano to Celia Cruz.

At the end of the century, Emilio and Gloria Estefan were at the peak of their success. They owned a mega-star house on Miami's private Star Island, while their business empire included the Crescent Moon label (and associated companies), a catalogue of 3,000 songs, plus assorted hotels and the Lario's mini-chain of Cuban restaurants. The couple also had an agreement with the Universal Television Group to produce Hispanic market TV films and – following Gloria's appearance alongside Andy García in a bio-pic of Arturo Sandoval – a co-production with Disney based on their own life stories was planned.

Finally, their solid support of the anti-return side in the case of the stranded balsero child, Elian Gonzalez, meant that their stock with the anti-Castroists was now riding high. This had not always been so, with accusations of ideological vacillation or ambiguity often circulating among the hard-liners.

⊙ **Mi Tierra**   Epic/Sony, US

Not all of the dozen tracks are winners, but those that are, notably the title track, are stunners. An extremely catchy tune and a lyric spelling out the sweet pain of an exile's memories, plus a cracking arrangement by Emilio Estefan and his Miami Sound machine partner Randy Barlow all help to maintain "Mi Tierra" as a perennial favourite on the dance-floor.

⊙ **Abriendo Puertas**   Epic/Sony, US

The writer of most of the tracks, a former Cali University medical graduate named Kike Santander, was told to think festive, and the result was ten light, tuneful, well-crafted tropical pop songs, their polished arrangements adorned with guest instrumentals by the likes of the young Colombian vallenato star Gonzalo "Cocha" Molina.

⊙ **Alma Caribeña**   Epic/Sony, US

Juanito Marquez and Cachao Lopez bow out for the third slice of Estefan tropicalia, replaced by a team of arrangers centred round

Emilio Estefan and Sal Cuevas on bass. Other guests include Yomo
Toro, Puerto Rican cuatro ace. Some good salsa, a lot of guitar-rich
bachata and ballad action, and another hit.

Hansel y Raul

Hansel Martínez, born in Morón, near Camaguey, and **Raul Alfonso**,
originally from Marianao, are veterans of several movements. During
the 1970s' charanga revival, which started in New York, they were

SONY TROPICAL

singers in the influential group **Charanga 76**, composing several of its biggest successes, notably "Regresaras", "Wanda" and "Ku-Ku-Cha". As a duo, they occupied the more traditional end of Miami pop salsa of the 1980s and it was during this period that the hit songs they co-wrote and sang enabled them to tour the world, taking in Colombia and Mexico, as well as Africa and the growing markets of France and Japan. They also penetrated the Latin showbiz MOR elite, singing for the Reagans at the White House with Tina Turner and Barry Manilow. In 1988, they "went on hiatus from one another", in part due to the imposition of a spell in jail on Martínez for cocaine handling, but came back in 1996 with a new album and world tour, which extended their global reach to new salsa territories such as Switzerland, Italy, Thailand and the Philippines. Their third major affiliation is with the hard-line anti-Castroists of Miami. Along with Willie Chirino, they are the most active musicians of this faction, organizing from their Brickell Avenue HQ events such as a counter-demonstration against Jane Fonda's rally to raise funds for Cuba or the picketing of Café Nostalgia in Calle Ocho.

⊙ **Hansel y Raul: Oro Salsero, 20 Exitos**   Polygram, US

A double CD containing all of the classics in their original versions, beginning with their first big hits as a duo, "Maria Teresa y Danilo" and "Con La Lengua Afuera".

⊙ **Celebrando**   Sony Tropical, US

Their 1995 come-back album, containing the big dance-floor success, "Bailala Pegaita", recorded with a new charanga led by pianist Alex Arias, featuring heavyweight session musicians such as Eddy "Guagua" Rivera on bass and Edwin Bonilla on timbales.

Alfredo de la Fé

The man who brought the electric rock violin to salsa, **Alfredo de la Fé** is a versatile and brilliant musician whose name crops up throughout the patchwork of Cuban diaspora music. He was born in Havana in 1954, the son of a musician, and claims to have seen his first violin, and known he wanted to have one, at age two. He was learning classical violin at the Amadeo Roldán Conservatory in Havana at age eight, and two years later obtained a scholarship to study in Poland. In 1965, his family moved to New York, where he continued his studies at the Juilliard School.

De la Fé was recruited from the classical world into that of salsa because of the need for violinists generated by the charanga boom of the late 1960s. **Roberto Torres**, the founder of the charanga Orquesta Broadway, used to frequent a record shop next door to a restaurant owned by de la Fé's uncle, and called the boy in to help out with Broadway's violin section. According to the British musicologist John Child, Broadway members were uncomplimentary, saying his playing was too classical, and José Fajardo, the violinist in whose band de la Fé next played, was also a harsh teacher. Instead of being discouraged, de la Fé listened and analysed until he had mastered charanga violin, and the rare solos he began to be permitted by Fajardo turned into highlights of the band's set, rivalling Fajardo's own soloing.

Throughout the 1970s, de la Fé played, either as a full-time member or as an occasional session man, with some of the most important bands in US Latin music. In 1972, he was hired by Eddie Palmieri's band, where he spent five years learning from the volatile and inventive pianist. He also played with the **Grupo Folklorico y Experimental** and its successor, the **Conjunto Libre**, on two of the

great bassist Cachao López's descarga albums, on many of Roberto Torres' SAR label productions, and with the band he later recalled as the hottest and best he'd ever been in, **Típica 73.** Típica 73, named after the year of its foundation, was a powerhouse of New York salsa and launching pad for numerous stars. With the band de la Fé began to customize his violin, adding wah-wah pedal and a range of other effects. He also participated in their controversial visit to Cuba in 1979 to play, record and – on returning – be vilified by the American Cuban exiles. De la Fé finished the 1970s joining Tito Puente's small

Alfredo de la Fé with customized violin and hair

group, the **Latin Jazz Ensemble**, and then making his first solo albums, from one of which, **Alfredo**, a disco hit, "Hot To Trot" was released.

In 1983, de la Fé was contracted to play in a club in Cali, Colombia, for a three-week residence which turned into a decade, during which his self-con-fessed minor cocaine habit turned into a life-dominating addiction. Nonetheless, he produced much excellent work, including an album of vallenata music and the song which became the Colombian pavilion's anthem in the Seville Expo 92. In 1995 he returned to working in the US and Europe, and by the end of the decade, having renounced drugs, was living in Turin, Italy, touring successfully with a new multinational band, and signed to the Latin division of the world music label, Ryko.

⊙ **Latitudes**   Ryko Latino, UK/US

De la Fé's first album of the new millennium acts simultaneously as a review of his past, with echoes of Eddie Palmieri in the beefy triple trombone section, or of the Tito Puente period descarga fireworks, and a manifesto for the future, with the eclecticism and polish of his new young 14-strong band, which is augmented to order by accordion, trumpet, tres, African djembé drum or Brazilian percussion. The best tracks are powerful, deep son montunos (one written by his father), where the searing violin reminds one of de la Fé's impact on Colombian bands such as The

Latin Brothers. There are also some faster salsa and timba numbers, a punchy danzón, jazz and a de la Fé invention, "batusalsa", in which he grafts Brazilian batucada percussion onto a salsa base.

Albita

Albita Rodríguez was born in 1962 to a couple of guajira singers from Las Villas named Martin & Minerva who specialized in performing the old *repentista* improvised verse-exchange. Although much of her youth was spent listening to American rock and funk, she followed her parents into **campesina** singing and, unusually for a woman, played the tres. She succeeded in becoming the new gener-

ation's Celina Gonzalez by imposing a modern young image on the old redneck guajira genre. In 1988 her debut album **Habra música guajira** was one of Egrem's biggest sellers, and she began to work in officially approved "velvet exile" in Colombia, a country of guajira-aficionados, where she recorded a major hit single "La parranda se canta".

In 1993, Rodríguez and her band walked over the US-Mexican border at El Paso, Texas, and arrived in **Miami** on tickets paid for by the radio station WQBA, which had heard of the group's defection. Although her repertoire and deep, melodramatic voice

were far from the Miami style, she rapidly attracted attention via
adroit image manipulation, moving from a cult cabaret show at the
Centro Vasco on Calle Ocho to the smart restaurant-club YUCA, in
South Beach. Renamed Albita, she recorded three albums which
were well received by critics but whose sales decreased successively
from the 100,000-copy debut. After a hiatus in 1998 and 1999, when
her record company and half the band deserted her, she came back
with a new album in 2000.

⊙ **No Se Parece A Nada**   Crescent Moon/Epic, US

Albita's successful US debut album, though some of the songs are
weak. Showcases the diva's powerful contralto and introduces her
eccentric selection of mambo rallying cries – including the "woah-
woah-WOAH!" that sounds distinctly as if she is falling off a ladder.

⊙ **Son**   Hipbop Latino, UK

The comeback album after Sony ditched Albita as uncommercial.
Includes a jaunty version of the Peanut Vendor got up in techno
colours with a rap interlude, and a moody "Veinte Años" that
reaffirms the pre-eminent suitability of Albita's voice to dramatic
Spanish-style ballads rather than dance music, although her blend
of Estefan-ized Cuban oldies and Miami pop-salsa still has some
mileage in it.

Café Nostalgia

The house band of the successful club of the same name. The nucleus of the group was formed by recent Cuban exiles: the leader Omar
Hernandez was bassist with the Havana jazz groups AfroCuba and
Cuarto Espacio before fleeing the island on a raft in 1994. Other
members jumped ship from dance bands or touring revues. The
singer Luis Bofill arrived via Germany and, like most of the group, did
odd jobs to survive - the guitarist was at one time a security guard at

Gianni Versace's Ocean Drive mansion. The group's repertoire consists of an eclectic mix of standards and descargas, and much late-night jamming with guests from the audience. In 2000, Bofill was replaced as singer by Nelson Trejo, a former member of the Orquesta Revé in Cuba.

⊙ Te Di La Vida Entera   Naïve, France

The first and best album, created in 1998, an original and successful attempt to create a "soundtrack" for the Zoe Valdés novel *La Douleur du Dollar*. A mixture of original 1950s and 1960s tracks and re-recorded modern versions by the Café Nostalgia house band augmented as required by top session men such as the ubiquitous bassist Eddy "Guagua" Rivera, an orchestral string section and even a harp. Features a wide range of classics, from the Bola de Nieve version of "Be Careful, It's My Heart" to a terrific updating of the Matamoros guaracha "Un Cubano En Nueva York", and even a Cubanization of Piaf's "Mon Manège A Moi".

8

After the Revolution

O n New Year's Eve 1958, the **Orquesta Aragón**, whose chachacha, "Cuba, Cubita, Cubera", was the big hit of Christmas, was playing at a Havana club named Las Aguilas. The atmosphere was tense, with rumours of the departure of **President Batista** circulating feverishly. At 3am, a radio newsflash confirmed the dictator's family had just flown to exile in the Dominican Republic: the country was leaderless, and **Castro's rebels**, who had taken Santiago, were now heading for the capital. Amid the panic, the Orquesta Aragón's dance was abruptly abandoned and musicians and revellers found themselves in the street, heading for home.

It was another week before Castro's arrival in Havana where he set up his headquarters in the Hilton Hotel (renamed the Habana Libre) and a further two years before Cuba's new government declared itself officially to be Communist. In the meantime, hundreds of Batista supporters had been shot in the dry moats around Havana's colonial castle, many of the middle and upper classes had fled, much

of the countryside had been redistributed to peasants or turned into State farms, and massive expropriation of US-owned assets had taken place. The US responded by breaking relations with Cuba and unleashing the inept CIA-backed **Bay of Pigs** invasion attempt by Cuban exiles.

New regime, new rhythms

At first, the new regime had a relatively restrained effect on popular music. Although the casinos and brothels and many cabarets and dancehalls were closed down, Cubans carried on dancing. The chachacha was still popular, as was the pachanga, a fast and funky new rhythm created by the bandleader **Eduardo Davidson**, which he introduced to New York when he went into exile there. This was a time of new rhythms (when the possibility of exporting them had not yet disappeared) and two of the most famous were both Afro-derivations – the **pilón** and the **mozambique**.

The pilón, meaning mortar, based itself on the up and down pounding movement of big traditional African food-pulverizing batons. Its creator was a Santiago singer and bandleader named **Pacho Alonso** who became a favourite of early 1960s carnivals with songs such as "Rico Pilón". Alonso visited France in 1962, followed – in an indication of the way things were going – by Czechoslovakia and the Soviet Union where his group, **Los Bocucos**, became the first non-classical musicians to play in Moscow's Tchaikovsky Hall. The Bocuco's star singer at this time was a young oriental-featured sonero named **Ibrahim Ferrer**, the co-creator of the pilón, who was pictured, in 1962, shaking hands with the Captain of a Russian naval ship, the *Aurora*. This was the time of the Cuban Missile Crisis, when Presidents **Kennedy** and **Kruschev** kept the world on tenterhooks following the American ultimatum to the Russians to remove nuclear

missiles from Cuba. Ferrer later recalled that the crisis precipitated the band's return home, and curtailed his own international career, although pictures of him in full pilón swing on the Cristal Beer float in Havana's carnival the following year show him looking decidedly cheerful about things.

The pilón lasted a couple of years with Alonso dreaming up variations such as the pilón-twist and eventually a short-lived successor, the upa-upa. It coincided with the brief burgeoning of another new dance rhythm, the mozambique. The creation of a folklorist turned popularizer from Havana, **Pedro Izquierdo**, known on stage as "Pello El Afrokan", the mozambique featured the massed percussion of a Santiago conga-line, a brass section, and chorus answering the lead vocal. Pello's most popular songs, notably "Maria Caracoles", were hugely successful throughout the 1960s, and the mozambique was taken up in the US by Eddie Palmieri, who recorded an excellent proto-salsa version of "Maria Caracoles".

The grand Cuban music hall

The most popular of all the new groups to spring up in the post-Revolution years, however, was a Cuban quartet adapting an American style. Attired in silk suits, pencil ties and sapphire signet rings, **Los Zafiros** (The Sapphires) took the doo-wop tight harmony vocal style of the Platters and Frankie Lymon and the Teenagers and creolised it, creating a virtuoso act, complete with razor-sharp synchronized dance steps. In 1962 Beny Moré's funeral in Havana was the scene of a massive public tribute, and with Ernesto Lecuona's death in the same year, it seemed as if an era had passed away. Los Zafiros, with their brilliant doo-wop rumbas, calypsos, ballads and sones and their incorporation of electric guitar (played by Manuel Galván) seemed briefly to fill the gap with a new Cuban sound for **the Beatles era**. In 1965, one of the

WORLD CIRCUIT

Los Zafiros, tropical doo-wop kings

last big Cuban shows in non-Communist Europe before the freeze, **The Grand Cuban Music Hall** bill, featured Los Zafiros, the Orquesta Aragón, Pello el Afrokan, Elena Burke, Jose Antonio Méndez and Los Papines.

In Paris, Los Zafiros played at the prestigious Olympia just after the Beatles and later claimed to have struck up a friendship with them.

The 1965 Grand Cuban Music Hall shows in Paris were tremendously successful, and on their return to Cuba the artists were feted

Clandestine rock

Needless to say, the Cubans were not immune to Beatlemania. Back in Havana, the Miami radio station WQAM was keenly listened to for its rock output, and a crop of clandestine groups sprang up – Los Kent, Los Gnomos, Los Jets, Los Hanks – who played at private parties. Their activities were clandestine because, as in Iron Curtain Europe, rock was seen as ideologically deviant, while long hair (like overt homosexuality) became a virtual passport to the forced labour battalions. It would be 1970 before this position softened enough to permit a rock group **Almas Vertiginosas** to play briefly at Havana Carnival.

by the authorities. However, despite the plaudits, many star musicians and dancers regularly used their privileged travel access to defect. The wave of Cuban musicians which left the country in the first years of the Revolution did so for a variety of reasons. A number of established stars, such as Olga Guillot, Rolando Laserie, Celio Gonzalez, Xiomara Alfaro and the Sonora Matancera, immediately realized that the new regime would obstruct their careers – especially financially. Others balked at the imposition of militia duty and the puritan atmosphere which, before long, invaded Havana in spite of Che Guevara's celebrated reassurance that the new regime would be "socialism with pachanga". The big gay showbusiness milieu was decimated and outré personalities, such as the wild **La Lupe**, soon became aware that Havana nightlife was no longer for them.

Serving the state

For all those musicians who opposed the Revolution there were just as many who supported it: men such as the bandleader **Julio Cuevas**, a long-standing socialist who had joined Cuban volunteers fighting on the Republican side in the Spanish Civil War, or the fílin star **José Antonio Méndez**, who immediately returned from exile in Mexico, and indeed the members of the Orquesta Aragón, who had operated as a sort of proto-socialist co-operative since the band's foundation.

Many ordinary musicians, as opposed to stars, considered life in pre-revolutionary Cuba had offered little that was worth losing with a change of regime. In the early 1950s, according to Aragón's leader, Rafael Lay, the band was offered a regular Sunday afternoon radio slot in Havana, which followed their established Saturday night concert in Cienfuegos. The radio fee worked out at two pesos per member (less than a dollar), for which they had to drive six or seven hours

through the night after the Saturday date and back on Sunday evening. Throughout the century, it had been normal for musicians to work at menial jobs as well as performing, and sickness pay or the provision of training was unusual. Decades later, many Cuban artists would praise the Revolution for giving them a steady living.

Whatever the musicians' political views, the Revolution soon began to effect major changes to their conditions of work, as well as to the content of the music itself. To begin with, the employing bodies were abruptly subsumed into the State. The record companies had their studios, master tapes and archives confiscated, and all recording and record distributing functions were placed under the control of a new entity, **Egrem**. The **Sabat family**, proprietors of Panart, the biggest Cuban label, had taken the precaution of smuggling copies of masters to their New York office before leaving for exile. Galo Sabat signed the transfer of the company over to the government and remained as manager for a year, during which time State-appointed advisers ordered cheap label paper from China, which was non-heat-resistant and curled off the discs, and wax from Poland, which broke the presses as it was the wrong quality. Forty years later, Egrem would still be using the Panart recording studios – patched and dilapidated like Havana's battered 1950s American cars – to record Cuba's own sporadic record output and later to rent out to foreign producers.

While the radio and television stations were nationalized and the content of their programmes monitored, the musicians became State employees – evaluated and graded periodically on a rating of A for a top virtuoso down to F, and either salaried at between 200 and 400 pesos a month, or engaged on fixed or indefinite contracts. All musicians had to belong to one of a chain of regional "empresas" named after historic musical figures such as the Empresa Ignacio Piñeiro or Adolfo Guzmán, which would authorize trips outside the country and

obtain the necessary visas, and also give the requisite permission to change groups or form new ones. Dismissal rarely happened; obliga-

Record Losses

The effect the troubled economy had on the record business was increasingly catastrophic: vinyl, cardboard, access to printing presses all became scarce. Egrem employees would have to queue for a batch of LP sleeves for a new release alongside a state clothing manufacturer wanting cardboard packaging for a consignment of underwear – neither permitted to go elsewhere, even if they could afford to. A top band might have to wait a year or more to record an album and, since official policy was to record all types of music (irrespective of ephemeral concepts like popularity), could then wait a further year to see the record released.

Individual State shops could not order records according to their own requirements, but simply received whatever goods were issued to them by the central industrial distribution body, and no mechanism existed for reporting back consumer demand. A popular record would sell out immediately, and then disappear from the shops, as a re-print, in the unlikely event that it happened, would take another year. Record sales for Cuban artists consequently became more and more meaningless, especially since, although in theory a system of fee plus royalties applied to record payment, royalties were rarely paid. A Kafka-esque parallel vocabulary of showbusiness awards and prizes existed. A "platinum disc" in Cuba brought no more financial success to its creator than a flop – it was simply a tag Egrem had decided to award – while a "No.1 record" had nothing to do with sales, but a vague impression of audience reaction to radio broadcasts.

tory retraining was the likely penalty for poor performance, and an expansion of the State-funded music schools ensured that free education was readily available.

One of the most profound changes created by the new system, whether for good or bad, was to break the strict link between consumption or purchase and artistic success. Traditionally, musicians receive the fruits of public popularity via bookings for shows and royalties on record sales. Under the Cuban model, most musicians received their modest salaries and were required to perform regularly, irrespective of whether there was public demand. At the same time, the record business became increasingly dysfunctional.

By this time, the Cuban economy, directed by the non-economist Che Guevara, was in trouble. America, once the buyer of 90% of Cuba's main crop, sugar, now embargoed the purchase of sugar or any other dealings with Cuba. The Soviet Union had saved the country from disaster by agreeing to buy Cuban sugar at a high rate while selling the country oil at a low rate. Nonetheless, the loss of trade, the outflow of capital and managerial expertise, and the sclerotic effect of a centralised State control meant that commerce within Cuba was grinding to a halt.

In some senses, Cuban music prospered. The mass State employment of musicians, combined with the lack of market forces, meant that hundreds of country son and trova groups kept playing, especially where there were tourists to be entertained. Cuba's increasing isolation intensified this effect, preserving in aspic a wide range of traditional styles. As Cuban-derived musics around the world evolved and mingled into hybrids like salsa, Cuba's hermetically sealed musicians remained unaffected. And the growing excellence of the health service meant that musicians lived longer, hence the 80 and 90 year old soneros rediscovered in the 1990s.

Tradition or innovation?

The first decade after the Revolution set Cuban music on a dual course of preservation and rediscovery of tradition, on the one hand, and experimentation, often involving the belated incorporation of outside trends, on the other. The first new musical genre to be directly associated with the Revolution – excluding the rash of songs which simply commented on the new regime – was **nueva trova**. While nueva trova was typically an acoustic guitar-accompanied song form, it also had links with a movement which sought to develop new musics combining traditional forms with innovative elements like jazz improvisation and electronic instruments. The nueva trova stars **Pablo Milanés** and **Silvio Rodríguez** both participated in the **Grupo de Experimentación Sonora of ICAIC**, the Cuban Institute of Cinematic Art and Industry. The aim of the ICAIC group, directed by Cuba's top classical guitarist, **Leo Brouwer**, was very much experimentation based on traditional forms, and the overlapping of its personnel with several similarly-minded groups was crucial in nurturing one of the most important strands of modern Cuban music. Another key member of this community was the **Orquesta Cubana de Música Moderna**, which was formed in 1967 around the percussionist **Guillermo Barreto** and led by saxophonist **Armando Romeu**, grandson of the great bandleader Antonio María Romeu. Guillermo Barreto had been a leading light of the **Quinteto Instrumental de Música Moderna** which transmuted into **Los Amigos** (featuring the great bassist Orlando "Cachaíto" López and the conga maestro Tata Güines). He was also a member of **Orquesta Cubana de Música Moderna**, the launching pad for several Cuban jazz stars, such as the pianists Gonzalo Rubalcaba and Chucho Valdés, the trumpeters Arturo Sandoval and Guajiro Mirabal, and the top trombonist and

musical director Juan-Pablo Torres. Like the ICAIC group, the Orquesta Cubana de Música Moderna had a close connection with the cinema. Chucho Valdés recalled that the orchestra or its members had been responsible for the soundtracks of every film made in Cuba up to the mid 1970s.

Emergence of new groups

In the early 1970s a school of new groups emerged from the double training grounds of nueva trova and experimental fusion. One of the

Irakere

first was **Grupo Manguaré**, formed in 1971, whose stylistic pool also included the Andean folkloric elements which, through the Chilean and Argentinian political folk revivalists of the 1950s and 1960s, had been such an influence on the original nueva trova singers. Thus Manguaré included charangos, the little armadillo-bodied Andean guitars, and Venezuelan cuatros in their line-up. The following year, **Grupo Moncada** (named after the barracks in Santiago which had been attacked in the early stage of the Castro insurrection) was formed. Moncada's aim was to combine the texts and melodies of nueva trova with traditional Afro-Cuban rhythm and modern progressive rock instrumentation. Then in 1973, Cuba's most famous and influential modern Afro-Cuban jazz group emerged from the membership of the Modern Music Orchestra. **Irakere** was the creation of the pianist **Chucho Valdés**, son of the great bandleader Bebo Valdés, and it reflected above all its founder's eclectic tastes: thus Afro-Cuban polyrhythms mixed with deconstructions of classic boleros and sones, alongsided passages of Mozart or rock, while extraordinarily brilliant soloing by Valdés and the star brass players Paquito D'Rivera and Arturo Sandoval shimmered through the weft. While Irakere featured electric guitar and bass, it also used traditional conga drums, and its fluency in avant-garde jazz was tempered by a strong grounding in dance rhythms. Irakere became immensely popular in Cuba and was soon impressing jazz festival audiences in Scandinavia, Italy and Germany, and finally the US, where the group played the Carnegie Hall in 1978.

The great success of Irakere not only set the scene for Cuba's continued pre-eminence in the jazz field in the 1980s and 1990s but ensured the creation of other genre-straddling groups. **Tema IV** made use of synthesizers for the first time in Cuba and also drew on new Western ideas of theatrical staging. The group metamorphosed

into **Síntesis**, one of the top progressive rock outfits of Havana. **Mezcla**, founded in 1985, were another group which aimed, once again, for a modern rock and progressive instrumental treatment of traditional rhythms.

Juan Formell and the Los Van Van years

The sky-rocketing arrival on the scene of Irakere, with their hit "Bacalao Con Pan", briefly eclipsed Cuba's biggest popular dance stars, **Los Van Van.** Formed four years before Irakere, and anchored more in pop than jazz, the group was the creation of bass player Juan Formell who had worked in the National Police Band, a variety of popular dance and cabaret ensembles, and, crucially, also spent a couple of years as arranger in the **Orquesta of Elio Revé**. Revé's band was a key institution in son preservation during the era of trova and experimentation. Revé, a Guantánamo-born timbalero, steeped in the son changüi, founded his own charanga in 1959 and, although it was twenty years before he achieved stardom, he immediately showed flair in instrumentation, arrangement and, above all, choice of personnel. Formell's arrangements in the late 1960s proved a high point of the Revé band's career, as did the presence in the 1980s of the keyboard player **Juan Carlos Alfonso**, who also went on to become a major star in his own right. Formell's contribution to the Revé band was twofold: modernizing and beefing up the old violin-led charanga format with electric guitars and a drum kit, and putting his formidable talent for catchy modern song-writing to use in creating the components of a new dance craze for Revé – the **changüi-shake**.

When Formell set up Los Van Van he applied the same formula, and incidentally took half of Revé's players with him. Indeed, at the very beginning of their career, Los Van Van played Formell's hits from the Revé repertoire and were regarded as a sort of temporary Revé

Julio Etchart

Juan Formell (third from left) and Los Van Van

offshoot. Formell's constantly progressing inventiveness soon established his new group's identity, however, and their first big success,
"Marilú" – a hybrid of tropicalized American rock trends of the period
– was a complete break with the son-bound tradition of Revé.

Van Van's songs often described and commented on changing life in
Havana. The 1974 "La Habana Joven" (Young Havana), for instance,
creates a picture of an idealistic young couple sitting on the lovers'
promenade of the Malecón, dreaming of their careers as teacher and
ship's officer in the brave new Cuba. With the recruitment to the band
of the virtuoso percussionist, José Luis Quintana, "Changuito", Van
Van came up with yet another new dance, the **son-go**, or songo. With
its complex, churning, heavy but syncopated rhythms on drum kit and
congas, it proved to be one of their most enduring creations. In the
1980s, the songo was taken up by Puerto Rican and New York bands

such as **Batacumbele**, proving itself to be one of the few examples of direct Cuban influence on the salsa scene at this time.

Further isolation

For Cuba the 1970s and early 1980s was a period of isolation abroad and economic crisis and tight political control at home. In the after-math of the Revolution, access to almost all Cuba's immediate neigh-bours had been barred, as a wave of Latin American nations broke diplomatic relations: Mexico remained the one major exception. Across Cuba, the **Comités de Defensa de la Revolución**, the CDRs, were set up in every street and apartment block in order to watch against counter-revolutionary infiltration, although in practice this often meant any kind of non-conformity. Musicians had to join in. Orquesta Aragón concerts would sometimes end early as members had to get back for "cederista" duty. Concerts were by now severely reduced in quantity: a clampdown in 1968 had closed most of the cabarets and economic collapse had finished the job.

Nonetheless, cracks in the Iron Curtain's Caribbean extension appeared from time to time. In 1976 the death of Spain's long-stand-ing dictator, General Franco, and the installation of democracy opened the Spanish market to the nueva trova stars. **Silvio Rodríguez** and **Sara González** performed in Spain and Rodriguez recorded there, in a move that was to mark the foundation of his financial success and an intermediate step in the rediscovery by Spain of the music of its old colony.

Cuban musicians also played in some of the newly independent, and ideologically sympathetic, states of Africa: the Orquesta Jorrín and the Orquesta Aragón both visited Tanzania, the Congo, Guinea and Mali. African musicians came to Cuba, strengthening the ances-tral links and musical bonds of their respective cultures. Among

Malian musicians who obtained grants to study in Cuba was the flautist and arranger **Boncana Maiga**, who later formed his Cuban-style band **Las Maravillas de Mali** back in Bamako.

A slight thaw

In the late 1970s, under conditions of mild thaw initiated by US President Jimmy Carter, occasional concerts by US artists took place in Cuba. The most spectacular was the Caribbean "jazz cruise" arranged by a US cruise company, Carras Lines, in April 1977. Reprogrammed at the last minute to stop in Cuba, the line-up included Dizzy Gillespie, Earl Hines, Stan Getz and Ry Cooder. The US contingent left New Orleans on the *SS Daphne*, booed by Cuban exiles, including Castro's sister, Juanita, and arrived in Havana to an ecstatic public welcome forty-eight hours later. For two days the illustrious Americans gave and attended concerts, and jammed with Cuban musicians such as Chucho Valdés, Arturo Sandoval, Paquito D'Rivera, and Los Papines. Ry Cooder went in search of **Miguel Ojeda**, the laúd player he had heard on rare imported recordings in Los Angeles. All of these men were to meet again later in dramatically different circumstances.

Two years later, another important American musical visit saw the **Fania All-Stars**, the leading lights of the New York salsa movement, play a central Havana theatre, in an event which was scarcely noticed by the Cuban public, but did attract a number of musicians curious to know what these Yanquis were doing with a new brand of Latin music which actually seemed to be based almost entirely on Cuban forms. Within months, an all star Cuban band, the **Estrellas de Areito**, had been convened under the direction of **Juan-Pablo Torres**, to record a series of highly polished but traditionally based tracks which were in total contrast to the Van Van/Mezcla progressive aesthetic then dominant.

The Cuban international rapprochement of the late 1970s, such as it was, did not last long. In 1978, when the Orquesta Aragón reciprocated with gigs in the US, two of their three New York dates at the Lincoln Center had to be cancelled after a bomb wrecked the hall following the first show.

At home the 1980s began in repressive style. Paquito D'Rivera left for exile in the US, helped by his new friend, Dizzy Gillespie, and became one of the most bitter critics of the Castro regime with endless stories of its excesses., Like all musical "gusanos" (worms), as defectors were called, D'Rivera's music was banned from the Cuban media. When the first edition of Helio Orovio's seminal *Diccionario de la Música Cubana* was published, in 1981, it contained no entries for many prominent musical defectors, a situation only remedied over a decade later.

Throughout the 1980s, the brilliantly successful dance music of Los Van Van and the equally lustrous jazz inheritance of Irakere continued to dominate Cuba's international image. Paquito D'Rivera shone in New York, joined by virtuosi such as the percussionist **Daniel Ponce**, who had left in the Mariel Boatlift, when 120,000 Cubans fled the island in an operation cleverly undertaken by Castro. At home **Arturo Sandoval** held the spotlight supported by the young pianist and Irakere graduate (and another Dizzy Gillespie associate), **Gonzalo Rubalcaba**, with his group **Proyecto**.

The son revival

During this time, the son tradition was in a sort of semi-dormancy in its homeland. In salsa-crazy New York, Puerto Rico and especially in Colombia and Venezuela, traditional Cuban son, mambo and guaracha were the immutable foundations of the new dance bands and the jazzy chord sequences and Earth Wind and Fire aesthetics of Cuban dance fashion were regarded as heresy.

In Cuba, however, tradition was not fully neglected. A thousand son quartets – ageing but salaried – still operated sporadically around the country and major players were still in touch with their roots. At Havana University a group of engineering students including **Juan de Marcos González**, a keen amateur guitar and tres player, and a young trumpet named **Jesus Alemañy**, found themselves much more attracted to the traditional sound of the old Septeto Nacional than to the currently fashionable Andean neo-folk and progressive fusion. In 1976 they formed the group **Sierra Maestra**, playing at first entirely acoustic instruments with the aim of re-creating the old styles. One of their first tasks was to seek out the old Septeto Nacional, then playing from time to time in Havana Central Library, in order to study their way of playing. Sierra Maestra became extremely popular, moving on from pure traditional re-creation to subtle new composition in an updated mode. De Marcos went on to create the **Buena Vista Social Club** phenomenon while Alemañy founded the successful international band **Cubanismo**.

At the same time as Sierra Maestra, another great rejuvenator of the son tradition, **Son 14**, appeared in Camagüey. The creation of Adalberto Alvarez, an outstanding arranger and composer, the band's strengths were its rich exciting conjunto playing and its remarkable sonero Eduardo Morales, known as "Tiburón" (shark).

By the mid-1980s, Havana's dance music scene was beginning to regain a suggestion of its former tropical allure. In 1983, the great Venezuelan salsero, **Oscar D'León**, played Cuba, galvanizing huge crowds with his deeply tradition-based but electrifyingly modern salsa. Los Van Van had a series of smash hits, memorably combining topical lyrics with a new more swinging sound. These included "Sandunguera", the song about the red-hot girl dancer "encima del nivel" (over the limit) and "Baile del Buey Cansado" (the Dance of the

Tired Ox) In 1989, the Orquesta of Elio Revé, which had in the meantime become one of the top attractions of Havana, visited Europe
under the auspices of the WOMAD Festival. The "world music" audience, a movement primarily composed of middle class under-forties
consumers from the industrialized nations, began to look to Cuba as
one of the prime new territories for musical investigation after Africa,
the favourite region of the mid-1980s. Meanwhile, at home in
Havana, the great popular dancehall La Tropical had re-opened in
1986 and a new sound was beginning to be apparent in the first performances of a dynamic new group, **NG La Banda**.

But things were to get much worse before the Cuban musical
renaissance could really gather momentum. The collapse of the
Soviet bloc and the withdrawal of Soviet aid to its former allies and
satellites meant that by the end of the decade, Cuba had lost 85% of
its trade, and almost all supplies of the cheap oil it relied on so totally. Castro declared an emergency austerity programme entitled the
Special Period in Peacetime, and the country plunged into a state
of penury, in which the flourishing of dance music would have
required a miracle.

Artists

Los Zafiros

Los Zafiros (The Sapphires) were a true Cuban pop phenomenon, a
group of self-destructive heart-throbs, formation-dancing out of the
barrios into the limelight and bringing the spectacle of swooning

female fans to post-Revolutionary Havana, before fizzling out amid alcohol and recrimination.

They came together in the working class Havana suburb of **Cayo Hueso** in 1962, with the aim of creating a modern harmony vocal quartet in the mould of American groups such as the Platters and the Ink Spots, but also in that of the well-established Latin vocal group tradition of Cuba's **Las D'Aida** and the Argentinian Los Cinco Latinos.

Only one of Los Zafiros had showbusiness experience: **Miguel Cancio** had sung upper register in the well-known quartet of Facundo Rivero. The other members were **Eduardo "El Chino" Hernandez,** a judo-instructing panel-beater, who sang tenor, the alto-voiced **Leoncio "Kike" Morina**, a clerk in a car rental company, and **Ignacio Elegalde**, who, prior to placing his remarkable soaring falsetto lead voice at the service of the Zafiros, had been a dancer in a group led by his aunt. The four Zafiros began to work with a neighbour, a professional composer and arranger, named **Nestor Milí**, who groomed them in close harmony vocal and slick synchronized dance routines. He also encouraged them to develop their repertoire to include ballads, American-style doo-wop numbers, versions of boleros, rumbas, Santiago congas, even calypsos and bossa-novas. It was Milí who introduced the final ingredient to the Zafiros sound, a single electric guitar prominent in the backing mix. At first played by **Oscar Aguirre**, the guitar role was transferred after a year to **Manuel Galván**, a Havana guitarist with a distinctively muted Duane Eddy bass twang of the sort which was later re-adapted in the 1990s for film soundtracks of the David Lynch school.

The Zafiros rapidly took off, first acquiring a residency in a Varadero tourist hotel, The Oasis, then beginning to record. Their first single, written by Nestor Milí, was a stunning combination of a

breathless conga percussion backing behind a lead voice answered by a chanting, train-klaxon-mimicking, doo-wopping chorus. Before they had been in existence a year, the Zafiros had stolen the show from Beny Moré at a concert in the Havana Libre hotel, and were receiving a deluge of offers from cabarets and television stations.

In 1965 the Zafiros were close to the top of the bill of the **Grand Music Hall de Cuba** show which toured Eastern Europe and ended up, amid great acclaim, in Paris. On their triumphant return to Cuba, however, the group's career lurched to a halt. Probably because of a reputation for unpredictability engendered by their hard drinking and quarrels, the Zafiros stopped being booked for major tours, and

spent a decade in lucrative but frustrating routine cabaret work before falling apart. Manuel Galván left in 1972, and six years later the group was no more. Ignacio Elegalde died in 1982, aged 39, from a brain haemorrhage, followed, a year later, by Kike Morína from cirrhosis of the liver. El Chino Hernandez out-lived

them by only a decade, while Miguel Cancio spent some years as a musicians' union administrator before joining his son Hugo in Miami in 1993. Manuel Galván continued working in Cuba, eventually becoming a beneficiary of the 1990s world music rediscovery of Cuban music, first as a member of the **Vieja Trova Santiaguera**,

then as a session guitarist with the various spin-offs of the **Buena Vista Social Club** project.

The Zafiros' story had an important sequel. In 1997, Miguel Cancio's son Hugo, who had been sent into Miami exile by his father via the Mariel Boatlift, produced a feature film, *Zafiros Locura Azul* (Zafiros Blue Madness), which was pioneering in that it was shot in Cuba with Cuban actors and crew, but on American money. The film rapidly became a cult in Cuba, spawning a clutch of Zafiros-homage groups, like Los Nuevos Zafiros and Los Zafiritos, and a rush to reissue rare Zafiros recordings in Europe.

⊙ **Bossa Cubana**   World Circuit, UK

A high quality reissue with good sleeve information and a full range of crazy blue delights: from the wah-wah choruses, rattling timbales and merengue brass of "La Caminadora", through the Creole Dion and the Belmonts of "Un Nombre de Mujer", to "Bossa Cubana", with Galván's guitar clicking away gutturally behind an irresistible brew of Yma Sumac bird-calls and rapid fire vocals – quite unlike the evanescent Brazilian bossa nova it's based on.

Pacho and Pachito Alonso

One of the most successful dance band leaders in 1960s Cuba, **Pacho Alonso**'s work was continued by his son **Pachito**, a leading purveyor of unpretentious Cuban popular entertainment to Latin America at the start of the 1990s.

Alonso Senior was born in 1928 in Santiago where he studied education while singing in amateur shows at the Coliseo theatre. After moving to Havana in 1946, he was given an introduction to the radio station Mil Diez and also met the Santiago-born bandleader **Mariano Mercerón**, a saxophonist with a finger on the pulse of modern son and danzón arranging, and with an ear for a hot singer. Alonso was

hired as vocalist in Mercerón's band, along with the two stars Beny Moré and Fernándo Alvarez. In 1954 he formed his own conjunto, which bore an assortment of names – among which were Los Bocucos (named after a type of Santiago carnival drum), Los Pachucos and Los Modernistas. Much of Alonso's composition and percussion arrangement was undertaken with the co-operation of **Enrique Bonne**, another Santiago-born musician, who worked with large groups of drummers, such as the fifty-strong **Tambores de Oriente**. The pilón, Alonso's great invention, was a bouncy rhythm characterized by a rap on the timbal on the third beat of every bar, accompanied by a hip-shaking dance incorporating hand movements mimicking the up and down pounding of a big mortar and pestle. Taken up by students at the University of Havana, the pilón became extremely popular during the 1960s, and Alonso continued playing and touring the Communist world for a decade.

By 1982, shortly before Alonso Senior's death, his son Pachito Alonso had stepped into his father's shoes. Pachito was born in 1960 and studied at the University of Havana in order to become a telecommunications engineer, but in his teens he was already helping run his father's band and produce its recordings before graduating to chief arranger.

In the late 1980s, Pachito Alonso reorganized the band, renaming it **Pachito Alonso y sus Kini Kini,** and decided to re-launch the pilón as an international dance craze, inspired by the world-wide popularity of the lambada. To this end, he built the band into a 20-member show, adding four Tropicana-style dancing girls with "daring hips" of the sort which "all men dream about", according to their English language publicity, and a pair of sisters, **Lourdes** and **Aymee Nuviola**, joining Alonso himself and **Jose Luis Arango** as lead singers. The pilón didn't quite reach the lambada's heights, but

Alonso built the group into a highly effective live act, touring Central and South America and winning sponsorship from both Coca Cola and Pepsi – an echo of the Cristal Beer backing his father had received thirty years earlier.

⊙ **Rico Pilón – Pacho Alonso**   Bis, Cuba

A good retrospective of Alonso padre, showcasing the trundling percussion, the trumpet-dominated blast of brass, prominent electric rhythm guitar and crooning vocals. The big hit "Rico Pilón" is there, of course, as well as other successful compositions by Pacho Alonso and Enrique Bonne, many with the rhyming popular catch-phrase titles Bonne liked to employ – "La Pianola de Manola", "La Chalupa de Upa Upa", "Yo no quiero piedra en mi camino".

⊙ **Ay! que bueno esta Pachito Alonso y sus Kini Kini** Hibiscus, France

Recorded by a French Antillean company, this early 1990s collection is a touch rough and ready in production and vocals. Nonetheless, it shows that Alonso junior had inherited a distinctive and exciting way with percussion and brass, which might have made the pilón an interesting part of the alternative tendency to 1990s timba.

Rumbavana

Little-known outside Cuba and Latin America, the **Conjunto Rumbavana** is nonetheless an important and prolific band which spawned the careers of several major singers, and succeeded in being an indefatigable creator of simultaneously modern, popular and truly son-based dance music during the lean years of the 1970s and early 1980s. Time and again in the press archives from this period, the name of Rumbavana stands out, playing in Lima at the Cuban Embassy's celebration of the Anniversary of the Revolution in Peru, starring in a Bogotá stadium or a nightclub in Barranquilla,

(Colombia's tropical music capital) or topping the bill, above "the explosive Gay Crooners", on a Havana Carnival TV broadcast.

Rumbavana was founded in 1956 in Havana by the percussionist **Ricardo Ferro**. The three trumpet section, which the conjunto format imposed, included **Manuel Mirabál**, who was later to achieve fame as "Guajiro" Mirabál, lead trumpeter of the Tropicana Orchestra and key member of the Buena Vista Social Club musician pool. Another Buena Vista star, **Raúl Planas**, joined as singer in the 1960s, while the bolero star Lino Borges was one of the founding vocalists.

Rumbavana rapidly became a fixture of Havana's nightclubs, and within a few years a favourite of carnivals throughout the island. In 1967, with the arrival of the pianist and composer **Joseíto González** as director, the group's success increased further, as González showed great flair in strengthening the repertoire, not only contributing many of his own songs, but nurturing young songwriters of promise like **Adalberto Alvarez**, an early protégé of Rumbavana.

In the 1970s, Rumbavana experimented with electric guitars in the line-up, but always remained closer to their traditional son, mambo and guaracha base than the more progressive groups. This aspect of their music was accentuated as they began to tour internationally and to share stages with great Latin dance bands from outside the island. Despite their failure to share in the 1990s world Cuban boom, Rumbavana retain a key position, antecedent to groups such as Adalberto Alvarez' and **Cándido Fabré's**, in the preservation of traditionally-based Cuban dance music.

⊙ **Lo Que le trae Rumbavana**   Declic, France

A collection of 1970s and 1980s Egrem-licensed tracks, the title number written by Cándido Fabré and five of the others by Joseíto Fernández, this album demonstrates the band's strengths, even though the sound is a little harsh. Rumbavana are sometimes cited

as predecessors of 1990s timba, and certain traits – the complex punchy brass charts, the thudding passages of bass drum-led breakdown – confirm this. And yet, the intensity and depth of the piano tumbaos, the hypnotic choruses, the traditional melodic base, also connect them with great conjuntos of the 1940s and 1950s from whose ranks they sprang.

Orquesta Revé

One of the most characterful of Cuban musicians, **Elio Revé** brought son changüí into the modern era, where it remains due in part to the efforts of his son Elio, who carries on the good work.

Elio Revé Senior was born in 1930 in Guantánamo, one of twenty-four children of a poor family of coffee-pickers. However, his father was an amateur bass-player, and the young Elio mixed with a host of the mythical names of Guantánamo son – uncle Julián Venao, Negra con Pelo, Mongolo, Felipe Radical, Cuatro Filos. By the time he was a teenager, he was an adept of santería music, dancing to the tumbas francesas of Santiago, and imbued with the old son changüí played on tres, maracas, marimbula and bongo. He took up the timbales and throughout his life always preferred goat-skin heads to modern plastic. Earning his living at any jobs available – railway stoker, ploughman, cane-cutter – he gradually found work as a professional musician and by the early 1950s had moved to Havana and gained experience in the band of **Cheo Belen Puig** and the **Orquesta Almendra**. In 1955 he started his own band, a charanga, but always keeping a dosage of rough changüí in the suave violin and flute format.

The Revé orquesta's first big success occurred in the 1960s, when the young bass-player **Juan Formell** modernized the band's sound, and for a while Revé was the toast of Havana. Formell soon left to form

Elio Revé whips up a storm

his own group, **Los Van Van**, however, taking a good proportion of Revé's musicians with him, and it was the early 1980s before Revé again hit the top. He did this by renaming the band **El Charangón** (Big Charanga) and going back to his roots. Revé replaced the drum-kit Formell had introduced with a trio of batá drums played by his brother **Odelquis**, hired **Papi Oviedo**, an excellent deep changüí tres player, and found a singer **"Padrino" Rafael** capable of reproducing the old-style nasal "voz de vieja" (old woman's voice) of Eastern country son.

By 1986, Revé's two most recent albums, **La Explosión del Momento!** and **Rumberos Latinoamericanos**, were top sellers. In

1989, Revé's orquesta was contracted by the WOMAD organization to tour European world music festivals, and WOMAD's Real World record label issued **La Explosión del Momento** in Europe – one of the earliest instances of what soon became a torrent of European releases of Cuban records.

Revé's international fame lasted less than a decade: in 1997 he was knocked down and killed by a car while standing beside the band's coach on a Cuban road. After a pause, the Orquesta Revé was taken over by his son **Elio Revé Jr**, a keyboard player, who continues to run the Charangón as a tight, rootsy, changüi-rich dance institution, and bark out his father's familiar fierce timbal-whipping cry of "Weaah!", like a Samurai eviscerating an enemy.

⊙ **La Explosión Del Momento!**   Real World, UK

An ageing but still wonderful set of tracks licensed from Egrem, showing that 1980s Cuba wasn't all Van Van and jazz-funk, and Tito Puente wasn't the only timbal ace in the world.

⊙ **Tributo al Maestro**   Egrem, Cuba

A posthumous "greatest hits", with some good tracks – notably "Rumberos Latinoamericanos" – not on the previous record.

⊙ **Changüi en La Casa de Nora**   Tumi, UK

A new Havana-recorded album of the Charangón as of 1999, under the tutelage of Elio Revé Jr, and sounding just fine – semi-acoustic, tight and exciting.

Los Van Van

If one band upheld Cuba's reputation for world-class dance music through the lean years of the post-Revolutionary period, that band was **Los Van Van**, the indefatigably creative rhythm turbine founded

by the bassist **Juan Formell**. Formell comes from a musical family originating in Santiago: his grand-father was a trumpeter and his father, **Francisco Formell**, a director of the Radio CMQ orchestra and arranger for Ernesto Lecuona. Formell was born in 1942, started his career in the National Police Band, and worked in the orquestas of Guillermo Rubalcaba and Peruchín before joining the charanga of Elio Revé in 1967. Formell's early influences were traditional son, popular Mexican harmony trios such as **Los Panchos**, and all the new US rock'n'roll and dance crazes. He seems to have been particularly impressed by the shake, because before long – having become Revé's arranger as well as bass guitarist – he was creating a new sound for Revé, the changüí-shake. He also experimented with the "afro shake" and introduced the delights of the straight shake to the romantic star Elena Burke, to the benefit of both their careers.

In 1969 Formell founded his new band, Los Van Van. The word "van" means "they're going", so the name had a resonance of "The Go Gos", but it was also a reference to the great event of that year, Castro's failed attempt to save the Cuban economy by marshalling the population to reap a record 10 million ton sugar harvest. "Ten million tons y van, van" (...and still going, still going) was the phrase the leader used in his speeches. The name, incidentally, explains in part why Los Van Van are so especially hated by the anti-Castroists of Miami, who regard the group as closely linked to the regime.

Los Van Van was, like the Revé orquesta, basically a charanga format, but to the violins and flutes Formell added electric guitar, his own bass guitar and American-style drum-kit. A vital founder-member of the 12-strong band was **César "Pupi" Pedroso**, born in 1944, son of a pianist, and, like Formell, steeped in traditional son and keen to experiment: his inventive keyboard work and prolific song composition was a major foundation of the band's sound. Other key players

were **José Luis Cortés**, "El Tosco", a virtuoso flautist who went on to found **NG La Banda** (see p.292), and **José Luis Quintana**, "Changuito", a brilliant drummer who managed to incorporate jazz-funk influences from Elvin Jones and Earth Wind & Fire's Maurice White into his essentially Afro-Cuban playing. The final outstanding personality of the early Van Van joined in 1974. **Pedro "Pedrito" Calvo**, a statuesque black vocalist and dancer, possessor of a luxuriant moustache over flashing white teeth, was born in 1942 and had earned his living as a shoe-maker as well as being part-time singer for the Orquesta Ritmo Oriental (in which his father had played). So popular was the dynamic Pedrito with the ladies that in 1984 Van Van came out with a song, "El Negro No Tiene Na" (The Black Man Hasn't Got Anything), denying gossip that the singer had contracted some disease from his multiple liaisons.

Over their first decade of existence, Van Van progressed from a heavily US-influenced sound, replete with elements previously unheard in Cuban music (three-part Western pop harmony vocals, touches of R&B, heavy reverb on voices) to a more Afro-Cuban dance style, which Formell christened songo, and which became about the only Cuban innovation of the period, taken up by American and Puerto Rican salsa bands who also began to cover Van Van songs.

Through the 1980s, Van Van's sound evolved and deepened: Formell abandoned the flute and added trombones to the mix, while Pupi Pedroso moved from the arsenal of curious Eastern European keyboards to a Yamaha synthesizer, and syn-drums now entered the percussion mix. This was a period of resounding dance hits for Van Van – like "Sandunguera" and "La Titimania" – but also an increasing flow of the social commentary lyrics linked to island-conquering catch-phrases, such as 1984's "La Habana No Aguanta Mas"

(Havana Can't Take Any More), referring to the flow of country-dwellers into the overcrowded city.

The 1990s saw Van Van at the forefront of the internationalization of Cuban music, and the changes in the Cuban music business occasioned by the country's economic situation. In 1989, Van Van had already recorded in Paris an album which was released in the UK by the Island label, and in 1992 they made their last record with the Cuban State company Egrem, **Disco Azúcar**, a reference to a discotheque in the resort of Cancún, Mexico, where they'd undertaken a three-month engagement. In order to strengthen their appeal, Formell brought in new members: handsome young singer and heart-throb **Mayito Rivera**; a progressive young keyboard player in tune with the new timba style, **Boris Luna**; and his son, **Samuel Formell**, who after a turbulent youth had turned out to be a first-class drummer. Although Juan Formell himself began appearing less on stage in person, Van Van were more popular than ever. In 1995, the band's song, "Soy Todo", with its chorus, "¡Ay Dios Ampárame!"(Oh God, Protect Me!), asking the orishas' help in the country's plight, was a massive hit, with concert halls full of dancers alternately doing the wriggling tembleque dance of the timba movement and mimicking the singer's movements – kneeling with arms upraised to the heavens.

By the end of the millennium, Van Van were still Cuba's top popular band, and had penetrated the US Latin establishment, playing from Puerto Rico to Miami (the latter only amid riot conditions) and obtaining, rumour has it, a rock star level advance from a US-owned company for their 1999 album, **Llego Van Van** (Van Van Is Here), which won them a US Grammy Award.

⊙ **The Legendary Los Van Van**   Ashé, US

All that the Van Van novice could possibly need: a beautifully produced double CD set of the most important and representative

tracks from 1969 to 1989, with a 105-page booklet in English and Spanish containing a first class historical and musical text by Rachel Faro, pioneering American producer of Cuban records, and superb archive photos.

⊙ **Llego Van Van, Van Van Is Here**   Havana Caliente, US

The 1995 Grammy winner, 12 sets of observations on the lives of the members of the group and the citizens of Havana from El Negro Esta Cozinando, The Black Man's Cooking (and ready to have his yucca tasted) to El Cheque (translation unnecessary, least of all to Cuban musicians). All eminently danceable.

⊙ **Colección Juan Formell y Los Van Van, Vols. 1 to 15**   Egrem, Cuba

For the Van Van fanatic, a complete re-edition of Egrem's Van Van tracks, from the first single, Marilú, to their early 1990s jibes at the lambada craze (Solo quería baila lambada, she only wanted to dance lambada).

Orquesta Anacaona

Another long-established Cuban musical institution, the **Orquesta Anacaona** has one major distinguishing factor, it is all-female and so are the stars who have passed through its ranks: singers such as **Graciela**, of the Machito and Mario Bauzá orchestras, **Omara Portuondo** and **Moraima Secada**. The name Anacaona was a reference to a female Taino warrior who resisted the Spanish conquistadors, and the group was created in 1932 during a craze for all-female bands originating in the US. Anacaona was originally a septet, formed from among the numerous sisters of the **Castro Zadarriaga** family of Havana, led by the eldest, **Concepción**, who had studied piano, guitar and saxophone. The members started playing together to fill in time while unable to follow classes at the University of Havana during a student strike against the Machado government.

The orquesta first played publicly in the Teatro Payret, and immediately captured the public imagination. A series of eminent male advisers began to rehearse and play with the Castro sisters, first **Alberto Socarras** in 1938, later **Rafael Lay**, Director of the Orquesta Aragón, and **Richard Egües**, Aragón's eminent flautist. By the 1940s, Anacaona was a highly professional and versatile group, able to function either as a charanga or a brass-dominated jazz band due to the multi-instrumental skills of its members, and in constant demand both at Havana cabarets and abroad.

In 1987, all of the original members of the band had retired, and the leadership was taken over by the bassist, Georgia Aguirre, who had

Lo que tú esparabas...

joined the orquesta with her sister Doris in 1983. With much arranging input from the new young pianist Janysett MacPherson Zapata, Anacaona updated its repertoire to include a cross-section of Latin dance rhythms, from merengue to timba, and, after a residency at the cabaret Papa's in the tourist resort of Marina Hemingway, began to attract bookings from abroad, particularly Spain,

where they toured extensively throughout the early 1990s. In 1998, they were engaged by the top French theatre director Jerome Savary to supply music for a tropical-soundtrack version of Molière's Le Bourgeois

Gentilhomme in Paris, following which they recorded an internationally distributed album for the French Lusafrica label.

⊙ Lo Que Tú Esparabas   Lusafrica, France

Anacaona's latest manifestation, recorded in 2000 in Havana, includes guest appearances by Richard Egües, Buena Vista's venerable crooner Raúl Planas, and a saxophone section beefed up by Ernesto Varona. The dominant sound of the record is a mix of light romantic salsa and a middle-of-the-road version of 1990s timba. Repertoire includes classic sones by Ignacio Piñeiro, Mario Bauzá and Marcelino Guerra, a few of the band's own songs, items by contemporary star writers such as Juan Formell and Manolito Simonet, and a jolly little number called "Il fait trop beau pour travailler" by the French jazzman Claude Bolling, rendered as a jaunty merengue.

Síntesis

One of the most successful members of the movement to extend post-Revolutionary new song into a more modern musical setting, **Síntesis** was created in 1976 by a Havana bass player, singer and arranger, **Carlos Alfonso**. Alfonso's contemporary references were Pink Floyd, Genesis and Emerson, Lake & Palmer. Under their influence he developed a three-part structure to his songs: a virtuoso instrumental interlude, followed by a sung text, and a lengthy and theatrical series of improvisations on electric guitars and synthesizers. The texts reflected the literary values aspired to by nueva trova with verses by the great Chilean poet Pablo Neruda, as well as songs by the nueva trova stars **Amaury Pérez** (a one-time member of the group) and **Silvio Rodríguez**, whose poetry was the basis of one of Síntesis' most successful albums, **El Hombre Extraño** (1992).

The third ingredient of the Síntesis mix was Cuban traditional music, including, unusually, some early pre-son elements, such as their set of variations on the old Hispanic zapateo dance form, and their version of a danza written by the classical guitarist Leo Brouwer. Síntesis were also enthusiastic participants in the movement to update Afro-percussion and santería rhythms, as their acclaimed 1987 recording **Ancestros** demonstrated. It was a sound that attracted a variety of labels from commentators, including ethno-music, ethno-rock, canción-rock, and beat Cubano, all of which Alfonso rejected as simplistic.

Síntesis' modest debut concert in Havana Cathedral Square in November 1976 was noted with approval by the Communist journal El Caimán Barbudo. From these relatively informal beginnings, the group went on to achieve great popularity within the island and in the 1980s became the modernizing face of Cuban music throughout Latin America.

⊙ **Ancestros Vols. I & II**   Mage Music, Spain

The group's 1987 Afro-investigation re-edited by the biggest Spanish label on the island in the mid-1990s. A set of songs to individual orishas sung in Yoruba and Arará, the work earned Egrem's award in 1989 for high artistic value, and remains one of the best examples of its genre.

Mezcla

One of Cuba's top progressive groups of the 1980s, **Mezcla** also has one of the country's most unusual leaders in its American founder **Pablo Menendez**. Originally Paul Menendez, he was born in Oakland, California, the son of the folk singer Barbara Dane, with whom he played guitar. Moving to Havana in 1966, he studied at the

Escuela Nacional de Arte and became a friend and musical collaborator with some of the original nueva trova stars. An original member of the **Grupo de Experimentación Sonora** of the Cuban Film Institute, Menéndez later joined the nueva trova-influenced ethnorock group **Síntesis** as lead guitarist and played in the jazz group **Sonido Contemporaneo**. before creating Mezcla in 1985.

Mezcla began in 1985 with a musical ethos which drew heavily on that of the Grupo de Experimentación, updating traditional Cuban forms – particularly Afro-Cuban percussion – and combining it with the lyrics and melody of nueva trova. The group's singer and keyboard player, **Sonia Cornuchet**, was much influenced by American folkrock, while percussionist **Octavo Rodríguez** was an avid researcher into Yoruban rhythm. Mezcla were important precursors of the move by nueva trova towards rock, and their bassist **Juan Antonio Acosta** and drummer **Juan Carlos Abreu** introduced a strong progressive rock input, having worked with the rock group **Los Magneticos** and the rock-trovador **Santiago Feliu**, respectively.

Mezcla's early live and television performances made them extremely popular, with the song "Nacimos del Fuego" (We Were Born of Fire) becoming a major hit – but only in the Cuban sense of attracting public approval since the album it came from was never

released. In the early 1990s, Mezcla began to play in Europe and the United States, and it was their successful mobilization of West Coast public opinion against the US State Department's refusal to grant members of the group visas which helped initiate the major influx of Cuban musicians to the US by the end of the decade.

⊙ **Fronteras de Sueños**   Intuition, Germany

This 1990 production, recorded in Cologne, gives a good picture of the Mezcla formula, and demonstrates why it wasn't this style (which Cubans regarded as modern and progressive) but the traditional and roots styles which came to appeal to the international market. Synthesizers, electric guitars, jazz-funk bass and saxophone, and Sonia Cornuchet's Joni Mitchell-like voice dominate the mix, although certain numbers, such as the big Cuban hit "Rio Quibú", possess a stronger, pan-Caribbean rhythmic feel.

Chucho Valdés and Irakere

Because of its great international success in the jazz world, **Irakere** was Cuba's most famous musical export in the 1970s and 1980s, while Jesús **"Chucho" Valdés**, its founder, remains the country's most renowned individual virtuoso.

Chucho Valdés was always destined for musical greatness. He was born in 1941 in the Havana suburb of Quivicán, the son of the eminent pianist and bandleader **Ramón "Bebo" Valdés**, creator of the "batanga" rhythm, and a member of the Tropicana Orchestra. Bebo Valdés taught his son piano and music theory and – since he seemed to have a liking for jazz – advised him to learn Cuban music first and then, separately, jazz, and not try to blend them until he was competent at both. Stories of Chucho Valdés astonishing listeners while not yet ten abound, and in 1957, having already refused offers

from the Tropicana amongst others, Bebo Valdés took Chucho on as pianist in the **Orquesta Sabor de Cuba**, a band he formed to back the star vocalists **Rolando Laserie**, **Pio Leyva** (later of Buena Vista fame) and **Fernando Alvarez**.

In 1960, when Alvarez became extremely successful throughout Latin America, Bebo Valdés moved to Mexico, and Chucho remained in Havana studying composition and playing with his own quartet and the orchestra of the Teatro Musical. In 1967,

"Chuchó" Valdés

Valdés junior was invited to join the **Orquesta Cubana de Música Moderna**, the elite grouping led by Armando Romeu. Among the other members were the saxophonists **Paquito D'Rivera** and **Carlos Averhoff**, the trumpeter **Arturo Sandoval** and the guitarist **Carlos Emilio Morales**. For four years Valdés performed with the Orquesta, while becoming increasingly involved in researching how the roots of Afro-Cuban musics coincided with jazz, an interest which led his composing toward the creation of an early work, *Misa Negra*, combining the two elements. At the same time, a smaller group of musicians within the Orquesta, led by Valdés, began playing informally together. Paquito D'Rivera, one of its members, later commented that they were motivated not only by a common interest in modern jazz, but by a desire to create a smaller, more mobile group that could travel abroad easily.

In 1970, encouraged by the enthusiasm for their music by Dave Brubeck, who they met at a jazz festival in Poland, Valdés and the ten founder-members of what was to become Irakere began giving concerts, and then recording together. It was 1973 before they acquired the name Irakere, which means sacred forest in Yoruba, and a further two years before they received permission to sever definitively their connections with the Orquesta de Música Moderna. So dramatic was their mass departure, each member was required to select a replacement, who had to be auditioned and accepted, before he could leave. Among the other founder-members of Irakere (in addition to Valdés, D'Rivera, Sandoval, Averhoff and Morales) were **Jorge Varona** (trumpet), **Carlos del Puerto** (bass), **Enrique Pla** (drum-kit) and **Oscar Valdés**, who sang and was also a key member of the adventurous but minutely researched Afro-Cuban percussion section. Later eminent Irakere alumni included **José Luis Cortés**, founder of NG La Banda, and the star percussionists **Orlando "Maraca" Valle** and **Miguel Angá Díaz**.

One of Irakere's chief influences was jazz, in particular bebop and the work of Dizzy Gillespie and Charlie Parker, although Valdés commented that since jazz still had an aura of imperialist music for the authorities in the 1970s, the group didn't use the term. In addition, they incorporated Afro-Cuban music, rock and the progressive funk sound of **Earth Wind & Fire**, an important influence in Cuba generally. Finally, the musicians' Conservatoire backgrounds came out in their occasional treatments of classical themes, such as the Mozart *Adagio* they often transformed into a show-stopper. Above all, Irakere was able to blend all of these elements with highly danceable popular music, as their first hit, "Bacalao Con Pan", amply demonstrated.

Irakere soon embarked on an international career establishing themselves as the ambassadors, par excellence, of modern Afro-

Cuban music. In 1976 they visited Scandinavia, Italy and Germany and by 1978 were playing at New York's Carnegie Hall, winning a Grammy Award the following year. In 1983, they made the first of many visits to Ronnie Scott's in London,.

At the same time, the membership of Irakere was fluctuating, a constant theme being the desire of members to maximize their individual potential as world-class virtuosi. In 1980, Paquito D'Rivera defected to the US, followed a decade later by Arturo Sandoval. By the late 1990s other members were leaving – Oscar Valdés to create the Afro-jazz group **Diákara**, Maraca Valle to form **Otra Visión**, Angá Díaz for multiple freelance projects. Chucho Valdés himself had long maintained a solo career parallel to Irakere and by the mid 1990s was playing less and less with the group, indulging in more high profile projects. An extremely successful stint with Roy Hargrove's group **Crisol** was followed in 1996 by a joint recording with his father Bebo, who had re-emerged from two decades of virtual retirement in Sweden. Meanwhile, the next generation of Valdés keyboard aces is coming along nicely – Chucho's daughter Liana is a classical pianist, while his son Chuchito is a frequent substitute for his father in Irakere.

⊙ **La Colección Cubana Irakere**   Nascente, UK

A good varied "best of" demonstrating the range of the band virtually within the first three tracks. The collection opens with a meditative duet between Chucho Valdés on electronic keyboard and D'Rivera's quicksilver soprano, which accelerates into a bracing jam. The second track is a joint effort by Valdés and Beethoven, full of dainty flute and keyboards colliding with jazz guitar, funk bass and rollicking brass. The album ends with a stew of Afro-percussion and boogaloo on "Misaluba" and the venerable Ernesto Lecuona's "La Comparsa" is dragged kicking and screaming into the late 1970s.

⊙ Colección Irakere, Vols. 1 – 11   Egrem, Cuba

For Irakere fanatics, here's the group's entire Cuban-recorded output from the Areito label, re-edited onto 11 CDs, each one bearing a small reproduction of the original sleeve. Begins with their first great hit, "Bacalao con Pan", from the 1974 album Teatro Amadeo Roldán Recital, and ends with "Santiguera", from the 1986 Quince Minutos.

⊙ Yemayá   Egrem, Cuba

A collection of Afro-Cuban-tinged pieces by Irakere, 1998-style, shows that the departure of so many of their star soloists has not undermined their position as the Beatles of Latin jazz – a title conferred on them by the Miami critic Nat Chediak.

⊙ Chucho Valdés: Invitación   Egrem, Cuba

This collection of solo piano pieces, based on themes by the great turn of the century Cuban composers Ignacio Cervantes, Manuel Saumell and José White, showcases the finesse and sensitivity Valdés is capable of expressing but culminates in a final piece in full Irakere mode.

⊙ Paquito D'Rivera Presents Cuban Jazz   Tropijazz, US

A Paquito D'Rivera-organized record, set up by the New York salsa entrepreneur Ralph Mercado, but notable above all for the musical reunion of Chucho Valdés and his father Bebo. Other great artists include old Irakere hands Carlos Emilio Morales, Carlos del Puerto and Miguel "Anga" Diaz, plus the unusual and enjoyable adornment of steel pans played by Andy Novell. The two generations alternate on pianist/arranger duties, and the album ends with a sparkling Bebo and Chucho duet on "The Peanut Vendor".

Paquito D'Rivera

Paquito D'Rivera, the man who Mario Bauzá once described as the only modern musician to play true Latin jazz, was born Francisco

Rivera, the son of a saxophonist and bandleader named **Tito Rivera**. Tito also worked as Havana representative of the Selmer brass instrument company and the earliest published photo of the young Paquito was a Selmer advert with the boy playing a saxophone, over the slogan "Even a child can play a Selmer." He fell in love with jazz through listening to his father's records of Benny Goodman, and took up clarinet and saxophone, studying at the Havana Conservatoire before spending three years in the Army. On demobilization, D'Rivera joined the same career path as Chucho Valdés, who became a close friend – a spell in the **Orchestra of the Teatro Musical de la Habana** followed by the **Orquesta Cubana de Música Moderna**.

Rivera was a leading light of **Irakere** from its foundation and, like Chucho Valdés, he began to receive offers of solo work as the group became famous. In 1976 he recorded with the Danish bass-player Niels-Henning Orsted-Petersen and the next year he was sought out by **Dizzy Gillespie** when the American star visited Havana. When, in 1980, D'Rivera decided to leave Cuba his critics accused him of being lured by offers of lucrative CBS contracts and stardom. D'Rivera retorted that Cuba was a culturally stifled police state. Having escaped from Irakere's minders at Barajas Airport, Madrid, by checking an empty suitcase onto the flight home, he went into exile first in Madrid and then New York where he began to work with fellow fugitive **Daniel Ponce** and the group of Latin jazz players centred around the brothers **Andy** and **Jerry Gonzalez**.

Over the following two decades D'Rivera consolidated his position as one of the aristocrats of the jazz world, working with artists as diverse as Mario Bauzá, Bebo Valdés, McCoy Tyner, Herbie Mann, Astor Piazzolla, Lalo Schifrin and the London Symphony Orchestra, Arturo Sandoval, and Dizzy Gillespie's United Nations Orchestra, the leadership of which he took over on Gillespie's death in 1993. A

relentless and vitriolic critic of the Castro regime, D'Rivera published his memoirs, entitled *Mi Vida Saxual* (My Sax Life), in 1998.

⊙ **Tropicana Nights**   Chesky, US

With a booklet essay by D'Rivera in which he accuses the Castro regime of decimating the Havana nightlife, and a cast of over two dozen, from New York session aces (trombonist Jimmy Bosch, conguero Milton Cardona and the young Barcelona-based singer Lucrezia) this 1999 production is a heady mixture of standards – "Siboney", "Mambo Inn", "El Manisero" – and D'Rivera compositions like the title track.

⊙ **Reunión: Paquito D'Rivera Con Arturo Sandoval**   Messidor, Germany

Recorded immediately after Sandoval's departure from Cuba, and featuring both men at the peak of their form, backed by a quintet including Danilo Pérez on piano and Giovanni Hidalgo on percussion.

Arturo Sandoval

In 1990, ten years after the defection to the US of Paquito D'Rivera, **Irakere**'s other great brass star, the trumpeter **Arturo Sandoval**, walked into the US Embassy in Rome and demanded political asylum. He had waited until his wife and children were with him on tour, he said, having determined to leave Cuba years earlier.

With his remarkable technique, capable of encompassing both ultra-fast soloing in the highest register, in the manner of Freddie Hubbard and Maynard Ferguson, and a mellow and sensitive style suitable for the boleros he also excelled at, Sandoval was already an international star. Born in 1949 in the small town of Artemisa, near Havana, he studied music at the Escuela Nacional de Arte, and in 1967 became one of the founding players of the **Orquesta Cubana de Música Moderna**, where he met his future fellow-member of

Arturo Sandoval

Irakere, which he joined after an interlude in the band of the Cuban Army General Staff.

With Irakere, Sandoval toured internationally and began to make contacts. The most important was with Dizzy Gillespie, his hero and model from childhood, whom he met when the great American trumpeter visited Havana as part of the cast of the "jazz cruise" in 1977.

In 1981, Sandoval left Irakere and set up his own group, with the pianist **Hilario Durán** as musical director. For a decade he combined this work with high profile collaborations, recording with Dizzy Gillespie on the highly regarded **To A Finland Station** in 1982, then guesting with Gillespie's United Nations Orchestra, and directing the Havana Festival of Latin Jazz.

After his defection, Sandoval moved to Miami, where he obtained a professorship at Florida State University, while his prolific recording

included the album **Reunión** with Paquito D'Rivera and the soundtrack of the film *The Mambo Kings*. He also worked with Emilio and Gloria Estefan, whose circle he rapidly entered playing on Gloria's seminal return-to-roots album **Mi Tierra**. In 1998 Sandoval became an American citizen, after a campaign in his support had petitioned President Clinton to override the rejection of his application by the Miami office of the US Immigration & Naturalisation Service who had turned him down on the grounds that he'd been a member of the Communist Party while in Cuba.

⊙ Flight to Freedom   GRP, US

The first album under Sandoval's own name after he installed himself in Miami shows him on pyrotechnic form, revelling in the company of Miami Latin stalwarts such as Ed Calle (ex Miami Sound Machine) and René Luis Toledo, and the pianist Chick Corea, who helped Sandoval set up the recording. Sandoval's classic stratospheric trumpet work contrasts with gentler tracks, such as "Samba de Amore" which he treats to a softer, more contemplative rendition on flugelhorn.

Estrellas de Areito

The Estrellas de Areito (Stars of Areito) was a supergroup assembled in 1979, by Areito Records (Cuba's second State label) for a

five-day recording session, inspired by the example of the New York salsa equivalent, the Fania All Stars. The instigator was an African record producer, Raul Diomandé, from the Ivory Coast, who specified that certain musicians known in Africa should be included to enhance export possibilities. Thus the singer **Rafael Bacallao** and flautist **Richard Egües** from the Orquesta Aragón were selected, along with Rafael Lay, Aragón's leader. Lay died four years later, so this was one of his last recordings, and the same applied to several other members of the Estrellas, making the project of particular historic importance. One of the ten lead vocalists was **Miguelito Cuni**, the sonero who most closely rivalled Beny Moré in the 1940s and 1950s, while the five-man trumpet section included **Félix Chappotín**, the father of modern Cuban trumpet playing. Both Cuni and Chappotín died within five years of the recording. Other great old stars included **Niño Rivera**, then aged 60, the tres player from the Sexteto Boloña and one of the most famous and influential treseros of the twentieth century, and **Tata Güines**, the conga star who had worked with Chico O'Farrill and Fajardo and been a founder member of the **Grupo Cubano de Música Moderna**.

The musical director of the Estrellas was another ex-member of the Grupo, **Juan-Pablo Torres**, the trombonist and regular Areito producer who would move to the US in the 1990s and eventually work with **Rubén González** in the pianist's post-Buena Vista period of fame. González was a member of the Estrellas, as were fellow Buena Vista alumni the timbalero **Amadito Valdés** and trumpeter **Manuel "Guajiro" Mirabál**. Included in the almost four dozen-strong cast were also representatives of the new generation, notably **Paquito D'Rivera** and **Arturo Sandoval**, then at their peak of Irakere popularity.

According to Amadito Valdés, the atmosphere in the crowded studio was remarkably free and animated. Between trips from the control

room to the small studio, Torres would write and distribute short guide scores, while the musicians vied with each other as to who could insert

the most outstanding piece of improvisation. In this they were encouraged by singer **Teresa García Caturla**, who orchestrated the whole enterprise – introducing soloists and adding "sabor" (tastiness).

In spite of its artistic excellence, the Estrellas de Areito project was not successful at the time, suffering from the poor production and distribution then endemic to Cuba. A version of the group toured Venezuela, where the Estrellas LP did well, but the record remained an enthusiast's secret until about 20 years later when the music reached an international public.

⊙ **Los Heroes**   World Circuit

Digitally re-mastered on two CDs, equipped with a superb booklet, rich in period photos and detailed information and containing full lyrics, the Estrellas' re-release is a beauty. Torres' combination of the violin section of a charanga with big band brass gives the music great depth and texture and the percussion is superb with bass tumbaos of pre-Van Van solidity imparting great depth and swing. Meanwhile, touches such as Niño Rivera's superb distorted amplified tres help whip up the excitement. The fact that the traditional structures of son or guaracha are adhered to in a descarga mode adds an intensity often absent from jam sessions.

Sierra Maestra

Sierra Maestra's place in Cuban music history rests on its key role in the revival of interest in traditional acoustic son, and also on the fact that it constituted the musical debuts of two men who went on separately to become among the most important creative forces of the late twentieth century – tres player **Juan de Marcos Gonzalez** and the trumpeter **Jesus Alemañy**. De Marcos was one of nine engineering students at the University of Havana who came together in 1976 to form a group to research and re-create classic son, which they felt was dying from lack of a new young audience. Alemañy, a music student and the nephew of a distinguished Tropicana orchestra trumpeter, **Luis Alemañy**, was recruited two years later. Sierra Maestra took its name from the mountain range which was both the refuge of Castro's guerrillas and the cradle of traditional son. The group went to the historical source for its style and repertoire, searching out surviving members of Ignacio Piñeiro's **Septeto Nacional**, particularly Raphael Ortiz, and unearthing vintage recordings. De Marcos began to study tres with Isaac Oviedo (father of Papi) at a time when the instrument had almost been abandoned by popular musicians.

Sierra Maestra began performing at a time when their fellow students were listening to mainly nueva trova and Chilean and Argentinian folk and political song. Their presentation – Afro haircuts and bell-bottom jeans – combined with their traditional, largely acoustic repertoire, was novel and immediately successful. They were invited to take part in the TV talent competition *Todo El Mundo Canta* (Everybody Sings), which they won, and in 1980 made their first LP for Egrem, **Sierra Maestra Llego con el Guajano Relleno**. In spite of the fact that the title track was an old Ignacio Piñeiro number from the 1930s (and that Los Van Van's modernism was then all the

rage), the record was a great popular success. Subsequent Sierra Maestra records included a co-production with the star Afro-Cuban singer **Celeste Mendoza**, and an album (now virtually impossible to find) recorded in the Congo in 1987 during a tour of Africa.

By the late 1990s, Jesus Alemañy had left to form his own group, **Cubanismo** (he was replaced by **Bárbaro Teuntor**), and Juan de

Marcos was fully engaged with his **Afro Cuban All Stars** and other projects. Nevertheless, Sierra Maestra continued with the same mix of three high quality soneros, **José Antonio Rodríguez**, **Luis Barzaga** and **Alberto Valdés**, and instrumental line-up of bass, tres, guitar, trumpet and multiple percussion, and a repertoire of mixed "anthological pieces" (classic songs) and new group-written songs in a traditional son style.

⊙ **¡Dundunbanza!**   World Circuit, UK

Sierra Maestra's first London-recorded album opens with their version of the New York salsero Willie Colón's "Juana Peña" and contains four songs from Arsenio Rodríguez, including the title track – a splendid vehicle for the high, exciting four-voice tight harmony choruses, plus de Marcos' densely-woven tres tumbaos and Alemañy's stratospheric trumpet.

⊙ **Tibiri Tabara**   World Circuit, UK

The follow-up to **¡Dundunbanza!**, recorded three years later,
featured legendary bassist Cachaíto López and Portuguese pianist
Bernardo Sassetti as guests. The new trumpeter, Bárbaro Teuntor,
proves a worthy successor to Alemañy, with a full, mellow tone, and
he also sings on a nice changüi with de Marcos' tres ringing out
behind him. The range of repertoire is interestingly expanded with
a smooth, modern canción-ballad and a calypso-like sucu-sucu.

Adalberto Alvarez/Son 14

Because of his influence on non-Cuban Latin musicians as a songwriter, and his role in preserving the continuity between son and
modern Cuban dance music, **Adalberto Cecilio Alvarez Zayas** is
one of the most important Cuban bandleaders of the last twenty
years. During this period, when the traditional salsa fans of New York,
San Juan and Bogotá asked who and where was the Cuban equivalent of Oscar D'León or José Alberto, the answer was Adalberto
Alvarez in Santiago.

Alvarez was born in 1948 in Havana while his parents were on a
visit from their family home in the central city of Camagüey. His father
led a son conjunto, **Avance Juvenil**, which performed throughout the
province with visiting star groups from Havana, and the young
Adalberto was often taken along to play clave or güiro at the side of
the stage, as the Sonora Matancera or the Orquesta Riverside filled
the Camagüey dance-floors.

When Alvarez chose to go to the Technical Institute of Aeronautics
to pursue his childhood ambition of becoming a pilot, his mother
warned him that his weaknesses at mathematics and for dance
music would ensure he didn't complete the course. She was right,
and Alvarez took up music instead, passing an audition for the presti-

gious Escuela Nacional de Arte where he studied music theory and bassoon. At ENA, Alvarez escaped the restrictions of a purely symphonic training by putting together an unusual orquesta típica playing son on bassoons, oboes, flutes and strings. Among the group's repertoire was a shake-cha, composed by Alvarez, the equivalent of the son-shakes Juan Formell was creating at the same time.

In 1972, Alvarez graduated and returned to Camagüey to teach music in the Provincial School of Art, by which time his songs were already attracting attention. "Con Un Besito Mi Amor" (With A Kiss, My Love) was the first of a number of songs taken up by the nationally popular band **Rumbavana**. Alvarez himself took up active performance, taking over leadership of Avance Juvenil from his father. At this time, his musical interests began to focus on non-Cuban salsa, and he spent hours tuning an ancient radio to Venezuelan and Colombian stations, which in the early 1970s were hotbeds of true salsa, with the Venezuelan Oscar D'León's first band, Dimension Latina, helping to make the smooth, rich sound of four-trombones immensely popular.

By 1977, Alvarez, with his songs being played nationally by others, determined to find a more high-profile vehicle, and succeeded in overcoming the morass of bureaucratic obstacles and moved to Santiago where he assembled a new band of 14 members. **Son 14** (a play on the meaning of son as a verb, "they are") were an immediate success and were spotted by the influential pianist Frank Fernández, who persuaded Egrem to record them without delay. Their first record, "A Bayamo En Coche", was a great hit, and was covered by a panoply of foreign artists, from Willie Chirino to the Dominican superstar Juan-Luis Guerra. Alvarez wrote the song on a trip from Camagüey to Santiago. The bus broke down in Bayamo by a rank of horse-drawn carriages, he reflected how nice it would be to continue

by horse and carriage, and by the time the journey resumed he'd written a standard of twentieth-century salsa.

Apart from Alvarez' song-writing and arrangements, Son 14's strengths included several outstanding individual musicians. The singer **Eduardo Morales,** known as "Tiburón" (Shark), was a fine charismatic sonero, adept at improvising, with a rough, memorable voice, while the tresero, **Pancho Amat,** was one of the best players of his instrument in Cuba – a classically trained virtuoso with remark-

Tiburón in full flow

able breadth of repertoire. For fifteen years, Alvarez and Son 14 enjoyed great success, travelling to Venezuela, where they played to a 70,000-strong stadium audience in Caracas, and Colombia, where they won over the citizens of Cali, one of the most salsa-mad cities on the continent. In 1983, when Oscar D'León made his sensational visit to Cuba, Son 14 was the group invited as support.

When, in 1984, Alvarez left Son 14 and moved to Havana, the group continued to be based in Santiago under the leadership of the bass player Jorge Machado, and then the trombonist Lázaro Rosabal. Tiburón Morales' continued presence, augmented on occasion by that of his son, **Marcos "Tiburón Junior"**, ensured Son 14 kept a high profile.

Alvarez formed a new group, **Adalberto y su Son**, retaining the important features of Son 14: strong vocals by the top soneros **Felix Baloy**, and subsequently **Jorge Luis Rojas "Rojitas"**; powerful brass; and a dense interplay of tumbaos on keyboards and tres. The latter was played by Pancho Amat until he left, whereupon Alvarez had the tres parts synthesized since he regarded Amat as irreplaceable.

Throughout the 1990s, Alvarez' reputation continued to grow. Known as "El Caballero del Son" (The Gentleman of Son), because of his dignified, non-sensational lyrics, he was more and more recognised as Cuba's most eminent writer of exportable dance music. In 1991, his album **¿Y Qué Tu Quieres Que Te Den?** was the biggest hit of the year in Cuba, recorded with Pablo Milanés' short-lived label PM Records. By the mid-1990s, Alvarez had acquired a new star singer, **Aramis Galindo**, and his daughter **Dorgeris** as pianist, and was at the front of the queue of Cuban artists singing with American companies. Alvarez' group ended the decade in Los Angeles, at the Vanity Fair party after the Oscars ceremony, with Robert de Niro,

Madonna and Monica Lewinsky reportedly dancing to the eagerly awaited new Cuban salsa.

⊙ Son 14 with Adalberto Alvarez   Tumi, UK

A classic collection starting with the doo-wop a cappella prelude to "Bayamo en Coche" and continuing through eleven more tracks of 1970s Santiago salsa, complete with fire engine effects, the ultra-fast sections (that Alvarez later realised were still too Cuban-Latin to be mainstream salsa), and Tiburón's rasping soneo.

⊙ La Máquina Musical, 20th Anniversary   Tumi, UK

A 1999 Son 14 production, recorded in Santiago's Siboney studio, featuring more raucous and exciting Tiburonisms – the singer wrote half the songs – including plenty of Cuban salsa.

⊙ ¿Y Qué Tú Quieres Que Te Den?   PM, Cuba

The great 1991 hit album, worth tracking down if at all possible for its knock-out title track, a plea to the orishas for help – Cuba certainly needed it at that point in time – with a rap-prayer, a great mass chorus and much melodic inspiration.

⊙ Jugando con Candela   Havana Caliente, US

A big-budget US-financed album, produced by a former associate of Sergio George, the brains behind top selling US Latin acts such as Marc Anthony and DLG. Alvarez's shot at international fame sounds a bit too much like exactly that. Although shades of salsa romantica blandness and DLG's MTV funk impart a sense of forced chart friendliness, songs like "Te Equivocaste" and "Solamente Tú" still show off Alvarez's gift for catchiness, and the band is on good form.

Guillermo and Gonzalo Rubalcaba

Another musical dynasty, the Rubalcabas, have achieved international fame in the work of the third generation star **Gonzalo Rubalcaba**,

the only Cuban pianist to challenge Chucho Valdés in outright virtu-osity.

The first member of the family to excel at music was Gonzalo's grandfather, **Jacobo Rubalcaba**, a composer and trombonist from the port of Sagua. Jacobo worked as a tailor while studying music and wrote well-known danzones, such as "Linda Mercedes" and "El Cadete Constitucional", and had a distinguished career as director of his own Charanga Típica before dying in a traffic accident in 1960. His son **Guillermo** took up piano, played with Enrique Jorrín and led the Charanga Típica of the Ministry of Culture, which eventually merged into the **Charanga Rubalcaba**, with Orlando Cachaíto López as its bass player. Still one of Havana's most active danzón bands, the Charanga Rubalcaba performs for Sunday afternoon danzón sessions at Havana's Tropical. Benefiting from the post-Buena Vista revival of interest in early Cuban dance music, Charanga Rubalcaba released a new record on the Spanish label Eurotropical in 1998.

Gonzalo Rubalcaba was born in 1963, into a household constantly visited by musician friends of his father – Frank Emilio Flynn, Antonio Arcaño and Pacho Alonso all dropped in regularly – and well stocked with worn jazz records. Gonzalo originally wanted to be a percus-sionist, but was steered, at first reluctantly, in the direction of the piano by his parents. He studied classical piano at the Amadeo Roldán Conservatory and the National School of Art, graduated brilliantly, and immediately embarked on a busy career. By the early 1980s, Rubalcaba had played within Cuba with the **Orquesta Cubana de Música Moderna** and **Los Van Van**, toured Africa with the **Orquesta Aragón,** and formed his own group, **Proyecto**, a septet containing members of the Charanga Típica of his father.

In 1985, Rubalcaba made the first of his important American jazz friends when **Dizzy Gillespie**, watching him playing in the bar of the

Hotel Nacional during the Havana Jazz Festival, commented that the young Cuban was the best pianist he'd heard in ten years and invited him to guest with his orchestra the following night. At the following year's festival, Rubalcaba met the famous bass player Charlie Haden, who had him invited to the Montreal Jazz Festival in 1989 and introduced his work to the jazz label Blue Note, who immediately signed Rubalcaba to a record deal, using the company's Japanese affiliate to circumvent US Cuban embargo legislation.

By the 1990s, Rubalcaba seems to have been recognised by the Cuban government as a potential world star and cultural ambassador for the country. By dint of his tactful behaviour and a certain suppleness on the part of the Cuban and American authorities, he became one of the first artists to achieve US residence while maintaining Cuban nationality and travelling regularly between the two countries. This was accomplished in two stages. In 1992 he moved to the Dominican Republic, which he had visited two years earlier to record as a guest on Juan Luis Guerra's great hit album **Ojala Que Llueva Café**. In 1993 he visited the US for the first time as pall-bearer at Dizzy Gillespie's funeral, followed by a second visit, this time to star in a concert at the Lincoln Center, where he impressed both US and Cuban officials by his refusal to talk politics. The Miami anti-Castroists, who only welcomed Cuban musicians who publicly criticised the Cuba regime, were not impressed and Rubalcaba's Miami concert debut in 1991 was attended by crowds of howling, spitting protesters. His residence in South Florida still attracts controversy, though not violence.

Musically, Rubalcaba's style – either solo, in trio with drummers such as Jack de Johnette and bassists of the stature of Charlie Haden, or in small groups with added brass and percussion – has alternated between avant-gardism (as in the synthesizer-dominated

"Giraldillo") and extemporising from a base of standards – danzón, fílin or the Beatles numbers he has made signature pieces.

⊙ Por Eso Yo Soy Cubano: Eurotropical, Spain
La Charanga Rubalcaba

Guillermo Rubalcaba's vintage charanga, recorded in 1998, with three violins and a cello as the swinging string section and the great Cachaíto still finding time to take care of bass duties. The twelve numbers comprise danzones (including "Pueblo Nuevo", the Buena Vista Social Club track attributed to Rubén González as composer, but here to Orestes López), a cha-cha-cha, sones, boleros, the classic Rudy Calzado guaracha "Kikiriki", and a "Cuban mosaic" kicking off with a rather nice "Manisero".

⊙ Mi Gran Pasión: Gonzalo Rubalcaba   Messidor, Germany

The younger Rubalcaba, recorded in 1987, with possibly the finest line-up of Proyecto – Horacio "El Negro" Hernández on drum-kit, Roberto Vizcaíno on Afro-Cuban percussion, Felipe Cabrero on bass, Lázaro Cruz and Reynaldo Melián on trumpets, and Rafael Carrusco on sax and flute. A gentler and more introspective recording than Rubalcaba's later hyper-fast progressive mode, **Mi Gran Pasión** contains beautifully updated danzones as well as themes from Tchaikovsky and state-of-the-art Latin jazz, Havana style.

9
The 1990s

Havana at the beginning of the 1990s was a mixture of romance and destitution as the economic collapse of the **Special Period** progressed. In the shops, bare shelves and long queues for the irregular deliveries of staples were the norm. Records were like gold dust: **Egrem**, which had been issuing up to a hundred titles a year in the mid 1980s, had difficulty making a dozen new albums in 1991. Power cuts were regular, petrol was almost unobtainable and, except in the tourist hotels, nightlife was drastically reduced. In the Tropical, bands still played on but rum was strictly for rich foreigners and Cubans were reduced to drinking a brown concoction of fermented vegetable peelings called "vino espumoso". **Prostitution** and acquiring foreign visitors as temporary lovers was beginning to be practised, but very discreetly: to be found by the police in possession of dollars was a crime punished by prison, and only dollars could buy anything worth having, in the special foreign currency stores reserved for tourists and diplomats.

A new market

For Cuban musicians, a tour abroad was a financial windfall, not for any salary boost – they were still paid their minuscule State peso wage – but for the chance to hoard some of the $20 a day living expenses,

and perhaps to sell a couple of boxes of smuggled cigars while on the road. At this time, Cuban bands working abroad charged a fraction of the fees of the big US or Colombian bands, and the musicians would often contrive, once out of the country, to play a few extra unofficial dates, not contracted with the State agency, for even less money.

For Cuban music, in short, things looked grim. And yet, the seeds were already sown which would end the decade on the highest note since the glory days of the 1950s. Firstly, **tourism** was increasing. In spite of the dilapidated and incompetent Soviet-era hotels, the numbers of foreign visitors to Cuba doubled between 1988 and 1993, to reach 600,000 a year. Most of these were younger and culturally curious. Cuban music was beginning to fascinate a new audience, not just the salsa-buying Latinos but European and Japanese "world music" fans.

Catering to this market was a growing number of small adventurous record companies. In Britain, the fledgling Earthworks label had put out an LP, **Viva El Ritmo!**, a compilation of tracks by Irakere, Son 14, Los Van Van and others, licensed from Egrem in 1985. By 1987, the World Circuit label, which would end the 1990s publishing the first 4-million-selling Cuban CD, had licensed and released Egrem's LP **Fiesta Guajira** by Celina Gonzalez. In Spain, the "new flamenco" specialists Nuevos Medios put out Beny Moré and Bola de Nieve albums in 1989 while in the US, the Blue Note label signed the brilliant jazz pianist Gonzalo Rubalcaba in 1995, sidestepping the US legal ban in dealing with Cuban artists by contracting him to a Japanese subsidiary, which then licensed the recording to the US parent company.

The increasing numbers of interested foreign record companies found a Cuban music scene divided into two broad areas. On the one hand, much traditional music was still being played unchanged – old son and trova quartets, charangas playing danzones – indeed, half the bands from the 1930s onwards seemed still to exist, at least

in name. These were regarded as ancient history by most young Cubans and by State cultural officials, but they were of great interest abroad. In 1989, the elderly ex-Compadres second voice, Compay Segundo, who has been adopted by the younger traditionalist Eliades Ochoa, travelled to Washington to appear at the Smithsonian Institute. The same year, the Orquesta Revé, a popular dance band but a traditionally based one, toured Europe with the WOMAD Festival organization. Interestingly, Cuban cultural officials had initially resisted the booking for Revé, apparently believing a progressive group like Irakere or Síntesis would be more appropriate than a largely black changüí outfit.

Timba time

The second strand of music was, in fact, a more progressive one. Later christened **timba** as a semi-marketing term in much the same way the name "salsa" had come into existence, this music was often referred to as "salsa Cubana". It was a fast, dynamic, complex music, jumpy and flash, full of street slang lyrics and catch-phrases, and its chief exponents were **NG La Banda**, the group founded in 1988 by **José Luis Cortés**, the flautist who had started his career as a founder member of Los Van Van, before joining Irakere. Both Van Van and Irakere were important influences on the timba bands, for their emphasis on jazz harmonies and improvization, speed, virtuosity and the staccato delivery of the breakdown rather than the measured hypnotic regularity of the classic salsa tumbao. Used intermittently by dance bands for decades as a general term for rhythm, the word "timba" came originally from the lexicon of rumba, particularly the old Columbia form, and Afro-Cuban dance and percussion were important components of the mix. So, paradoxically, was the soft ballad-based romantic salsa of the 1980s, at the opposite end of the spectrum.

La Charanga Habanera

The great success of NG La Banda, "la banda que manda" (the band that commands) as they referred to themselves, was soon repeated by a dozen new bands all more or less in the timba wave, although varying quite considerably in their music. Soon after the formation of NG La Banda, **La Charanga Habanera**, a long-standing group in traditional charanga format, was redesigned by its leader **David Calzado** with the characteristic timba accelerated keyboard riffs, double-thudding bass drum and, the group's trademark, acrobatic break-dancing routines by the singers that incorporated increasingly suggestive moves.

As the new bands became popular, their audiences' dancing evolved with the music. The despelote spread like wildfire – essentially a new version of the old Cuban shake of the 1960s or pelvic-thrusting pudín beloved by Orquesta Revé fans in the 1980s, the dance involved the frenzied wriggling hip and shoulder action known as tembleque when the groups went into the instrumental breakdown. Through the development of timba and despelote, Cuban popular dance maintained its distance from US/Puerto Rican/Colombian salsa dance, the same distance which had separated the jive-like turns and group formations of casino, the dance of the Van Van generation, from the rest of the salsa world.

By the mid 1990s, the Charanga Habanera had been challenged by several top newcomers: **Manolito y su Trabuco**, **Giraldo Piloto y Klimax**, the suaver **Issac Delgado and Paulito FG**, and finally, **Manolín**, known as **El Médico de la Salsa**, the Salsa Doctor, as he had qualified in medicine before taking up music. In addition to their music, the timba performers were identified strongly with their lyrics – cynical, aggressive, reflective of the wheeling, dealing and hustling world of modern Cuban city life, and so full of slang and double-entendres as to be unintelligible even to non-Cuban Spanish-speakers. By the time the international record industry began to look seriously at the world sales possibilities of timba, the impenetrability of the texts and the excessive length of the flashy, solo-filled numbers were seen as a disadvantage. Cash-strapped Cuban radio may have had plenty of airtime for 16-minute tracks, but the airwaves of the world dictated four minutes, and artists like **Manolín** and **Issac Delgado** began to devote their efforts to shortening their records and making them accessible.

In addition to timba, another younger music was germinating – rap, or hip-hop, a lo Cubano. Just as their older brothers and sisters

YOURI LENQUETTE

Issac Delgado and Manolín, el Médico de la Salsa

surreptitiously listened to Celia Cruz, Willie Chirino or Gloria Estefan on the radio from Miami, so young Habaneros were tuning in to rap stations, and even, when weather permitted, to Florida TV programmes like *Soul Train*, gazing agog at the likes of Public Enemy and Grand Master Flash, and break-dancers spinning their stuff. Before long, Cubans would be following Puerto Ricans and other Latino youth in creating their own rap.

A new deal

The chance for thousands of high quality State-trained musicians to tour, record, and generally come in from the cold wasn't long in arriving. In spite of their official disdain for perestroika, and the "Socialism or Death!" banners in the streets, Cuba's rulers realized survival depended on adapting to economic reality. The signal for change was delivered by Castro in his October 1991 report to the 4th Congress of the Communist Party. Measures would be taken to stimulate foreign exchange earnings, with certain areas, including culture, given priority. At the same time, "self-financing", whereby a State enterprise generates, uses and invests its own profits, as opposed to "budget financing", where it simply runs on its State-allocated funds, and passes any profits directly back, was to be extended "whenever possible and suitable." As in post-Iron Curtain Europe, where Army divisions abruptly diversified into tourism, there was a sudden flurry of shadowy new companies owned partly by the State and partly by individuals. Some of them bore the title S.A. – the Spanish equivalent of Ltd (Limited Company) – which stands for Sociedad Anónima but which Havana wags translated as "Socios y Amigos", implying "Associates & Friends" of the regime. Among the new entities were two record companies, Artex, formed by the State artists' touring agency in 1989 (and soon renamed Bis), and PM Records, which was the label operated by Cuba's first non-governmental cultural enterprise, the Pablo Milanés Foundation. The latter was set up by the nueva trova star on the proceeds of his international success and employed sixty people on a range of activities, including radio and video production, and book and magazine publishing.

In Cuban embassies abroad, commercial attachés used to representing one monolithic State exporter now found themselves con-

fused as to whose interests to promote. The official line was that socialism was holding firm, and there was no competition, as all companies paid the same rates. Already, though, the Pablo Milanés Foundation commented that artists might prefer to use their services, as they were smaller, more flexible and more internationally-minded.

In 1993, Cuban economic legislation took an even bigger leap when, first, the possession of US dollars was legalized, and, second, a limited degree of private enterprise was allowed. This was the beginning of the paladares, the little family-run front parlour restaurants, and the spare rooms for rent in citizens' houses. Within months, half of Cuba was looking for ways to make a buck. The peso was now – more than ever – only useful for buying rations and the dross of Cuban manufacture. Los Van Van, faithful chroniclers of Cuban street life, brought out their song "Un Socio" (A Partner) about a Havana hustler, with long experience of house swapping, cigar peddling and bread and cheese broking, looking for a foreign partner for a new business idea.

The linked areas of tourism and music were among the first to respond to the new possibilities, and the British, Canadians, Italians and – above all – Spanish were the most eager new socios. Spanish hotel chains such as Sol Melia and Kawama Caribbean, in partnership with the Cuban State, began a massive programme of modernizing the old hotels and building new ones. Foreign airlines began scheduling new flights into Havana and the beach resort of Varadero to help Cubana's over-stretched and antiquated Ilyushin jets bring in the flow of European package tourists.

The Spanish were also the biggest players in the music game. In 1994, Kawama Caribbean converted the old Copa Room of the Hotel Riviera, a once-glamorous circular cabaret opened by Ginger Rogers, into **El Palacio de la Salsa**, a swish modern dance club for tourists and those few Cubans with the requisite $15-$40 entry fee.

In 1991, NG La Banda, the timba founders, whose last Egrem LP had been licensed to the venerable Madrid company Fonomusic, now signed a three-CD deal with the Barcelona company **Magic Music**. One of the first albums was **La Bruja** (The Witch), whose title song referred to the new social category which came to typify 1990s Cuba – the jineteras, or girls trading sex more or less directly to tourists. Magic Music also signed La Charanga Habanera, while another Spanish company, Eurotropical, a new imprint of the Tenerife-based Manzana Company which had been catering to the big Latin music audience of the Canary Isles for fifteen years, snapped up Manolito y su Trabuco and Giraldo Piloto y Klimax.

By the mid-1990s, a new brand of young Cuban dance music star was beginning to emerge in Havana, half in and half out of the old system. Although obliged to obtain permissions and exit visas through the State empresas, the new stars negotiated and kept their own fees for foreign work, of which they were in theory obliged to pay a modest proportion to the State in tax. They even had a Cuban version of the advertising sponsorship deals available to the stars of the capitalist world.

In search of old stars

If one part of the international audience, and all young Cubans, looked to timba for their entertainment, another segment of the world market was thinking retro, and traditional. Once again Spain led the way. In 1992 the Spanish celebrations of the 500th anniversary of Columbus' discovery of the Americas had focused public interest on the music of Spain's former colonies, of which Cuban music was the most prominent. The Seville Expo provided further occasion for concerts.

In 1992 the Spanish rock star **Santiago Auserón**, former leader of the top group Radio Futura, embarked on his own Columbus-style

quest for the roots of Cuban music, preparing a series of compilation albums of classic old recordings entitled **La Semilla del Son** (The Seed of Son). Among the artists he met in Cuba was the veteran guaracha star "El Guayabero" and the recently formed group of old soneros **La Vieja Trova Santiaguera** (see Chapter 2), both of whom were invited to tour Spain. In 1994 Auserón, with the support of the city of Seville, organized a series of concerts in and around the Andalusian capital, putting together great old soneros and flamenco performers. Among the Cubans invited was Compay Segundo, who found the Spanish as delighted with his characterful singing and playing as he was with Madrid's Basque lunch clubs and the Andalusian cortijos near Huelva, where he went to see if he could find traces of his own Spanish family roots.

The idea of rediscovering eminent old Cuban musicians began to gather pace. In 1994 in Miami, **Cachao López**, the great exiled bass player, recorded his magnificent **Master Sessions** albums under the auspices of the actor Andy García, while in Germany, the label Messidor assembled an oldies super-group around the Swedish-resident bandleader **Bebo Valdés**.

The Buena Vista phenomenon

In Havana, **Juan de Marcos González**, the tres player and founder of the 1980s son revival group Sierra Maestra, was thinking along similar lines. De Marcos' idea was to assemble a band of great old musicians from the 1950s, to record new versions of their classic repertoire. In 1996 he got his opportunity. **Nick Gold**, the proprietor of the London company World Circuit, arranged to record a fusion album in Havana with **Ry Cooder**, the Californian ethno-retro-bottle-neck-guitar ace, playing alongside Malian and Cuban musicians – the whole project to be co-ordinated by Juan de Marcos.

Buena Vista socializing

Gold and Cooder arrived in Havana in March 1996 to find that the Malian musicians had been unable to arrange visas and couldn't come, so they set about recording anyway, in Egrem's old Panart studio on the **Calle San Miguel** which, in spite of its decrepitude, the World Circuit team regarded as atmospheric and capable of producing exactly the sound they wanted. De Marcos and his wife Gliceria busied themselves around Havana, recruiting musicians such as **"Cachaíto" López**, Havana's most eminent bass player and son of the late Orestes Lopez, **Amadito Valdés**, former timbalero with the Estrellas de Areito and the Cuarteto D'Aida, and **"Guajiro" Mirabál**, the Tropicana Orchestra's lead trumpeter. All of these still worked regularly but they also sought out performers who had stopped doing so, like **Ibrahim Ferrer** who had passed a number of years since his

retirement cleaning shoes to eke out his small pension, and **Rubén González**, once pianist for Arsenio Rodríguez, who hadn't had a piano since his instrument had been destroyed by woodworm. All of them accepted the modest fees offered, as did the bolero diva **Omara Portuondo**, who was brought in from the adjacent studio where she was by chance recording her own album.

Three records were made in these sessions, featuring selections of historic sones, boleros, guarachas and danzones: one by a small group including Ry Cooder, another by a larger band led by Juan de Marcos González, and finally a set of instrumentals showcasing the piano of Rubén González. The first album was christened **Buena Vista Social Club**, after one of the tracks, a danzón written for the eponymous dance club by either Cachaíto López' father Orestes or his uncle Israel "Cachao". Nick Gold chose the title, feeling it encapsulated perfectly the atmosphere of the music, and furthermore didn't require translation for the Anglophone world music market.

Buena Vista Social Club, the first CD, was released the following year. Elegantly packaged and well marketed, the record began to sell at once, as did the following two CDs. The release, a year later, of a feature-length documentary film of the Buena Vista musicians by the German director **Wim Wenders** reached so many more potential purchasers that, by the end of 2000, the seven CDs (which by then comprised the Buena Vista series) achieved total sales of over seven million copies.

The Buena Vista success made stars out of its participants, and helped boost the pay disparity of Cubans as compared with other Latin musicians: suddenly **Ibrahim Ferrer** and the **Afro-Cuban All Stars** were commanding the same concert fees once reserved for US salsa acts like Celia Cruz. Egrem began to re-issue old recordings by Buena Vista members, as did a number of the European licensing spe-

cialists, often with the words Buena Vista attached to the titles. Buena Vista was, however, an external phenomenon, not a Cuban one. Until World Circuit donated the masters of the records to Egrem at the end of 2000 to release on cassette, the Buena Vista series had not been distributed inside the island, and those Cubans who had heard of the fuss about Ferrer, Segundo, et al were mystified that such a thing should be happening to singers they had long forgotten about.

Other musical exports

Not all Cubans were pleased by the success of the Buena Vista Social Club oldsters. At the most extreme level a theory circulated that the adulation of pre-1959 artists and music was a way of negating the successes and cultural advances of the Revolution. Some musicians simply felt irritated that Cuba's modern music was being overlooked by the focus on the past. In 1998, a riposte to the Afro-Cuban All Stars was organized in the form of a modern super-group called **Team Cuba**, bringing together in one show some of the top names of timba and new Havana dance music: Juan Formell, José Luis Cortés, Adalberto Alvarez, Paulito FG, David Calzado, Issac Delgado and Manolín. The band gave several mass concerts in Havana and then headed for France, where what was to be a "monumental manifesto" of timba in Europe began at the Théatre de la Mutualité in Paris. Unfortunately, the concert was an under-publicized and badly organized flop and Team Cuba made its way home, leaving a huge deficit in its wake.

In fact, the Havana music scene had its share of reverses as well as successes in the late 1990s. The recording facilities continually improved. Egrem opened a brand new studio in Miramar to supplement the ancient Calle San Miguel facility, Silvio Rodríguez invested part of the 6 million dollar cost of another state-of-the-art studio, Abdala. Egrem's Siboney studio in Santiago and Artex's in

Cienfuegos, radio and Cinema Institute recording studios all worked regularly. Private individuals began to find ways to install portable mixing desks and computers in their homes. By 2000, Juan de Marcos González could invest part of his Buena Vista and Afro-Cuban All Star earnings in a small studio in his new seaside bunga-low from which to run the Havana end of his new company, Ahora Productions. The trend-setting Pablo Milanés Foundation, however, in spite of star Spanish sponsoring committees and Milanés' own high status within the regime, didn't last long. In 1995, Milanés announced that the foundation was closing down, blaming attempts by the Cuban Ministry of Culture to control its activities. Within three years, the nueva trova star was back in business, adding his Pablo Milanés Studio to Havana's booming infrastructure.

The continuing boom in tourism provided work for hundreds of minor musicians in the cabarets and bars of the new hotels, while the new big salsa clubs, the **Palacio de la Salsa**, the **Cecilia**, the **Café Cantante**, the **Casa de la Música** in Miramar and others advanced economic liberalization to the point where the top groups who played there could keep a large proportion of the door money, and thus earn well inside, as well as outside, the country. Before long, however, the government balked at the extent of Havana's rebirth as a 1950s-style pleasure destination, especially the retinues of erotically attired jineteras (and male jineteros, as gay sex tourism boomed) who flocked to the new clubs. The Palacio de la Salsa reverted to a cabaret, and the big disco Ashé in the next door Melia Cohiba Hotel, Havana's plushest VIP accommodation, was closed down overnight and converted into a sort of Latin Hard Rock Café.

Musicians were also reminded of the limits to self-expression. Although the replacement of the ageing hard-line bureaucrat **Armando Hart** as Minister of Culture by **Abel Prieto**, a youthful long-haired

writer, was generally hailed as a liberalizing move, the government showed it might tolerate rich musicians, but not rich and outspoken ones. **Manolín, El Médico de la Salsa**, whose song "Arriba de la Bola" had once been used as the Cuban equivalent of a party political broadcast, intercut with footage of a Castro speech, found his 1997 single "Amigos en Miami", an appeal for friendship between Cubans and exiles, much less to the authorities' taste, and claimed to have been frozen out of the media and public performance for two years as a result, after a visit from a Party official to find out what he was up to. At the same time, the Charanga Habanera's groin-thrusting was deemed to have crossed the boundary into obscenity, and the group was told they would be denied an exit visa for six months as punishment.

The US market

In one area of activity, Cuban musicians made spectacular advances in the 1990s – breaking into the American market. At the beginning of the decade, strictly applied US legislation requiring visiting Cuban musicians to be engaged solely on minimally-paid cultural exchanges kept out all but a handful of artists. By 1997, dozens, from jazz stars Chucho Valdés and Irakere to salsero Issac Delgado, were playing US concert halls and festivals, and **Cubanismo**, ex-Sierra Maestra trumpeter **Jesús Alemañy**'s new group, was able to spend the best part of a year touring the country, with school workshops and outreach programmes as a concession to cultural exchange. Even in Miami, where spectacular protests still occurred sporadically – crowds of exiles spat and jeered at audiences arriving for Gonzalo Rubalcaba's concert in 1996 and Los Van Van's in 1999 – more discreet Cuban concerts took place without incident.

The US record industry also began to work with Cuban artists. From the early 1990s, "world music" independents led by Qbadisk

Jesús Alemañy of Cubanismo

had licensed Cuban recordings, but the Latino companies were neither interested in Cuban dance music – out of synch as it was with international salsa – nor prepared to do business with the musicians, unless of course, they chose to defect. In 1993, Ralph Mercado, proprietor of New York's leading salsa label, RMM, was reported as commenting he could never contract a Cuban artist while Celia Cruz, his biggest star and a leading anti-Castroist, was alive. Two years later, Jerry Masucci, founder of the original salsa label Fania, was in Havana signing up Adalberto Alvarez and Juan Carlos Alfonso via a Panamanian front company. The year after that, Mercado visited Cuba

via the Dominican Republic (direct links with the US were still almost non-existent) and made similar deals with Issac Delgado and Paulito FG. The rapprochement had a dual effect, musically, if a minor one. New York salsa arrangers such as Mercado's musical director Isidro Infante began to integrate the jumpy, jazz-inflected sound of timba into some of their productions, while certain Cuban bands began to produce records in the international salsa mould: Juan Carlos Alfonso, the leader of the top group Dan Den and a Revé alumnus, recorded a pure Colombian salsa album in Cali for Masucci's Nueva Fania label. Nonetheless, Cuban dance music ended the 1990s, as it had entered it, largely distinct from international salsa.

Cuba in the 1990s was not just timba and classic gold, however. The jazz descarga was renovated by the brilliant young flautist **Orlando "Maraca" Valle**, traditional son was not confined to disinterred oldsters and fifty-year-old songs but was also performed by younger groups such as the Septeto Santiaguera who wrote new songs in the old styles.

Cuban rap

There was also Cuban rap, bubbling semi-clandestinely out in the barrios early in the decade, achieving official recognition in the middle of it, and emerging at the end, via Spain and France, as a potential hit genre. The derivation of rap in Cuba, as elsewhere, has a more complex genealogy than appearances might indicate: **Cachao López** has claimed that he used to include rhythmically spoken improvisation in the lucumí dialect, equivalent to rap in his view, in descargas half a century ago. Later, mainstream Cuban bandleaders were affected by the general fashion for inserting rap sections in songs: a fine example is the rap-prayer to the orishas in Adalberto Alvarez' "¿Y Que Tu Quieres Te Den?" in 1991.

Rap, as modelled on the black urban American chart version, however, performed and consumed by an equivalent Cuban sociological sector to its American audience, dates from the early 1990s. It was first taken up by predominantly black youths living in the big run-down estates of new apartment blocks in the suburbs of Havana, especially Alamar, where the Festival of Rap came into existence in 1995. Interestingly, the authorities quickly accepted the new rappers, permitting a radio show, *El Rincón del Rap* (Rap Corner), in 1994 and facilitating the festival the following year. This would presumably not have been the case were Cuban rappers not as supportive in their lyrics of the political system as they are, confining their social criticism to sardonic reflections on the tribulations of jineteras, and other topics regularly addressed by groups such as Van Van and NG La Banda.

Early rap groups made do with cobbled-together assemblages of mikes and portable cassette decks, and their range of sampled music was extremely limited. A major virtue to follow from this necessity was the distinctiveness of the genre, with old sones and guarachas, Afro-Cuban percussion and santería influences prominent in the mix, whereas many young Cubans would probably prefer a more heavily US-modelled sound.

By the mid-nineties, a degree of professionalism was entering the rap scene. The first rap festival was won by **SBS**, a trio from the Parraga barrio whose recipe centred on sexually suggestive lyrics, over a musical cocktail of salsa, merengue and hip-hop. SBS became the first rap group to record, and, in 1997, the first to sign up to a foreign label, the Spanish Magic Music. Rap theorists and entrepreneurs began to emerge, such as **Ariel Fernández**, who promoted concerts and wrote on rap in the Communist cultural publication *El Caiman Barbudo*, and **Pablo Herrera**, a lecturer at the University of

Havana, who managed **Amenaza**, another success story from the 1995 festival. Amenaza gained first prize in the 1997 festival, and then decamped to France, where two of the members joined what was to become the first widely distributed Cuban rap outfit, **Orishas**. In 1998, Herrera visited New York, where a benefit concert was arranged to raise funds for rap and hip-hop recording equipment to be sent to Havana.

By the end of the decade, Cuba was estimated to possess 200 rap groups, 150 of them based in and around Havana, and the outside world was beginning to take a serious interest. The 1999 rap festival included 32 groups, and two acts from the US, Black Star and Dead Presidents, attended. In Paris, the group Orishas, consisting of two Cubans resident for some years in the city and two newly arrived Amenaza members, recorded a strikingly successful debut album which was circulating widely in Havana the following year in pirated cassette form. Orishas returned in triumph in December 2000 to perform.

Fin de millennium Cuban music, then, comprised an impressive range, from the deepest of country changüi to the most urban of rap and timba, all exporting itself busily. There was even teen pop. The Havana pop-rock band **Moneda Dura** (Hard Cash), whose 2000 debut album was one of the hits of the year in Cuba, had the record released in Spain.

At the same time, a 23-year-old Havana TV presenter and fashion acolyte named **Raydel** found his way to Paris, where his clean cut good looks and MTV-friendly voice earned him a contract with the record division of France Television to perform a ditty named "Hey Arriba", a Gypsy Kings meet Ricky Martin summer dance single of the sort beloved of French soft drink commercials. El Che's dictum that Cuba must embrace socialism with pachanga still had mileage, it seemed: as the socialism shrank, the pachanga expanded to fill the void.

Artists

NG La Banda

If Los Van Van was the key Cuban dance band of the 1970s and 1980s, their 1990s equivalent was **NG La Banda**. NG stands for Nueva Generación and the specific aim of the band was innovation, to bridge the gap between more intellectual, concert hall music – as played by Irakere – and the popular dance market. The members of the new group were music graduates of either the Escuela Nacional de Arte or the even more elite Instituto Superior de Arte, acutely conscious of their lengthy training and resultant virtuosity, and intent on bringing a new sophistication to dance music.

The founder and leader of NG was **José Luis Cortés**, a singer and flautist, born in 1953 in Santa Clara, who had been an early member of Los Van Van, before joining Irakere in 1980. The group gradually came together between 1985 and 1988 with its various members taking time out from their permanent employment (with Irakere, Pachito Alonso's band, the Radio & Television Orchestra, the Tropicana) in order to rehearse and record together.

The musical structure of NG included piano and keyboards, a drum-kit as well as Afro-Cuban percussion, and a brass section (almost all ex-Irakere) composed of three saxes and two trumpets. The brass instruments, called metales in Spanish, became so renowned for their pyrotechnic breaks they acquired the nickname "los metales de terror", and the entire thrust of the music was hectic and constantly shifting, with percussion breakdowns, signature changes, dance routines by the chorus – all the characteristics of timba. While NG's music revelled in complexity and virtuosity, their

lyrics came from the street. José Luis Cortés and star vocalist, **Tony Calá**, performed tough, slang-filled songs, often broken up with sections of rap, which aimed to speak directly to young dance fans from the barrios while the lighter, more romantic numbers were left to **Issac Delgado**. The barrios themselves were often the subject matter for NG songs, as in their great rumba-based hit "Los Sitios Entero" (The Whole of Los Sitios) about the tribulations of the Los Sitios district. Other favourite NG topics included santería, with songs like "Santa Palabra" and "Papa Changó", and social problems such as jineteria (dealt with in "La Bruja").

Because of the brashness and street slang of the songs, José Luis Cortés acquired the nickname, El Tosco – tosco means crude – and NG La Banda experienced establishment criticism and a ban on radio play for some tracks. The dance constituency loved them, however, and the front line of singers and musicians, dressed in boots and berets, brilliant colours and gold necklaces, would energetically demonstrate the steps of the successive new dance crazes, such as the limón, based on their huge hit of 1993, "Echale Limón" (meaning, roughly, what the hell).

By the mid 1990s, a clutch of rival timba bands, all heavily in debt to NG La Banda, existed, including two formed by members of NG, singer Issac Delgado and Giraldo Piloto, their drummer and joint

composer. "La banda que manda" (the band that commands), as NG referred to themselves, had become a fixture of the Cuban musical establishment, in demand for work with other artists, such as the singer Malena Burke, Elena Burke's daughter, with whom they recorded an album of modernized classic boleros and sones, and the new young discovery of 2000, Osdalgia, whose debut album was produced by José Luis Cortés.

⊙ **Cuban Masters: NG La Banda**   EMI Hemisphere, UK

A collection of mid-period NG, from a half-dozen albums released between 1994 and 1997. The opening track, "Papa Changó", a José Luis Cortés composition, like most of the songs on the album, acts as a virtual menu of NG characteristics – a jangling, restless keyboard riff, bass guitar zooming and popping feverishly, percussion in constant overdrive, a series of juddering horn flourishes breaking, rather than building, momentum, a rap section, a son section, a choral section, a clap-along section, all interchanging at high speed. New listeners should not attempt the tembleque at home without prior medical advice.

Issac Delgado

"El Chévere de la Salsa" ("the great guy of salsa" would be an approximation of the tag), **Issac Delgado** emerged as the best bet for international success to appear from Cuba's 1990s salsa/timba scene. The stylistic path he took diverged, however, from the frenetic timba approach of his one-time employers **NG La Banda** towards a mellower, romantic salsa style, with overtones of bolero and new song, particularly in his choice of material, which included songs by Pablo Milanés and Pedro-Luis Ferrer.

Born in 1962, Delgado took up music as an amateur while still at school. At the age of 16 he had the good fortune to be taken on

board as singer by the pianist **Gonzalo Rubalcaba** who was then setting up his band **Proyecto**. Delgado stayed for two years and Rubalcaba became a close friend finding time to play and arrange for him even after the pianist had become an international jazz star.

In the 1980s, Delgado worked with the group **Galaxia** and with **Pachito Alonso** before becoming a founder-member of NG La Banda. When he left NG in 1992 to set up his own group, he took with him the percussionist and composer **Giraldo Piloto**, while Gonzalo Rubalcaba played piano on, and directed, his first two albums, **Dando La Hora** (Telling The Time) and **Con Ganas** (Wanting). Both albums were recorded in Venezuela, the first for Pablo Milanés' PM Records, the second for the New York based independent Qbadisc.

Delgado also spent much of his first two years playing in Mexico (at the Disco Azúcar in Cancún) and Spain.

In 1994, Giraldo Piloto having left to form his own more timba-oriented group, Delgado flirted with censorship in his song "El Año Que Viene", with its implication that things needed to be improved in Cuba, which, despite being a successful TV theme, was unable to get radio play. Two years later, Delgado was in the vanguard of Cuban artists breaking into the US market, signing with RMM, the label of New York's major salsa entrepreneur Ralph Mercado. The resulting album,

Otra Idea, exhibited a marked move towards American pop-salsa blandness, in keeping with Delgado's stated aim of making timba internationally commercial. Delgado's US venture proceeded patchily: in 1998 he became the first Cuban artist to play a commercial club date in Miami, when the Zafiros film producer Hugo Cancio booked him for his Onyx club. Two years later, he negotiated an end to his RMM contract, claiming that his work had been inadequately promoted. RMM retorted that they had had to let him go because their star performer, Celia Cruz, objected to sharing a label with a pro-Castro Cuban.

Without a record contract, Delgado broke further Cuban business ground in 2000 by raising his own finance from foreign investors to record a new album speculatively in Havana's Abdala Studios, which was, once again, directed by Gonzalo Rubalcaba. At the end of the year, the record was released by Ahí-Namá, a California-based independent, and "El Chévere de la Salsa" was once again ahead of the game and in the news.

⊙ **Con Ganas**   Qbadisc, US

The Chévere de la Salsa's early 1990s product is light salsa, influenced by the thumping electric bass and busy brass of timba, but distinct from it. More than half of the 14 songs are written by either Delgado or Giraldo Piloto, while the remainder include a 1990s-style chachacha by Juan Formell, pieces by the nueva trova stars Amaury Pérez and Pablo Milanés, and a chunk of salsa romantica written by Delgado's old boss, José Luis Cortés.

⊙ **La Formula**   Ahí-Namá, US

The record opens with a piece of salsa-funk, complete with prominent electric rhythm guitar, continues with a slice of salsa romantica and, in track 4, quotes from the chorus of "Hotel California", albeit ironically. The song in question is "El Solar de La California", a portrait of a historic block in old Havana, co-written by Juan Formell. The final track, a catchy bouncing

cumbia, was particularly well received in Cuba, proof that Delgado's new sound isn't just for export.

Paulito y Su Elite

Paulito is a key member of the coterie of young pop stars who transformed the face of Cuban music in the 1990s. At the end of the decade, Paulito was the hip young tropical singer who could be seen extolling the merits of Cristal Beer and the beaches of Varadero in TV clips on the video screens at Havana's new international airport.

Born Paulo Fernández Gallo in Havana in 1963, he studied industrial design at a technological institute before taking up the clarinet in his teens. He turned to singing when he realized he could never afford his own instrument and in 1986 was hired as a chorus singer by **Adalberto Alvarez**. He was a founder member of Juan Carlos Alfonso's new group **Dan Den**, before moving to **Opus 13**, a progressive jazz-rock group in the mould of Irakere. In 1992 he left to set up his own group, trading as **Paulito and his Elite**, which immediately scored a major hit with the song "Tú no me calculas" (You don't read me right). Paulito's style was similar to that of Issac Delgado – light, romantic and not overly timba-frantic. His experience in the heavily son-based Dan Den, however, had instilled a capacity for a sonero's improvisation, and this stood him in good stead, allowing him to indulge in son-competition against **Cándido Fabré**, the master of the genre, on television, and build up a publicity-generating rivalry with **Manolín**, "the Salsa Doctor".

In 1996, having already released one CD on a Spanish label, Paulito signed to Nueva Fania, the re-launched company of Jerry Masucci, the father of New York salsa, but, like Issac Delgado with RMM, later complained that his work was not properly promoted. He

ended the decade pioneering the concept of joint venture by artists, putting his own money into a project with Egrem to record a new album, **Una Vez Mas Por Amor** (Once More For Love), which mixed romantic salsa, gentle timba, international tropical pop, and a surprising piano-backed reprise of an old Carlos Gardel tango.

⊙ El Bueno Soy Yo   Edenways, France

Paulito's 1996 Fania album, released in Europe by a French company and recorded in the old Egrem studio in Havana. All the songs were composed by Paulito who, along with his Elite boys, is on fine form. The record is a good example of slick middle-of-the-road Cuban dance music as it feels its way into the mainstream of international salsa.

Manolín, el Médico de la Salsa

Known as **El Médico de la salsa** (the Salsa Doctor), because he graduated in medicine before turning to music, **Manolín**'s real name is actually Manuel González Hernández. With his elder brother Lázaro, Manolín formed a band as a teenager, but didn't take up music as a career until he finished medical school in 1992. Starting as a singer in the cabaret of the Hotel Capri, he then moved with his own band to a regular slot at La Maison, a complex of luxury shop, restaurant and cabaret at Miramar. Manolín's performances were very well-received, and he began to be invited as opening act for stars such as Los Van Van and NG La Banda at plush new timba haunts such as the **Palacio de la Salsa** and the Café Cantante. Initially seen as a curiosity by the other bands (he appeared on television with a white coat and stethoscope), he rapidly began to overtake the stars in popularity. His secret was less his rather unreliable voice than his sheer charisma and the lyrics of his songs. As a songwriter, he demonstrated an unerring ability to generate catch-phrases which

gripped the public imagination. With Manolín churning out the songs, and his keyboard player and arranger **Luis Bú Pascual** clothing them in bracing timba-funk instrumentation, El Médico's first album, **Una Aventura Loca** (A Crazy Affair), sold enough copies in Cuba to earn its author $4000 – very serious money for a debutant Cuban singer in 1994. Two years later, its sequel, **Para Mi Gente** (For My People), recorded with the Spanish-owned label Caribe, did even better and gave rise to the huge hit "Arriba de la Bola" (On Top of the Ball), which was taken up by the government for use in television propaganda clips.

For a year, Manolín was the hottest act in Cuba, and was even called in to the office of the powerful Minister of Foreign Relations Roberto Robaina to be congratulated on his success. The approval of the authorities rapidly turned to cold shouldering (so he claimed), when, in the following year, his song "Tengo Amigos en Miami" was banned from airplay. At the same time, Manolín began a series of prolonged visits to Miami which led to reports in the Florida press that he had defected, whereas, according to El Médico, he was merely trying to obtain work and a new record deal. During 1998 and 1999, Manolín and his band played seasons at two Miami clubs, Amnesia and Starfish, with the musicians lodged unsatisfactorily in a cheap motel while arguments broke out over fees, and his Spanish record label refused to release him from his contract. At the end of 2000, Manolín had left his band in Miami and returned to Havana, where he borrowed Paulito F.G.'s musicians for gigs, before disappearing again to Mexico.

⊙ **Para Mi Gente**   Ahí-Namá, US

Manolín's second album, containing the huge hit "Arriba de la Bola". The phrase implies "on top of the situation", and in it, Manolín taunted the famous Cuban bands who had left Cuba to

work abroad, with the assertion that they had left the field to him, thus provoking an outbreak of angry ripostes from his rivals. Manolín's band provides a slightly ragged but exciting salsa-timba backing, with blaring horns and a nice mixed male and female chorus.

Bamboleo

Of all the timba generation, **Bamboleo**, a late-comer, offered the most varied, inventive and unformulaic music. The group was founded by **Lázaro Valdés**, a keyboard player and arranger with an impeccable pedigree: grandfather, Oscar, was the percussionist of the Orquesta Cubana de Música Moderna, his great-uncle Vicentico was a bolero star, while his father played piano for Beny Moré and his uncle Oscar was the singer and Afro-percussion specialist of Irakere. Lázaro studied violin and piano at the Escuela Nacional de Arte, working for the important jazz player Bobby Carcassés as well as for Amaury Pérez. His immediate pre-Bamboleo career was preceded by five years as the keyboard player for **Pachito Alonso**'s Kini Kini.

Bamboleo came into existence as a result of a failed attempt to create a quite different group. Valdés was approached by the Spanish label Caribe to set up a band to back an all-female group they intended to create based on the model of the famous Mulatas de Fuego of the 1950s. The auditions failed to come up with enough suitable mulatas, and the project was shelved, leaving Valdés with the nucleus of a group, and the notion of using female singers. He recruited **Vannia Borges**, an art school trained oboist who had worked in an all-female group, the Cuarteto D'Capo, and was then with Pachito Alonso, and **Haila Monpié**, a cabaret dancer; he then added a duo of male singers, **Rafael** and **Alejandro Leberra**, and put behind them a nine-piece band com-

posed of two saxophones, a trumpet, bass, keyboards, drum-kit and Afro-Cuban percussion.

The band made their debut in February 1995 and were immediately successful. This was partly due to the dynamism of their act and the excellence and distinctiveness of their arrangements, but it was also helped by Valdés' clever image creation. The two girl singers' shaven heads, in particular, seemed daringly modern to Cubans, while their album sleeves, produced by the American company Ahí-Namá, were smart, moody and modern, by the standard of Havana cover art direction. The haircuts had in fact occurred partly by chance: Vannia Borges had posed as model for the cover of a record by the group AfroCuba, for which she'd had the word Cuba shaved into her hair, and the only way to remove it had been to shave her whole head. Valdés realised it was an eye-catching new look and had Haila Monpié do the same.

⊙ **Yo No Me Parezco A Nadie**   Ahí-Namá, US

Bamboleo's second American release comprises nine songs written mainly by the prolific timba composer **Leonel Limonta**, who is also Bamboleo's manager. From the stentorian brass assault of the opening number, the music stands out from run-of-the-mill timba, due not only to the outstanding brass writing, but also to the irresistible piano tumbaos, the solid, swinging bass and the intensely rhythmic percussion, the whole reaching a level of excitement rarely achieved by 1990s bands.

Juan-Carlos Alfonso and Dan Den

One of the most famous modern practitioners of son-based salsa as opposed to timba, the keyboard player and bandleader **Juan-Carlos Alfonso** was a rock fan in his youth but developed into a salsero under the influence of the bands he played in. He was born in 1963 in

the town of Bejucal, in the province of Havana. His father was a musician and both Juan-Carlos and his sister María de los Angeles (who also pursued a musical career) studied with a prominent local teacher. Juan-Carlos graduated from the Conservatorio Alejandro García Caturla and began a decade's intensive work as pianist and keyboard-player with the **Conjunto Colonial**, a popular band led by the 1950s bolero specialist Nelo Sosa, then the **Orquesta**

Sensación, another long-established dance band, and finally, in 1984, with the **Orquesta Revé**. Elio Revé's band was at that time poised to break through to great national acclaim with his revitalized changüí-influenced roots charanga, and Juan-Carlos Alfonso's keyboard work and arrangements became a vital part of the band's success. He also established himself as an important songwriter, producing several of Revé's biggest hits, notably "Yo sé que tu sabes que yo sé" (I know you know I know) and "Mas joven que mañana" (Younger than tomorrow).

In 1968, Alfonso left Revé and created his own group. The name **Dan Den** was onomatopoeic, based on the sound of the cowbell in Bejucal's carnival comparsa percussion, and, indeed, the group

made its first public performance at the Bejucal Carnival. With its New York-style three trombone brass section and regular piano and bass-led salsa sound, Dan Den rapidly acquired an audience in Mexico and Colombia where the band toured extensively in 1992. In 1993, Dan Den won the Best Tropical Band prize at the Fería of Cali, Colombia's salsa capital, which is a highly significant accolade from one of Latin America's most fanatical and knowledgeable salsa cities.

⊙ **Salsa en Ataré**   Tumi, UK

This 1997 Cuban-recorded album followed Alfonso's brief relationship with the New York salsa label Fania, consists of eight songs by the maestro and one by Mo Fini, proprietor of the Tumi label. Rich, deep trombones, first class timbales, bass that manages to combine old school salsa steadiness with flights into timba territory and great keyboards all make for an excellent sound. Ataré is a popular neighbourhood of Havana, and the title song is both a warning and an invitation.

David Calzado y la Charanga Habanera

The most talked about band in Havana in the late 1990s, partly because of the controversy surrounding their allegedly obscene act, **la Charanga Habanera** started life in 1988 as a classic charanga, made up of a violin and flute section, with bass, piano and percussion, and playing a traditional charanga repertoire of chachachas and light salsa. It was formed by **David Calzado**, a violinist with a similarly conventional background. Born in 1960, Calzado was from a musical family – his grandfather had been a trovador in Santiago and his father Sergio was a member of the Orquesta Estrellas Cubanas. After graduating in music from the Escuela Nacional de Arte in 1978,

Calzado spent ten years gaining experience of a variety of musical roles. He played with his father's band and with the Orquesta Ritmo Oriental, arranged and produced records for Egrem, before, finally, taking over as first violin of the orchestra of the Tropicana. It was at the Tropicana that he was approached by the French Riviera casino, the Sporting Club of Monaco, who wanted a charanga-style band to play a summer season in the Club's cabaret. Calzado put together a band, which was re-booked annually for the next five years, during which time the Charanga Habanera performed as support for stars such as Whitney Houston, Barry White and Charles Aznavour, and Calzado studied European entertainment and staging.

In 1993, Calzado re-launched the charanga, reducing the violin section and adding brass, acquiring a new repertoire of songs and extravagantly jumpy timba arrangements, dressing the musicians in an assortment of baggy hip-hop streetwear and African sapeur-style couture outfits. Calzado also choreographed their whole act with interludes of breakdancing and demonstrations of rather lewd new steps: the pelota, in particular, had decidedly onanistic over-tones. For all of this, and for their sexually explicit lyrics, Charanga Habanera were feted by the public but also attacked. Calzado defended himself by pointing out that sexual double-entendres had been a part of Cuban popular music since the days of Miguel Matamoros. This did not prevent Calzado's group from being banned from performing or travelling abroad for six months as a result of a particularly outré performance at a youth festival in 1997.

In 2000, following an unsuccessful participation in the Team Cuba French mega-concert, the Charanga Habanera split up. The majority of its members stayed together, renaming themselves **Charanga Forever**, while Calzado kept the name Charanga Habanera and put

together a new, younger group, composed of session musicians and the timbal prodigy Julien Oviedo, aged only 15.

⊙ **Pa'que se entere La Habana**   Magic Music, Spain

A bounding, jangling blast of street timba, containing big hits such as "Super Turistica" and "El Temba", the latter heavily criticized for its theme of elderly tourists and young Cuban sex objects. The sleeve picture, of a 100-dollar bill with Benjamin Franklin transformed into a pirate, was part of the disc's considerable appeal.

Manolito y su Trabuco

One of the timba groups most attached to son and guaracha roots, **Manolito y su Trabuco** are also unusual among 1990s groups in being led by a tres-player, even though tres rarely features in their arrangements. Manuel "Manolito" Simonet was born in Camagüey and took up music as a pastime in his early teens, teaching himself tres by watching one of his uncles, an amateur tresero. He continued with the guitar and bass, finally taking private lessons to add piano to the list. At age 14, he put together his first group, the **Conjunto Safari**, of which members would later join Irakere, the Orquesta Revé and, in two cases, Manolito's grown up hit band Trabuco. Although Manolito studied to be an engineer, his musical sideline eventually took over; he was recruited to the **Orquesta Maravillas de Florida**, which was an old and nationally successful charanga based in the town of Florida, in Camagüey province. Manolito stayed with the Maravillas for five years, graduating to director, during which time he acquired a reputation for innovative arrangements, adapting brass charts for the violin section, and also writing his first successful songs for the band.

In 1993, Manolito created his own band, in enhanced charanga format, mixing a violin and a cello with a flute, two trumpets and two

trombones for richness of sound. Manolito y su Trabuco's appeal relied, in part, on the relative simplicity and earthiness of their presentation as compared to the showiness and virtuosity of some of the timba groups, and they soon began to achieve national success with songs such as "La Parranda" (The Party) and "Caballo Grande" (Big Horse). By 2000, the band was signed to Eurotropical, the biggest Spanish company working in Cuba, and their song "La Boda de Belen" (Belen's Wedding) was one of the biggest hits of the year. At the same time, Manolito's songs were being increasingly taken up by major non-Cuban salsa acts, such as the Puerto Rican star Victor Manuelle, who made his "El Aguila" (The Eagle) into an international hit.

⊙ **Para Que Baile Cuba**   Eurotropical, Spain

Manolito on top form, with "La Boda de Belen", the salsa number about the extravagant barrio wedding party that had half Cuba dancing at the end of the millennium. Unlike the repertoire of almost any other new 1990s star band, the songs are described as guajiras, guaguancó-sones, sones montunos (a dying genre among 1990s dance musicians) and salsas. There's even an old number by Ignacio Piñeiro, as well as two by Van Van's Cesar Pedroso – a major Manolito influence.

Cándido Fabré

One man almost alone kept the traditional charanga in the popular musical sphere in the 1990s. **Cándido Fabré** is a sonero and composer from Manzanillo, the old town at the head of the Cauto valley, the Eastern heartland of country son. Immersed in music since childhood, Fabré began performing in local fiestas at age 13 and by his late teens was a full-time member of a group of Manzanillo entertainers named **El Combo Samurai**, which he left in 1983 to join the **Orquesta Original de Manzanillo**.

The Original, though regional, was a highly respected charanga, composed of top flight musicians, who had evolved a polished sound and repertoire of sones and chachachas which, while traditional, managed to attract a modern audience and obtain national radio and TV work. Fabré became an important member of the group as his gift for son improvisation blossomed – the musicologist Lucy Duran reported that when she visited Manzanillo to research the Original's music, Fabré improvised an entire song from the stage describing every detail of her visit. Linked to this skill was a formidable facility for song-writing – the Original's repertoire began to fill with Fabré's varied compositions – not only of sones but rumbas, boleros, and, unusually in Cuba, merengues. As both the Orquesta's and Fabré's reputations spread, artists outside Cuba began to take up his songs, not always with the intention of paying author's rights, according to Fabré, who on more than one occasion improvised sones on stage demanding to know why a certain US-based singer was using his work without acknowledgement the fact. By the mid-1990s, Fabré reckoned to have written over one thousand songs, and stars of the stature of **Celia Cruz**, **Oscar D'León**, **Willy Chirino** and **José Alberto** were among those who had recorded them.

In 1993, Fabré took the logical step of setting up his own band, **Cándido Fabré y su Banda**, which was a fourteen piece charanga in the mould of the Original. Signed to the UK label Tumi, the band took advantage of the world interest in Cuban music to tour internationally and release three successful albums outside Cuba.

⊙ La Habana Quiere Guarachar Contigo   Tumi, UK

Another batch of songs by the one-man Tin Pan Alley, mostly dedicated to the subject of dancing, like the title track which name-checks all the top rival bandleaders from Paulito to David Calzado, and throws in a tongue-in-cheek homily on the practice of speculation (presumably financial) to boot. The band swings furiously, the maestro's voice is in good shape and, by track 4, a bouncy little

number with the hint of soca or merengue that often lurks within Fabré's music, he's convinced us of mass dancing having broken out in the streets of Liverpool at the instigation of his charanga.

Giraldo Piloto y Klimax

Another member of a musical dynasty, **Giraldo Piloto Barretto** is the son of the Giraldo Piloto who formed one half of the immensely influential song-writing team **Piloto y Vera** in the 1950s. The young Piloto's uncle was **Guillermo Barretto**, the eminent percussionist who founded Los Amigos, the group which turned into the seminal Orquesta Cubana de Música Moderna, and his aunt was Barretto's wife, the Afro-Cuban singing star **Celeste Mendoza**.

Giraldo Piloto graduated in composition, arrangement and percussion from the Escuela Nacional de Arte in 1980 and started his professional career as a percussionist in the orchestra of the Tropicana. In 1988 he was a founder-member of **NG La Banda**, where he played a major role, not only as percussionist but also as songwriter and arranger. Piloto was regarded as the chief creative force behind NG La Banda's seminal 1990 album **En La Calle**, and thus was one of the original architects of timba. In 1992 he left NG to set up **Issac Delgado**'s new band and to be the sound designer on Delgado's 1994 album **Con Ganas**.

The following year, Piloto decided the time was ripe for the creation of his own band, and **Klimax** was born. A thirteen piece, with a piano as well as keyboards and a brass section of two trumpets, tenor saxophone and trombone, Klimax mainly plays Piloto's own compositions (mostly love songs with a tough sexy modern approach) in a style which develops a song from a simple romantic opening through progressively complex arrangements and jazz harmonies into an all-guns-blazing timba finale. Klimax's debut album, **Mira Si Te Gusta**, on the veteran Canarian label Manzana, was an immediate success, and their

second, **Juego de Manos**, sold over 100,000 copies in Europe, making the group one of the top selling timba acts outside Cuba.

⊙ Mira Si Te Gusta   Eurotropical, Spain

A classic of timba with the title track – a story of murky barrio desires – comprising a virtual checklist of mid-1990s Havana musical components. Rapped out against a fast chanted chorus, a clatter of percussion, harsh angular horn passages, jazzy keyboard chords, and a bass which rapidly abandons any initial resemblance to a classic salsa tumbao, the song ends on an exhortation to get down and dance.

Vocal Sampling

"Six Cuban Bobby McFerrins", as they have been described, the members of the a cappella group **Vocal Sampling** created the most unusual music of Cuba in the 1990s. Their act consists of simulating the sound of an entire band, percussion and all, with their voices, cupped hands and inflated cheeks. Certainly influenced by the singing of McFerrin, and by the virtuoso Cuban doo-wop of **Los Zafiros**, the sextet spent much of the decade travelling the globe, attracting everywhere the same press comment, that it was impossible to believe they didn't have a hidden instrumental tape providing part of their sound, so realistic were their instrument impressions. While this was exaggeration in the case of their brass simulations, the human bass and percussion effects were remarkable, and the overall musical quality very high.

The original members of Vocal Sampling were all students at the Escuela Nacional de Arte in Havana in the 1980s. An informal group began to coalesce around a composition student, **René Baños**, whose preferred listening – American crooners of the Sinatra school and doo-wop – was merged with Cuban classics and gospel into a

CRISTINA PIZA

Vocal Sampling

deconstructed and painstakingly reassembled vocal repertoire practised in after-classes get-togethers. In 1990, the director of a Belgian
music festival, on a percussion research trip to Havana, heard them
by chance, became their manager and arranged their first visit to
Europe, where they were contracted by the WOMAD Festival organizers. In 1993 they recorded an album in Germany which was taken up
by the major US label Sire and released in 1995. The same year Vocal
Sampling's US concert debut occurred, as a result of a mass petition
of the State Department, who had initially denied the group visas, by
the members of the Contemporary A Cappella Society of America.

Following the US tour, Vocal Sampling re-formed, hiring new members with classical vocal training, and incorporating more new num-

bers, including songs written by René Baños, into their repertoire. The original members, Baños and **Abel Sanabria**, the "percussion" expert, remained, joined by Oscar Porro, who specializes in the bass parts, and **Reinaldo Sanler**, **Jorge Nuñez** and **Renato Mora**, who share a range of instruments, bird-calls, train sounds and much else between them.

⊙ **Live in Berlin**   Ashé, US

The Vocal Sampling show as of 1998, recorded by German radio at the Heimatklänge Festival in Berlin. Four songs by René Baños, whose voice strongly resembles Willy Chirino's, plus a selection of classics. These include "El Tren", by Rafael Cueto, complete with sirens, hissing steam and wheels bumping on rails, "La Negra Tomasa", and one of the finest versions of Silvio Rodríguez' "Fabula De Los Tres Hermanos", rendered in lovely six-part harmony.

Jóvenes Clásicos del Son

A 1990s equivalent of the son revivalists Sierra Maestra, the **Jóvenes Clásicos del Son** (Classic Young Soneros) were founded in 1994 and three years later nominated Best Cuban Group of the Year in Egrem's annual prize distribution. Their founder and director is **Ernesto Reyes Proenza**, a double-bass player and former member of the band of Cándido Fabré, the foremost repository of modern son excellence in the 1980s and 1990s. Reyes wanted a smaller, more mobile group than Fabré's with which to evolve a classic son-based repertoire capable of integrating discreet advances in harmony and instrumentation. He opted for a traditional septet format, with bass, guitar, tres, trumpet, congas, bongos and maracas.

The first member to join Reyes was **Sergio Pereda Rodríguez**, an engineering graduate and percussionist with a decade of musical experience, first touring the old Soviet empire in a group called

Muralla, then as bass voice in the a cappella group **Vocal Sampling**. With Pereda on board as bongo-player and second lead vocalist, the Jóvenes Clásicos next acquired their lead singer, a young Havanero named **Pedro Lugo**, whose mellow, supple voice had been trained by informal rumba gatherings and membership of the Conjunto of the late Felix Chappotín. The percussion roles were filled with the arrival of **Juan Manuel Hernández "Lolo"**, a conga player chosen for steadiness rather than virtuosity, since, in Ernesto Reyes' opinion, too much contemporary timba percussion was hyperactive and undisciplined. Three Santiago musicians completed the line-up: **Carlos Manuel Céspedes**, a guitarist with a background in nueva trova, **César Hechavarría**, a self-taught tres player who had played occasionally with the Cuarteto Patria after leaving the army, and **Raudel Marzal**, a trumpeter trained at art school with experience of two Santiago roots son groups, the **Septeto Turquino** and the **Sonora La Calle**.

⊙ Fruta Bomba   Tumi, UK

In 1997, the Jóvenes Clásicos released their first international album on the British Tumi label. A fresh, lucid reappraisal of traditional son for palates jaded with timba, full of the soft tones of acoustic bass and the metallic ones of the tres, plus some savoury

singing. Cándido Fabré contributes two songs, including the lovely old-fashioned minor key "Ya se durmió la guitarra", and there's a nice Compadres-style duet on "La Flor y La Hoja Seca", and more modern song-writing gets a look-in with a number by David Alvarez, the rising young trova-pop composer.

Orlando "Maraca" Valle

While certain Irakere graduates went on to found timba in the 1990s, others carried the flame for Cuban jazz. One of the most successful of the latter was **Orlando "Maraca" Valle**, Cuba's best contemporary flautist. Valle was born in Havana in 1966, one of five brothers who all went into music. The eldest, **Moisés**, (known as Yumurí), who became a popular singer, relates that their father tried to dissuade almost all of them from choosing dance music as a career. In the case of Orlando, however, who wanted to be a baseball player, the parental persuasion was in favour of music.

Valle studied music theory at the Instituto Superior de Arte and also received tuition from **Rafael Carrusco**, Gonzalo Rubalcaba's flautist, and **Raul Valdés**, a flautist with the National Symphony Orchestra. He began work in the band of **Bobby Carcassés**, the well-known jazz singer and multi-instrumentalist, with whom he visited Panama in 1987, and then joined **Emiliano Salvador**, the short-lived pianist posthumously recognised as one of the great names of Cuban jazz. When Valle later formed his group, **Otra Visión**, its name was in part an homage to Salvador's Nueva Visión, as the pianist was a major influence.

In 1988, Valle was hired by **Irakere** to replace **José Luis Cortés**, who had left to form NG La Banda. After six years with the most prestigious band in Cuban jazz, the young flautist branched out on his own, and soon became one of the most internationally active of

Cuban musicians. His first notable recording project was a descarga album named **Pasaporte**, with the star conga-players, **Tata Güines** and **Miguel "Angá Díaz"**, followed by his own first solo album, **Formula Uno**, with guests including Chucho Valdés and Richard Egües. In 1996 he formed his group, Otra Visión, the alternative vision being that of a modern Cuban music incorporating all the old genres, that was different from the uniformity of timba. A series of intelligently planned and well-received albums followed: **Formula Uno** and **Havana Calling** employed numerous past and present members of Irakere; **Sonando** used a highly eclectic cast of guests including Compay Segundo, Pio Leyva, Barbarito Torres and the Muñequitos de Matanzas.

In addition to running his own group, Valle undertook a number of high-profile freelance jobs, forming part of Jesús Alemañy's **Cubanismo** band for two international tours, producing and directing the recording in Havana of several tracks for the Cabo Verdean singer Cesaria Evora's album **Café Atlantico**, as well as guesting on records by Frank Emilio Flyn and Orlando Poleo. In the latter part of the 1990s, he based himself in Paris, where he had married a French flautist Céline Chauveau, a former student of his, who joined Otra Visión as second flautist, producer and manager.

⊙ **Descarga Total!**   Warner Jazz, UK

Released in 2000, Descarga Total fizzes with energy and class, and very little pure jazz. Maraca is still in updating-the-classics mode, but this is far from a cruise through the oldies on automatic pilot. The already excellent band is augmented by star guests including the timbalero Changuito, tresero Pancho Amat, brother Yumurí on vocals and string sections of the Tropicana and National Symphony Orchestra. The material is varied and beautifully chosen, from the opening high energy descarga and a superb modern danzón to "La Pelea", one of the few wholly

successful incorporations of rap into son, and "Pa Gozar Pilón", a dance-floor killer and possibly the best version of the pilón rhythm on record.

Buena Vista Social Club

One of the greatest successes of the century in Cuban music, **Buena Vista Social Club** is a remarkable record, performed by a group only temporarily together, named after a tune of uncertain authorship dedicated to an institution which no longer exists. The social club was once exactly that, based in a turn of the century villa in the residential suburb of Buena Vista in Havana, and used for dances and other events. In a scene from Wim Wenders' Buena Vista film documentary, the 89-year-old trovador **Compay Segundo** is pictured in his check jacket and Panama hat, sitting in the back of a 1950s American convertible searching for the Club, and being informed by neighbours that the place had long gone.

The title was chosen by **Nick Gold**, proprietor of the record company World Circuit, who was one of the three prime movers behind the 1997 record. The second was **Ry Cooder**, the American guitarist. Cooder's previous experience of Latin music included considerable work with Tex-Mex musicians in the 1970s, and an interest in Cuban music nurtured by listening to tapes supplied by friends such as Chris Strachwitz, the founder of Arhoolie Records, in the 1960s. The guitarist had visited Cuba twice before: once as part of the 1977 "jazz cruise" with Dizzy Gillespie et al, and a second time in 1996, shortly before the Buena Vista recordings, when he'd guested on the Chieftains' **Santiago** album with the Galician bagpipe player Carlos Nuñez. The final Buena Vista organizer was A&R consultant **Juan de Marcos González**, the former tres player of the group Sierra Maestra, who brought in the cast of musicians and singers.

Although 20 artists took part in the recording of the album, including Cooder and his son Joachim, whom his father inserted as an
additional percussionist, a nucleus of half a dozen achieved personal
fame as a result. Foremost among these were the singers **Ibrahim**

Ibrahim Ferrer (left) and Rubén González (right) with Nick Gold

Ferrer and **Omara Portuondo,** and the singer-guitarists **Compay Segundo** and **Eliades Ochoa** (all of whose biographies feature on other pages). In addition, two other musicians, both established top professionals in Cuba, added a major new international dimension to their careers. These were the bassist **Orlando "Cachaíto" López** and the trumpeter **Manuel "Guajiro" Mirabál.**

Cachaíto López is the son of Orestes López, joint inventor of the mambo and nephew of Orestes' brother, Israel "Cachao". Born in 1933, he entered the music profession in his teens and spent almost half a century in important popular bands including Arcaño's Maravillas, the Orquesta Riverside, the Charanga Rubalcaba and the Orquesta Cubana de Música Moderna, while also playing in the National Symphony Orchestra, teaching in the Guillermo Tomás conservatory and serving on the Ministry of Culture's evaluation committee for popular orchestras. Following his roles in Buena Vista Social Club and the allied Afro-Cuban All Stars album, Cachaíto became a key member of the touring bands of Ibrahim Ferrer and Omara Portuondo. In 2001 his own album of descargas was part of the third wave of Buena Vista releases.

Luis Manuel Mirabál Vázquez, better known as **"Guajiro Mirabál"**, was born in 1933, the son of the director of the municipal band of the town of Melena del Sur in Havana province. From the age of 18, he too pursued an intensely active musical career, playing in the Conjunto Rumbavana, the Orquesta Cubana de Música Moderna and for long periods in the orquesta of the Tropicana cabaret, under the directorship of Armando Romeu and latterly of Demetrio Muñiz, the multifaceted trombonist, arranger and producer who also joined the cast of the Buena Vista Social Club for subsequent ventures. Mirabal is also a teacher, and, away from popular music, a member of both the National Revolutionary Militia's ceremonial squad and the General Staff band of the Cuban Army. In this capacity, too, he is no

CRISTINA PIZA

"Guajiro" Mirabál

stranger to important audiences, having played for the welcome ceremonies of numerous visiting Heads of State.

The Buena Vista Social Club, strictly speaking, only existed for the duration of one record, although the phrase "Buena Vista Social Club presents" prefaced certain albums by individual Buena Vista stars which followed the huge success of the album (it sold over 4 million copies). Although the record passed almost unnoticed in much of Cuba, and only achieved Cuban release four years after the rest of the world, its stars eventually received the ultimate accolade, a meeting with Fidel Castro following a concert in honour of the Head of State's birthday in 2000.

⊙ **Buena Vista Social Club**   World Circuit, UK

The recording sessions went like a dream, apparently, with the musicians hitting it off instantly, jamming together and swapping ideas for songs to include. The 14 tracks have the relaxed spontaneity of old friends running through a bunch of favourite standards – Sindo Garay's "La Bayamesa", Guillermo Portabales' "El Carretero", Maria Teresa Vera's "Veinte Años". "Chan Chan", the song which made Compay Segundo virtually a household name in parts of the world, kicks off proceedings, and Cooder's presence seems to have crystallized an interesting side investigation on "Amor de Loca Juventud" and "Orgullecido", both numbers in which Compay Segundo gets to demonstrate the "influencia americana" – early jazz and music hall – which extended to Cuban music in the early decades of the century.

Juan de Marcos González & The Afro-Cuban All Stars

Juan de Marcos González was born in Havana in 1954 into an Afro-Cuban musical family. His father was a singer and a member of the

abakuá society Ireme Ita Ipo, and de Marcos grew up imbued with abakuá music, rumba and British and American rock. It was not until 1978, by which time he had graduated as a hydraulic engineer and started building dams, that de Marcos turned to music seriously. For years increasingly interested in traditional son, he set up the influential son revivalist band **Sierra Maestra** (see p.263) with which he worked for over fifteen years.

In 1994, when Sierra Maestra signed to the World Circuit label, de Marcos began the association which led to the creation of the Buena Vista Social Club project. The first of the three albums recorded in the 1996 session which gave birth to the Buena Vista album was de Marcos' own pet project, the assembling of a big band of some of the great names of the past to make a sophisticated new recording of the repertoire of the 1940s and 1950s. The personnel of the first **Afro-Cuban All Stars** record overlapped that of Buena Vista – the two dozen players and singers included **Ibrahim Ferrer**, **Rubén González**, **Cachaíto López**, **Guajiro Mirabál** and the laúd player **Barbarito Torres**. Other important instrumentalists included Demetrio Muñiz on trombone, the trumpeter Luis Alemañy, uncle of de Marcos' old Sierra Maestra partner Jesús Alemañy, and Miguel "Angá" Díaz on congas. In addition to Ferrer, lead vocals featured three important old singers and one younger sonero. **Pío Leyva**, born in 1917, was a gravel-voiced fun-loving son montuno expert who had worked through the 1950s in all the top Havana cabarets with bands from the Orquesta Riverside to the Conjunto Caney, and written songs such as "Francisco Guayabal", made famous by Beny Moré. **Raúl Planas**, born in 1933, had sung during the same period with the Sonora Matancera, partnering Celia Cruz and the Conjunto Rumbavana. **Manuel Licea**, known as "Puntillito", had been the most individually famous of all the Buena Vista singers with the

Juan de Marcos González and Pío Leyva

exception of Omara Portuondo. Born in 1927, he had emerged from a period with the orchestra of Julio Cuevas and the Sonora Matancera, a star of TV and cabaret, and retired in the early 1980s. The last of the Afro-Cuban All Stars singers was **Felix Baloy**, a powerful roots sonero, born in 1944, who had built a solid reputation over twenty years work in the bands of Elio Revé and Adalberto Alvarez, amongst others.

The success of the **Afro-Cuban All Stars** CD led to a series of world tours for Juan de Marcos and the band, and to a sequel, **Distinto, Diferente**, released in 1999. This time the cast list was

extended: over 50 artists took part, including important new names such as **Maraca Valle** on flute, **Guillermo Rubalcaba** and **Frank Emilio Flyn** on piano, **Angel Terry** – who led the Tropicana Afro-Cuban percussion ensemble on an abakuá ritual drum tribute to de Marcos' father – the bolero star **Lino Borges**, and Los Van Van's **Pedrito Calvo**. The new album aimed to bring the repertoire more up-to-date, with a timba arrangement admitted among a number of new songs, several written by de Marcos.

The success of his Buena Vista and Afro-Cuban All Stars projects transformed de Marcos from merely a successful group leader to a major figure in the Cuban music establishment. Moving to a new house near the beaches east of Havana, he set up a small home studio and his own production company, Ahora. One of its first productions was the debut album **Baila Mi Son** by Félix Baloy, which was released on the Tumi label in 2000.

⊙ **A Toda Cuba le Gusta**   World Circuit, UK

The better of the two All Stars albums, this first volume opens strongly with Cachaíto's rock solid bass, a powerful laúd figure, and a majestic blast of brass arranged by Demetrio Muñiz ushering in Puntillito's supple voice. The rest of the ten sones,

guaguancós and guarachas are meticulously arranged, played (and annotated in the usual World Circuit manner) and de Marcos also includes rarities such as the mozambique "María Caracoles", sung for the first time since his 1960s pilón and mozambique heyday by Ibrahim Ferrer.

Ibrahim Ferrer

Ibrahim Ferrer was plucked from impoverished retirement for the **Buena Vista Social Club** recordings when Ry Cooder asked for a "soft-voiced singer" and Juan de Marcos González thought of the old vocalist from the Pacho Alonso's Bocucos who had performed for the first time for several years the previous summer at Havana's Carnival. As a result of the Buena Vista gig, Ferrer achieved the greatest level of fame he had ever experienced in his 80s, and released his first solo album to international acclaim.

Ferrer was born in 1927 in the town of San Luis, near Santiago, at a social club dance (so he insists). His mother died when he was twelve, and he worked as a street vendor, and later as a carpenter and a docker, to support himself. At the age of eighteen he began to sing in a cousin's amateur band, **Los Jóvenes del Son**, and then a succession of other small groups until he was hired in 1955 by the **Orquesta Chepín-Chovén**. This was an important group, founded by a violinist and bandleader Electo Rosell (nicknamed Chepín) and pianist Bernardo García Chovén. Starting as a quartet, the group had grown by the mid-1950s to a skilled and popular fifteen-piece band, based in Santiago but appearing throughout the country, as well as on national radio. Ibrahim Ferrer was the Chepín-Chovén orquesta's singer at their peak of popularity and became identified with Chepín's song "El Platanal de Bartolo", one of their greatest hits.

In 1961, Ferrer moved to Havana and joined a group he had already sung in years earlier, **Los Bocucos**, led by Pacho Alonso (see p.237). During the 1960s zenith of the Bocucos, he was the singer responsible for their boisterous carnival repertoire, in particular the pilones and mozambiques – the Afro-percussion dance crazes of that period. In the 1980s, he worked less and less and by 1996 was retired, living with numerous grandchildren in a narrow little flat in the Cayo Hueso district, on a State pension augmented from time to time by jobs including shoe cleaning.

Ferrer's role in the Buena Vista Social Club recording, and on tour subsequently, was one of the most remarked upon, and his duet with the misty-eyed **Omara Portuondo** was a key scene of Wim Wenders' film. Ry Cooder produced his debut album, released in 1999, with a large orchestra of suitably eminent musicians, conducted and arranged jointly by **Juan de Marcos González**,

CRISTINA PIZA

Ibrahim Ferrer, a star at 80

Demetrio Muñiz and the octogenarian **Genero Jiménez**, once arranger for Beny Moré.

⊙ **Buena Vista Social Club presents Ibrahim Ferrer**   World Circuit, UK

Having waited 60 years to record his first solo album, Ferrer certainly wasn't stinted on facilities. The full string and brass sections of the Tropicana provide swathes of background for lush boleros such as "Herido de Sombres" and "Silencio", Omara Portuondo and Teresa Garcia Caturla are the duetting partners, and Manuel Galván, former Zafiros guitarist, brings some authentic 1960s electric twang to the two Zafiros ballads included. Not only Ferrer's first record, but his first appearance as a romantic singer after a career devoted almost exclusively to keeping dancers on the move.

Rubén González

Like Ibrahim Ferrer, **Rubén González** was a surprise beneficiary of the Buena Vista Social Club recordings, in that there was no plan to promote him as a solo artist. González, who had been retired for years, was brought in at the suggestion of Ry Cooder, who had heard his playing on old records. The pianist was delighted, mainly to get his hands on an instrument, as his own, an American-made combined piano and pianola that his parents had bought in the 1920s, had finally been devoured by termites during the preceding decade. Put in front of a piano, González' arthritis disappeared and he played unstoppably, arriving every day at the studio before it opened and sitting down to play the moment it did. Once the decision was made to record a solo album, it was done in two days. Within a year, González was touring the concert halls of the world, while a chorus of international jazz critics rivalled each other in superlatives.

Prior to this, González had never been a well-known figure in his own right, and had only recorded one solo album in his long career. He was, however, a distinguished instrumentalist. He was born just outside the town of Santa Clara in 1919 and studied piano as a child at the conservatory of the nearby city of Cienfuegos. Evidently he was keen even then and, despite the handicap of living so far away that he could only visit Cienfuegos once a month, he easily outstripped his fellow students.

González began to study medicine, but after several years abandoned it for music, playing first with Cienfuegos groups and then,

moving to Havana in 1941, to play with nationally known bands such as the orquesta of Paulino Alvarez, the Hermanos Castro, house band of Radio Progreso, the orquestas Siboney and Riverside, and the conjunto of Senén Suárez for a residency at the Tropicana. In 1943 he was the pianist for a time for **Arsenio Rodríguez**, preceding "Lilí" Martínez, Arsenio's most famous pianist. With these bands, González covered virtually the whole repertoire of Cuban popular music, from foxtrots, waltzes and danzones to the deep conjunto son of Arsenio Rodríguez. In the early 1960s he joined the band of Enrique Jorrín, creator of the chachacha, shortly after the genre's actual invention, and remained with the Jorrín band for the rest of his career, taking

over the directorship at one point, which he didn't like. His last notable recording projects before Buena Vista were the sessions for the **Estrellas de Areita** (see p.260).

⊙ **Chanchullo** World Circuit, UK

The sequel to González' sensational debut, Chanchullo relies on the same basic commodity, namely González' extremely fluid and elegant playing, wheeling and pirouetting around the traditional chord structures of the songs but never abandoning them. From the deliberate showmanship of the first track, it is clear that González is revelling in his new acclaim. There's an expanded version of the line-up on the first record, but slightly more adventurous material. Whereas the first album comprised almost exclusively the most standard of standards, Chanchullo branches out into interesting directions such as the terrific "Choco's Guajira", a sombre and exciting son montuno featuring a superb tres solo from Papi Oviedo.

Papi Oviedo

The latest generation of an important Cuban tres family, **Gilberto Oviedo La Portilla** was no spring chicken by the time he embarked on a solo career, whence his nickname **Papi** (or Papy), a sort of equivalent of the American "Pops". He was born in 1937 and worked for a variety of other bandleaders into his 50s. Papi's papi, **Isaac Oviedo**, a well-known tres player, was born in 1902, and left his native Matanzas to settle in the capital in 1926. The younger Oviedo started his musical life as a percussionist, playing conga drums to accompany his father at country fiestas throughout the province. Throughout this period, Isaac Oviedo supported his family by working night shifts in a hospital, while his son sold sweets and cleaned shoes to bring in extra cash.

YOURI LENQUETTE

Isaac Oviedo went on to lead two notable bands, the **Septeto Matancero**, while still in Matanzas, and the **Quinteto Típico**, led by Graciano Gómez, with whom he played throughout Cuba, Puerto Rico and the US. He also became a successful songwriter, noted for son montunos such as "Engancha Carretero".

By his mid teens, the younger Oviedo had also changed to tres, learning from his

Papi Oviedo and his tres

father and eventually acquiring an instrument as a present from his mother. He began to play in local groups, then graduated to the band of the nationally known bolero singer Orlando Contreras. Throughout the 1950s and 60s he was variously tresero in the **Conjunto Típico Habanero** of Manuel Furé, the band of Enrique Pérez, another bolero specialist, and the conjunto of **Chapottín Junior**, the group led by the son of the famous trumpeter Félix Chapottín.

In 1980 Papi Oviedo was hired by the bandleader **Elio Revé**, then reforming the band which was about to bring him his greatest Cuban

fame. Oviedo became a rare example of a tres player in a charanga-format band, and a key ingredient in the vital, Afro-steeped changüí sound of the **Revé Orquesta**. In 1995, Oviedo left Revé to form his own band, with which he released his first solo album, **Encuentro entre Soneros** (Meeting of Soneros) the following year. Oviedo's Soneros turned out to be a tight and rootsy conjunto with a deep, dark acoustic bass, bongo, congas and a pair of trumpets providing sparse but effective support for the homely vocals of **Cristina Azcuy**, a young Celia Cruz lookalike, **Osvaldo Montalvo**, a guajira specialist, and **Miguel Martínez**, an excellent young sonero. By the end of the 1990s, his international career also included membership of the touring band of **Omara Portuondo**, by now a world star, and collaboration with the Congolese singer and guitarist **Papa Noel** on an Afro-Cuban fusion project.

⊙ **Encuentro Entre Soneros**   Tumi, UK

The mix is held together with unobtrusive power by the metallic tones of Oviedo's tres which, unlike the highly ornate playing of treseros of the school of Pancho Amat, relies much on simplicity, space and rhythmic intensity. A pair of sones by Isaac Oviedo are included, as well as a version of the Compay Segundo chestnut "Chan Chan".

Jesús Alemañy and Cubanismo

The second member of the 1970s son revival group **Sierra Maestra** to emerge as a leading force in the internationalization of Cuban music two decades later was **Jesús Alemañy** who followed a similar path to his colleague **Juan de Marcos González**. Born in 1952 in Guanabacoa, the old Afro-Cuban satellite town to the east of Havana, he studied trumpet at the local Guillermo Tomás music school and was recruited to Sierra Maestra in 1978 shortly after the

group's formation. With the other members, he began to undertake research into roots son which involved tracking down and learning from the old Septeto Nacional members: thus Alemañy found himself taking tuition from **Lázaro Herrera**, "El Pecoso", the original Septeto Nacional trumpeter, and on occasions sitting in with the Septeto.

Throughout the 1980s and early 1990s, Alemañy played and travelled with Sierra Maestra, honing his solo skills as the only brass player in the band. He also played in the Tropicana orchestra, of which his uncle Luis Alemañy, and later his cousin Luis Alemañy Jr, were members, and intermittently with **Gonzalo Rubalcaba**'s new group **Proyecto**. By the early 1990s, he had acquired all-round expertise, mastering the piercingly high registers beloved of Cuban trumpeters and becoming equally at home as an improviser or a melodic lead trumpeter – two roles which rarely mix.

In 1994, Alemañy married the UK musicologist and broadcaster **Lucy Duran** and moved to London, where he worked with locally-based Latin musicians such as the Colombian timbalero **Roberto Pla**. In 1996, supported by the UK-based record company Hannibal, he returned to Havana to record an album which had as its aim a similar idea to that pursued by Juan de Marcos González with the Afro-Cuban All Stars – that is, to re-create the classic styles and repertoire of the 1940s and 1950s with modern recording techniques and state-of-the-art playing. Alemañy's principal collaborator was the pianist **Alfredo Rodríguez**, a veteran of classic Cuban bands such as the Sonora Matancera who had emigrated to the US in 1960, worked with the greats of US salsa and relocated to Paris in 1983, since when he'd been a central figure of the European Latin music scene.

Composed of skilled Havana session musicians, some of whom were, or soon would be, important figures in their own right – Tata

Güines, "Angá" Díaz and "Maraca" Valle – the recording band was christened **Cubanismo** by Joe Boyd, the head of Hannibal, who felt the name was clear and memorable for the non-Latin listeners he saw as the potential market. Largely instrumental, and packed with rhythm and forceful brass solo-ing, Cubanismo's debut record did indeed appeal to the world music market, selling 100,000 copies in the US alone. Two follow-ups, **Malembe** and **Re-encarnación**, also sold well.

Cubanismo soon began to tour with equal success. Their first live concert took place in 1997 in New Orleans and they were in the forefront of the wave of Cuban nationals touring the long-off-limits US. By intelligently interspersing their concerts with public workshops, school demonstrations and lectures and thus amply fulfilling the "cultural exchange" criteria of US visa legislation, they succeeded in spending almost half of 1999 on a multicity tour throughout

the country. They also obtained official sponsorship from New Orleans City Hall for the recording of their album, **Mardi Gras Mambo**, a collaboration between Cubanismo and New Orleans

musicians which triumphantly re-examined the old connections between the Crescent City and Havana in a modern context.

⊙ **Malembe**   Hannibal, UK

Cubanismo's second album exhibits the same mix as its debut: high intensity descargas, based on sones and guaguancós, but also disinterred 1960s dance rhythms, including the pilón. Maraca Valle again has a major wind role, as does uncle Luis, Yosvany Terry on saxophones and Guajiro Mirabál, but dominating proceedings are the commanding, crystal-shattering tones of Alemañy himself.

⊙ **Mardi Gras Mambo**   Hannibal, UK

Cubanismo's masterpiece to date, a wholly successful combination of Cuban big band son and mambo with New Orleans soul and rock, harking back to the days when the two cities were close culturally and in transport links. An inspired choice of songs, beautifully conceived arrangements and some excellent US performers, in particular the wonderfully high but husky-voiced John Boutté, make this among the best fusion records ever made.

Pancho Amat

Along with Juan de Marcos González of Afro-Cuban All Stars fame, and Papi Oviedo, **Francisco "Pancho" Amat** was a member of the most influential trio of tres players of the 1990s. Born in 1950 in Güira de Melena, a country town near Havana, he came from a poor family – his father was a street charcoal seller – and embarked originally on a career as a teacher, studying mathematics and education, but at the same time taking classical guitar lessons at the Ignacio Cervantes conservatory.

As a student in the late 1960s Pancho Amat became involved in the nueva trova movement, then at its peak, and the linked vogue for

Andean music – a major influence on nueva trovadores. After a visit to Chile, he took up the charango, the little Andean armadillo-bodied guitar, and in 1971 joined **Grupo Manguaré**, the newly formed political/new song/pan-Latin folk group, with which he performed for a dozen years, touring extensively in Latin America and Europe. It was Martin Rojas, the nueva trova stalwart, who suggested he diversify from charango to tres, which Amat did with such dedication and energy that he rapidly became a sought-after virtuoso tresero. Amat's classical background, and the cultural prestige accorded to nueva trova practitioners as opposed to soneros, enabled him to invest the tres with something of the cachet of a concert instrument, on a par with the classical or jazz guitar. By the mid 1990s, Amat had worked with dozens of major Cuban artists and institutions, including the National Symphony Orchestra, the Conjunto Folklorico Nacional, the guitarist Leo Brouwer, Pablo Milanés and Silvio Rodríguez, Richard Egües and other members of the Orquesta Aragón.

In 1995 he released his first solo album, **Son Por Tres**, while his career took on a greater international dimension, including tours as part of **Cubanismo**, work with The Chieftains and **Ry Cooder**, and close co-operation with the new Spanish re-discoverers of Cuban music, notably Joaquín Sabina and the rock star Santiago Auserón (aka Juan Perro).

⊙ **De San Antonio a Maisí**   Resistencia, Spain

A lavish solo album by Amat, accompanied by a new group dubbed El Cabildo Del Son, released in 2000. Top quality production, excellent booklet with the complete lyrics of every song, among them an interesting rarity, a 1932 son by Miguel Matamoros about a certain cocaine-loving Celina, "a lascivious and sensual woman of Bacchus". The traditional septet line-up (with a list of star guests, including Santiago Auserón and Silvio Rodríguez) help to showcase Amat's highly ornamental tres playing which is full of

expert trills and runs. It's a style reminiscent of the violao guitar found in Portuguese fado, and quite distinct, for example, from Papi Oviedo's playing.

Orishas

The first Cuban rap act to make serious inroads into mainstream showbusiness did so in Paris, appropriately enough, as France is not only the biggest producer and consumer of rap outside the US, but also the home of a distinctively melodic style not entirely derived from the American model. Two elements came together in Paris to form the group: a pair of home-grown Havana rappers and a trio of Paris Cubans who had been working in various musical modes for several years. The Habaneros were **Yothuel** and **Ruzzo**, two members of **Amenaza**, one of the leading groups in the first wave of Cuban rap. In 1998, helped by an exchange programme sponsored by the Cuban cultural organization **Hermanos Saenz**, Yothuel and Ruzzo arrived in Paris (the third member of the trio made his way to Norway). There they began to look for hip-hop scenes they could connect with, and soon made their way to the club night featuring the **DJ Niko**, a young Cuban active in the Paris hip-hop milieu for some years, where they were invited to guest.

Niko, Ruzzo and Yothuel were then contacted by another Paris-based Cuban, **Livan**, a DJ who had worked in the Paris independent *Radio Nova* since arriving in 1995 and then run Latin nights at the "dancing" below La Coupole brasserie. In 1999 he had participated in the Franco-Cuban tropical dance album by the act known as **Sergent Garcia**, which had included a rap number entitled "Afrocuban Orishas Underground". The final member of the group which became **Orishas** arrived with **Roldán**, a classically trained singer and guitarist who had studied music at Havana University, and

worked as a music teacher for six years, playing in the evenings in hotels in a traditional son group named Ricoson. Aware that the future was extremely limited, he came to Paris, where he joined a similar group to his Cuban band, this time called Sabor de Son, playing among other places at Livan's Coupole Latin nights.

A demo cassette produced by Orishas persuaded EMI to back the group, and in 1999 they returned to Havana to record samples of santería music and other material. Back in Paris, a number of professionals were brought in: **Angá Diaz**, who was based in Paris, added congas

and other percussion, while French session players provided strings, piano and touches of brass. With Niko's programming and the Colombian producer Mario Rodríguez putting together the final mix, the album **A Lo Cubano** came into existence. Its intelligence, funkiness and musicality immediately attracted attention from European media and public, and within a year the album was selling internationally, and being circulated on copied cassettes in Cuba. In autumn 2000, a live version of Orishas, with turntables, Afro-Cuban percussion and three rappers, accompanied by a recorded backing, began touring, reaching Havana in December.

⊙ **A Lo Cubano**   EMI Chrysalis, UK

Ironically for a rap record, the undoubted success of this debut album stems, to a large extent, from its melodiousness and its slow paced but intense sense of rhythm. Like Compay Segundo's "Chan Chan", which Orishas sample into their new adaptation "537 CUBA", virtually all the tunes are winners, due either to the very effective singing of Roldán, or to a range of atmospheric keyboard riffs, which lurk memorably behind even rap sequences. Sounds of Havana, a babalawo (santería priest) adapting his prayer obligingly to a rhythm track, and much else drift through the mix, the boys rant mellowly on about barrio life, and the general effect is mesmerizing and a sophisticated antidote to the empty flash of much timba.

Carlos Manuel

The first new princeling of Havana nightlife to make a bid for international recording success in the new millennium, **Carlos Manuel** was born in 1974 in the capital and acquired his earliest musical influence from his parents' amateur activities – his father played guitar and his mother sang in a choir. With his parents he listened, above all, to romantic music on the radio: the programme *Nocturno* in particular provided him with a foundation in the boleros and ballads he later drew upon for his repertoire. In his late teens he began to listen to Silvio Rodríguez and Pablo Milanés and took his initial steps as a professional singer with the nueva trova group **Mayohuacán**, with whom he experienced his first taste of mass public approval, when the group's version of the Pedro Luís Ferrer song "Carapacho pa' la Jicotea" became a major hit. In 1996, he was approached by the top Colombian salsa band Guayacán with an offer of a lead singing role, but at the last minute he signed instead to **Irakere**, with whom he spent a year touring internationally with a season at Ronnie Scott's in London and shows at the Playboy Festival in Hollywood.

PALM PICTURES

Manuel used his time with Irakere to save money and acquire instruments – a second-hand Roland synthesiser, an electronic keyboard – and by the late 1990s was putting together a band with former friends from student days. The group, **Carlos Manuel y su Clan**, soon forged a reputation in the Havana clubs, obtaining a Friday residency at the Café Cantante and a Sunday gig at the Havana Café. In October 2000, their recording of "Malo Cantidad" (Real Bad) a jaunty if dated ragga-timba hybrid – with that key attribute of a Cuban hit, a very catchy chorus phrase – became a huge hit, making Manuel temporarily the #1 singer on the island. Manuel's recordings were originally unreleased on disc, being disseminated directly from master tape via the radio, but by the end of the year he had been signed by the British label Palm Pictures.

⊙ **Malo Cantitad**   Palm Pictures, UK

The Clan's debut CD, a patchy but sporadically entertaining
exercise in Cuban pop/dance music, is very representative of its
time. Blending classically frenetic timba jumpiness with judicious
touches of romantic balladry and elements of rap, rock, Jamaican
ragga and the New York Latin funk of the influential DLG, the
music sometimes suffers from the common timba syndrome of
starting at such a pitch of desperate striving that there's nowhere
to go but down. At times, though, the band hits a salsa-like groove
and almost convinces, and the songs, especially if you're in a
position to get all the references to Havana life and other hit songs
of the 1990s, are certainly catchy.

Glossary

aché/ashé grace, power, or luck, imparted by the Afro-Cuban orishas.

agogo bell-like metal percussion instrument used in santería ceremony.

akpwon solo singer of santería ceremonial music.

batá sacred drum used in lucumí santería ritual.

bembé santería drum and dance ceremony.

bocú drum used in Santiago carnival comparsas.

bolero genre of romantic song, rhythmical but ballad-like, originating in Santiago.

bombo big drum used in carnival processions.

bongo small drum, played in joined pairs, used in early son groups and later central to salsa and Latin jazz percussion.

boogaloo (also **bugalú**) hybrid genre of Latin and US black music created in New York in 1950s and 1960s.

botíja earthenware jug bass played by blowing into the neck aperture.

cajón box-shaped percussion instrument originally constructed from salt-cod case.

changüí early form of rural son.

charanga group composed of piano, percussion, bass, violins and flute.

cinquillo rhythmic structure of Haitian origin.

clave the basic rhythm of Cuban dance music and the wooden peg percussion instrument (played in pairs) used to keep rhythm.

columbia one of three genres of rumba.

comparsa carnival parading group.

conjunto son group format typified by that of Arsenio Rodríguez in the 1940s, featuring one or more trumpets.

conga style of music and dance peculiar to Santiago carnival; later used outside Cuba as a synonym for the tumbadora drum.

corneta china cornet-like instrument of Chinese origin used in carnival.

danza eighteenth century Cuban salón dance music based in part on the French contredanse.

danzón more powerfully rhythmic development of the danza, created by Miguel Faílde in the late nineteenth century.

danzonete further development of the danzón, featuring a vocal part, created in the 1920s.

décima Spanish-origin verse form of ten octosyllabic lines.

descarga (literally "discharge"), a jam session.

diablo term primarily used by Arsenio Rodríguez, equivalent to mambo.

diana introductory vocal section of a rumba.

estribillo chorus of a song.

estudiantina (literally "student"), applied to "orquesta" to mean an early son-related group composed of young musicians; common in the late nineteenth century.

filin Hispanicisiation of "feeling", applied to a genre of music affiliated to trova, and influenced by US vocal jazz, created in Havana in the 1940s.

galleta large flat drum used in Santiago carnival conga groups.

guaguancó one of the three styles of rumba.

guajira Cuban country music, influenced by son but not synonymous with it.

guaracha lively, satiric song form originating in nineteenth century theatre entertainment, and later incorporated into salsa.

guayo perforated and ridged metal cylinder rubbed with a stick, forming part of changüi percussion.

güiro percussion instrument comprising a ridged gourd, rubbed with a stick.

habanera nineteenth century instrumental genre related to danza, widely adopted in Spain and Mexico.

ireme costumed dancer in abakuá ritual and in carnival, also known as diablito (little devil).

kinfuiti sacred drum of Congo origin, played using friction via an internally attached cord.

laúd small metal-stringed lute-like instrument used in country music.

mambí nineteenth century fighter for Cuban independence from Spain.

mambo fast syncopated instrumental part of a danzón; subsequently a new genre of dance music based on this movement, especially popularised by Pérez Prado.

maraca percussion instrument composed of seed, or shot-filled hollow gourd on handle

marímbula instrument composed of plucked metal blades, based on the African sanza or m'bira.

montuno adjective, connected with, or coming from, the mountains; the improvisatory second part of a son.

mozambique dance genre based on massed Afro-Cuban percussion; created by Pello El Afrokan in the 1960s.

orisha divinity, also known as santo (saint) of the syncretic religion of santería.

pachanga fast dance genre created in the early 1960s.

pailas early term for drums known as timbales.

pilón type of conga drum; dance rhythm of the 1960s.

pregón song based on a street-seller's cry.

punto a style of guajira song, divided into sub-styles: punto libre, punto fijo, and punto cruzado.

quinto improvising drum in rumba.

rasgueo multi-finger strumming style of Spanish guitar technique.

repique improvisation on a percussion instrument.

rumba African-based style of song, percussion and dance comprising the sub-genres columbia, guaguancó and yambú.

sandunga applied to dance-music to indicate spiciness or hotness; thus a sandunguera is a spicy, hot female dancer.

santería syncretic religion based on worship of African-derived divinities combined with Catholic elements.

shekere percussion instrument consisting of shaken gourds covered with cowrie-strung net.

son Cuba's major musical genre, originating in Oriente in the nineteenth century.

soneo improvisation of a sonero, or son-singer.

songo 1970s dance rhythm popularised by Los Van Van.

timba originally a rumba term, adopted in the 1990s as a name for modern Cuban dance music.

timbales pair of shallow kettle drums.

típico (literally "typical"), often used to mean traditional.

tres small guitar with three double metal strings.

tumba francesa percussion genre originating among Haitian immigrants.

tumbao rhythmic structure composed of riffing on bass and piano.

tumbadora tall vertical drum also known internationally as a conga.

vacunao (literally "vaccination"), the male pelvic thrusting motion in rumba dance.

yambú one of the three genres of rumba.

yuka drum used in Bantu-derived fiesta music.

zapateo heel and toe-tapping rural dance style of Spanish origin.

zarzuela light opera of Spanish origin.

Selected Reading

Olavo Alén Rodríguez, *From AfroCuban Music to Salsa* (Piranha, Germany, 1998).

A single CD packaged inside a well illustrated and erudite 170 page book (in English) by the head of the Havana-based Centre for the Investigation & Development of Cuban Music. Particularly strong on Afro-Cuban and Hispanic roots.

Cristóbal Díaz Ayala (ed.), *100 Canciones Cubanas del Milenio* (Alma Latina, Spain, 1999).

A visually striking box set containing four CDs of largely pre-1960s music, with a fascinating book which provides details (in Spanish) of the background to a hundred of Cuba's most important songs, their writers and performers.

Tony Evora, *Orígenes de la Música Cubana* (Alianza, Spain, 1997).

Only available in Spanish, this is a particularly rich and thoughtful exposition of the historical, musical and social conditions which formed the basic genres of Cuban music.

Radames Giro (ed.), *Panorama de la Música Popular Cubana* (Letras Cubanas, Cuba, 1998).

While occasionally toeing a visibly Cuban ideological line, this is nonetheless an excellent collection of articles on the different genres of Cuban music by an interesting selection of authors – not all academic. Only available in Spanish.

Helio Orovio, *Diccionario de la Música Cubana* (Letras Cubanas, Cuba, 1992).

Orovio's work is dry and purely factual, but an unequalled source of information on hundreds of musicians untraceable elsewhere. Currently only available in Spanish but soon to appear in English published by Tumi Records.

Fernando Ortiz, *Los Instrumentos de la Música Afrocubana* (Letras Cubanas, Cuba, 1995).

Ortiz' classic work is a fascinating and enlightening journey deep into the history and lore of Cuba's peoples and their cultural expression. Republished also as a set of individual booklets but only in Spanish.

Al Pryor, Jack O'Neil and Nina Gomes, *Cuba: I Am Time* (Blue Jackel, US, 1997).

Beautifully produced four-CD box set with non-rigorous but excellent 110 page booklet in English. Packed with illustrations and interviews, plus a wide range of music – from historical to contemporary.

Maya Roy, *Musiques Cubaines* (Actes Sud, France, 1998).

For French-speakers, an accessible and broad-based account of Cuba's music up to the late 1990s, particularly strong on Afro-Cuban culture.

Sue Steward, *Salsa* (Thames & Hudson, UK, 1999).

A lively, and enticingly illustrated, account of the wider world of Latin dance music, with Cuba at its core.

John Storm Roberts, *The Latin Tinge* (Original Music, US, 1979).

This pioneering and classic analysis of the arrival and spread of Cuban and other Latin musics in the US is particularly strong on the early New York scene.

Index

Stay in touch with us!

ROUGHNEWS is Rough Guides'
free newsletter.
In three issues a year we give you
news, travel issues, music reviews,
readers' letters and the latest
dispatches from authors on the road.

ROUGH GUIDES: Travel

ROUGH GUIDES: Mini Guides, Travel Specials and Phrasebooks

MINI GUIDES

Antigua
Bangkok
Barbados
Big Island of Hawaii
Boston
Brussels
Budapest
Dublin
Edinburgh
Florence
Honolulu
Lisbon
London Restaurants
Madrid
Maui
Melbourne
New Orleans
St Lucia

Seattle
Sydney
Tokyo
Toronto

TRAVEL SPECIALS

First-Time Asia
First-Time Europe
More Women Travel

PHRASEBOOKS

Czech
Dutch
Egyptian Arabic
European
French

German
Greek
Hindi & Urdu
Hungarian
Indonesian
Italian
Japanese
Mandarin
  Chinese
Mexican
  Spanish
Polish
Portuguese
Russian
Spanish
Swahili
Thai
Turkish
Vietnamese

AVAILABLE AT ALL GOOD BOOKSHOPS

ROUGH GUIDES:
Reference and Music CDs

AVAILABLE AT ALL GOOD BOOKSHOPS

100

Essential

CDs

Eight titles, one name

ROUGH GUIDES

Sorted

ROUGH GUIDES

Will you have enough stories to tell your grandchildren?

©2000 Yahoo! Inc.

Yahoo! Travel

Rough Guides
on the Web

www.travel.roughguides.com

We keep getting bigger and better! The Rough Guide to Travel Online
now covers more than 14,000 searchable locations. You're just a click
away from access to the most in-depth travel content, weekly
destination features, online reservation services, and an outspoken
community of fellow travelers. Whether you're looking for ideas for
your next holiday or you know exactly where you're going, join us online.

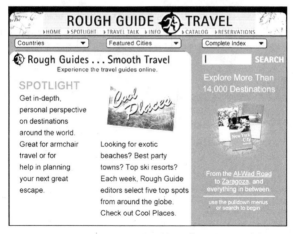

You can also find us on Yahoo!® Travel (http://travel.yahoo.com) and
Microsoft Expedia® UK (http://www.expediauk.com).